This is a story of intrigue, mayhem, and violence. A story of smuggling from a sleepy village in the heart of Kent in the 1700's, based loosely on true events. They started life as ordinary hard-working people who were pushed into a life of crime by other gangs, high taxation, and the way of life at the time. Now it seems no one could stop this gang who had a bad reputation eventually turning to murder to help their cause, they were in the end, beaten by their own confidence.

This book takes you on a journey from the gang's point of view, the friendships within the gang, their wrong doings were in fact taken for granted by them, in their eyes they could do no wrong, just so they could live their life the way they wanted.

Acknowledgements

Thank you to my wife, for the long evenings of reading and listening to these stories unfold over the period that it's taken. The fun of searching the internet and many books researching and in bringing these characters back to life to tell the story that has been told many times before.

Mr. Eddie Lee Sampson, for invaluable information and help when I was stuck for information.

The self-belief that I could write a book in the hope that people will read it and enjoy being taken back to the 1740's to when smugglers ruled the south of England and made it their own.

Chapter 1	The change begins.	Page 1
Chapter 2	First light	Page 29
Chapter 3	Etchingham	Page 59
Chapter 4	A large haul	Page 76
Chapter 5	Richard Hawkins	Page 84
Chapter 6	Shoreham by sea	Page 97
Chapter 7	Choose your friends wisely	Page 113
Chapter 8	Montivilliers	Page 117
Chapter 9	Pevensey landing.	Page 136
Chapter 10	A spy in our midst	Page 143
Chapter 11	The chance encounter	Page 153
Chapter 12	My prize	Page 156
Chapter 13	Sandwich	Page 163
Chapter 14	The Wingham Gang	Page 173
Chapter 15	Goudhurst	Page 191
Chapter 16	The Three brothers	Page 206
Chapter 17	Poole Custom House	Page 213
Chapter 18	Galley and Chater	Page 222
Chapter 19	The Trial	Page 248
Chapter 20	Cook	Page 285
Chapter 21	William Fairall	Page 278
Chapter 22	The Chase	Page 282
Chapter 23	Out in the sweet air	Page 290
Chapter 24	The last one	Page 295
Chapter 25	A new life	Page 298
-	A Smugglers Song	Page 301

This story is loosely based on true events and starts with a notorious criminal organisation involved in smuggling throughout southeast England from Kent through to Dorset from 1735 until 1749. They were the most infamous criminals of their time and would put fear into anyone who crossed them, and outsiders who got too close just disappeared without trace. No one was safe from their wrath, and woe betide anyone who crossed them. Just their name would send a shiver through the hearts of ordinary god-fearing people, they were: -

The Hawkhurst Gang
A smuggler's story.
Holkhurst Genge
Chapter 1
The change begins (1730)

The inn keeper was wiping the bar of spilt stale ale. The fire crackled and spat out sparks leaving a trail of smoke, close by the fire the inn keepers dog sat nervously watching the embers landing nearby and giving each dying ember a sniff as it landed. The room was dusky and dimly lit; candles cast eerie flickering shadows creating movement where there was none. A group of men sat near the fire trying to keep warm as they drunk ale and spoke about their day's work with the occasional sound of laughter to keep their spirits high, pipe smoke creating a haze and filled the air and wafted around the room from where they sat.

The door burst open as if like a sail that had been caught by the wind, the hinges creaking from lack of oil, and in with the wind and leaves came a shadowy figure, silhouetted against the setting sun. Forcing the door shut against the wind, he turned, paused to catch his breath, looked up and removed his hat and wiped his brow. Through strained and weathered eyes, he looked around, his eyes growing accustomed to the dim candlelit room of the old bar, the leaves finally settled where the wind had taken them. The old wooden beams showing the age of the inn, which to him has always played a part in his life like an old friend. He looked around the room, anyone who was unfamiliar would stand out, even in this dim light, trust and friendship is a hard thing to come by, keep your friends close and your enemies closer.

All eyes were looking at the figure as they all looked up to see who entered their domain, creating a hush that came over the men, the smoke had cleared but soon returned back to the haze as they stared at the figure.
The leaves blown in hardly had time to settle before a voice broke the silence from another part of the room.
"Is that you William?"
The voice came from a darkened corner lit only by a single candle placed on the table. The voice had a certain tone, one of confidence of unquestioning obedience about it.
"Yes" the reply came," it is I", I said lifting the lantern I was carrying to extinguish the flame. It didn't sound like my voice, as the cold had got in too deep, I needed warming up, as I moved nearer the fire and placed the lantern on the hearth with a few others that had already been placed there. The hush turned to murmurs again as the men carried on about their business.
"John" again came the voice from the corner, above the murmur, "two ales over here when you are ready, this time fill them up". "Looks like you'll be needing to throw some more logs on the fire as well".
With the first command John the bar keep, stopped what he was doing and cleaned out two tankards with what looked like an old dirty rag.
I rubbed my hands together close to the now dying embers of the fire, trying to get the feeling back into my fingers, I undid my coat so I could feel the heat getting into my body, a tingling sensation came over me as I could feel the warm blood coursing its way around my frozen body, the dog looked at me wagging its tail in anticipation that it was getting something, he only got a stroke and a pat on the head before the voice was heard again.
"Come over here William and sit down, rest your weary bones", came the voice again, eagerly trying to pull me away from the little heat that the fire was giving out.

I reluctantly pulled myself away from the fire and moved slowly towards the voice, my eyes getting used to the dim light as I sat down on an old stool and pulled myself closer to the ale-stained oak table that the figure was sitting at, the flickering light from the candle shed enough light for me to see his face now from the candle set on the table, it was Arthur Grey.
We both looked as each other before turning towards John who was filling two tankards with ale, "the last ale he gave me wasn't full", Arthur said, "let us hope he fills it this time", with some anticipation in his voice.
How is everything, I hope everything is good with you"? Arthur said in a much quieter voice.
"I am well as can be in this cold", I said.
"And feels like it will only get colder as the winter months draw in", Arthur said.
I looked towards Arthur, his face showing signs of being weathered from being outside in the cold, like lines on a map. Mine must have looked pretty much the same with this cold.
"Are you hungry lad, would you like John to get you something to help with the cold"?
Although Arthur had this way about him, one that you wouldn't push too hard for fear of turning him against you, to his friends he did have a softer side, but still, you would still be wary of him. I have seen both sides of him and I know which side I'd rather be on.
John came over with the tankards full of ale, he was trying his hardest not to spill a drop.
He placed the tankards on the table, reaching down to collect the few coins that were placed there by Arthur for the ale.
"Much obliged", John said, touching his brow and tipping his head as a mark of respect as he lifted the coins and placed them in the top pocket of his shirt, making his way to the fire to throw a few logs on the fire, as he did a mass of sparks flew up the chimney causing the dog to sit up in alarm.
"Did you want something to eat William"? asked Arthur.

"I will have something to help warm me up if John has anything", I said, now finding my voice. Before I could say another word.
"John", shouted Arthur, "do you have anything that will warm this frozen lad up after being outside in the cold"?
John stood up from the fire, wiping his hands still with the same dirty rag, "We do have some leftover soup that my wife made today, and what is leftover of the bread she baked in the oven this morning if that would be good enough", said John.
"That will do for me", I said, "that's more than I have at home".
"That will warm you up, take the chill out of your bones", said Arthur.
With that John turned and disappeared into the shadows behind the bar.
The inn has been part of our lives for as long as we can remember, we have spent many nights here with our friends reliving our stories and speaking about the past. John the bar keep is a good friend to us and we've enjoyed each other's company on many occasions drinking till the cock crows at sunup, then had to stagger home while everyone else went about their day's work, that wasn't always an ideal situation as Arthur had a butcher shop to run and I had work to get to work. I work as a carpenter, it is good work and people rely on me as I am the only carpenter in the village, it gives me an income, enough to keep the roof over my head and my belly full, but not enough for luxuries that I would have liked to have, would be nice to get another horse and a better cart to carry wood around, I thought to myself.

Just then John returned with a bowl of steaming soup and a large lump of bread. He placed them on the table along with a wooden spoon, giving it a quick wipe over with the rag he had been carrying around with him. I looked at it through the steam, not quite knowing or failed to ask what soup it was, the steam hit my nose, it did smell nice, and for my hungry stomach this was good enough, I handed over a few meagre coins for the pleasure,
"Thank you Will", said John, again the coins disappearing into his top pocket.
Arthur had a look in his eye as he reached into his pocket and pulled out his pipe and a small leather bag tied with a cord, I could see his thoughts were elsewhere as he had a blank stare, so I didn't disturb him as he sat there with his tankard of ale. He opened the leather pouch and reached in and filled up his pipe with tobacco he found in there, then got up and moved towards the fire.
The dog decided it was either hot enough now by the fire or try its luck at getting a free meal as it came over to sit by me, it looked up at me as if he'd never been fed, then laid down, still not taking its eyes off me waiting for any morsel of food that might come its way.
The soup wasn't that bad, I was still trying to work out what it was, beef, lamb, it was hot and tasty, I called over to John, "John, what's in this soup"? I asked.
"Rabbit", he said, "I caught them this morning as they were eating my cabbages in the yard, pesky things rabbits, but they make good eating".
Arthur returned from the fire after lighting his pipe from a piece of wood that he got from the fire.
"I'm glad you came in tonight William", Arthur said breaking the silence, "I've been doing me some thinking".
"You know I've been thinking of giving up my shop, I've mentioned it to you a few times?"
"Yes, I do", I answered wiping my mouth.

"There's a group of men that keep coming to my shop every now and then, they have been taking more of my money and goods, I'm finding it hard to keep on the straight and narrow, seems I'm working long hours only to have my stock and money taken from me whenever they feel like it, I can't go on like this, so something has to change. I've been in touch with the customs to see if there is anything that can be done, but they don't seem to be interested in my problems, neither the local mayor or magistrate when I told them, and I can't fight them off by myself, there's too many, they did it when I had my shop in Marden, not so much mind, but it's happening even more now since I opened the shop here in Hawkhurst.
"Can't you get a few people to help fend them off"? I said.
"I never know when they are coming in lad", he said scratching his head.
I've been doing some thinking", he said placing the pipe to his lips, making a sucking noise, I watched as his face glowed from the embers in his pipe.
"What's that"? I said taking a mouthful of bread, realising that it was not as tasty as the soup but, filling none the less.
Arthur was a big man and someone you wouldn't cross, but I know of the problems he's been having with a group that's been going around demanding money and goods, not just Arthur but the whole village. I've heard of people getting set upon if they don't hand over what they ask for, and you can't fight off a group of them, if Arthur has had enough, it's because the gang have been coming round for a long time and seems no one can stop them, it must be hard for him to keep doing what he's doing just to line their pockets with his hard work.
Arthur took a mouthful of ale and looked across the room at the group of men sitting by the fire, "well more like Thomas and I have been doing some thinking", he said, taking another puff on his pipe filling the air with smoke.

Thomas Kingsmill was a shady character younger than Arthur, and again someone you didn't want as an enemy, he was good friends with Arthur and have known each other for years, grew up together.

He spends a lot of time in Rye and frequents the Mermaid Inn, seems to make it his own from what I've heard, him and his brother George have gained a reputation in there. He likes it here too and spends a lot of time with Arthur, I've seen them drinking till sunrise.

Arthur was the bigger man of the two, and Thomas would always show him respect.

When they get together, they'd pick on people and ridicule them in such a way that it'll either clear the bar or cause a fight to which the outcome is assured. They change when they are together, no one seems safe from their vile comments.

So, whatever it is that they have been talking about I'm sure that I'm not going to like it.

"Enough is enough, I've been asking around and from what I hear, think these men come from the Hastings area, going from village to town, causing trouble wherever they go, taking whatever, they like, and no one seems to be able to stop them from doing what they do, helping themselves to people's money and goods. At first, I thought it's not right, but then I got to thinking how easy it would be to give up my trade, my shop, and do the same as them, no one would know if we kept it a secret and we could make a lot of money doing so, we don't see many customs men round here and seems they are not interested in the likes of us anyway, so, Thomas and I have been thinking about going into business together with a few others, but this goes no further, I want you to keep this quiet, between ourselves like, until we have got things sorted out", he said taking another puff on his pipe.

I listened intently, this didn't sound good, I thought to myself.
"I take it we can have your trust in this matter"? he said, looking directly at me.

"Err yes", I said, a bit hesitant, as if he caught me off guard, my mind was wild with images of what he was saying to me, "You can trust me; I won't say a word". I said sipping my ale. "I've been keeping this from you for a while, but we've started up a gang of our own, and been organizing a few things, ways of making money on the side so to speak, we've been selling the wool from the sheep around here, getting it off the local farmers and giving them some of the money, the taxes are far too high for them to make any money, so we have started selling it to France where they pay a pretty penny and more for it. This is why you haven't seen me around the butcher's shop for a while, so, as I said I've decided to give that up and let my sister Elizabeth take over the business, she can do it just as well as I can, this will leave me to do as I want, make extra money and the shop will be there still in case things go wrong, I couldn't see myself being a butcher for the rest of my life, not after what I've seen, and know what I can get".
"Are you sure?" I said, "you've spent years trying to build that shop up, you've done your apprenticeship too, it'll all be for nothing".
"Don't worry, it's not as if I'm giving it up all together, I can still go back anytime and work with my sister, she's been working with me for a long time, she knows one end of a cow to the other so she'll fit right in, besides if the shop goes then the locals might get suspicious, and it'll also be a good place to store a few items. After seeing what this gang have been doing and the way they are making a name for themselves around here, we thought that we would like to be a part of that. We have a plan of how to make some extra money for ourselves and getting a better life, this has been involving a lot of people that we know, some old friends, friends that go back a long way, and so far, we have been doing quite well out of it, so secrecy will be the word. I didn't think that I'd be doing something like this, but I thought if they can get away with it then so can we, do you understand"? Said Arthur.

He now turned to face me, now with the lines on his face showing more deeply, I've seen that look before, a very stern look, he sent a shiver down my spine, I've seen it many times but never directed at me, normally he saves that look for his enemies and people that have crossed him.
"Yes", I said, "I understand".
My smile disappearing, as I soaked up his words.
"I will let you know more details as and when I need you to know", said Arthur taking another puff on his pipe, and staring around the room to see if anyone had been listening to our conversation.
This all sounded a bit worrying to me, but as I know Arthur's temperament, I thought it a wise decision to do as I was told and follow orders, for now.
"Don't worry", he said, "this is far bigger than you can realise, than we can all realise", we have got a lot of members in the gang as I've said, and getting more joining us, but first thing we are going to do is to sort this gang out that keep on intimidating us and the Village, and make sure they don't return, enough is enough, it's going to be our turn from now on and get them to stop bothering us, but for now I think I've told you enough, we can let you know more when we find out who they are, as for now, I'm off", he said, getting a last puff on his pipe and drinking the last of his ale.
"Be in here tomorrow, before sundown, he said, wiping the ale from his mouth,
"I will tell you more then, just keep this to yourself".
I think he wanted to tell me more, but seemed reluctant, almost testing me to see my reaction or if I was trustworthy or not, but he seems to have forgotten where we have come a long way together; he should know me better, I was thinking to myself.

With that he stood up, he was a giant of a man, and with the low beams of the Inn, made him look even bigger, he made towards the fire tapping his pipe over the fire then stooping down to pick up a lantern which John keeps for the regulars to use. Picking up a piece of burning wood, he lit the lantern, the dog by my side stared up at him as if he had something to offer, he waved to John and bid him goodnight and moved towards the door, stooping to avoid the beams, placing his hat on his head and turning up his collar, with one hand on the solid oak door, he turned and looked across the shadowy figures in the room, grabbed the rim of his hat as he looked at me as a way of goodbye, looked again around the room as if to see if he was being followed, before disappearing into the night air.

I had now finished my bread and soup, the dog disappointed with no scraps returned to the slowly dying fire, and there was I thinking I had a friend, I smiled lightly to myself, trying to forget the news I'd just been given.

It was getting late, the soup had done its job on my stomach and warmed me up, I finished my ale with my mind now full of thoughts about what had been said. I too moved near the fire, I bid good night to John and told him to thank his wife for the soup, I rubbed my hands near the fire, warming them one last time, I reached down to pick up my lantern and grabbed a burning stick to light it, the dog looking up at me wagging its tail, still expecting to get something for its trouble,

"You won't want to eat this", I said throwing the stick back on the fire, the dogs eyes followed it. I turned up my collar as protection against the wind, I walked towards the oak door, not looking forward to going back out into the cold night air, I thought. I turned the handle of the heavy oak door and pushed passed the wind trying to get in as I made my way out into the cold night air with my lantern trying to light my way. My horse complained as I climb into the saddle, but soon settled into a trot towards home.

The way was dark, just the odd lights of lanterns in windows, how warm and inviting each one looked as I made my way home.
I reached my house, it looked cold and unwelcoming after being in the warm Inn, puddles filled the road that led from the village, overhanging branches were scraping against me eager to remove an eye if I wasn't careful, the lantern offering little way of lighting the way, I was cold but with my belly full I was happy to get home, one last job before going to bed was to feed my horse and bed him down for the night, ready for the morning, my fingers now frozen with the cold undoing the harness, the warmth of the soup slipping slowly from my body.
I finally got through the door, the fire was out as I'd been out all day, it was so cold, I lit it again using the flame from the lantern, after a while the heat from the fire started to fill the room after putting more wood on it than I normally would, another job, I thought, I need to cut more wood and dry it out, but in this weather that was going to be hard. I made myself a hot drink and sat by the fire sipping it, thinking about what had been said in the Oak and Ivy.
What plans had Arthur to make more money, who were the other members of this gang that he had started up with Thomas, what if we got caught, this led to more thinking and this made me tired.
I lay back in my chair by the fire, placed a large old sack over my legs, my head full of thoughts and drifted off to sleep.
The following morning, I awoke to the cockerel crowing his morning song.
"Sometimes I wish that cockerel wouldn't make that noise so early", I said to myself.
My body stiff from where I had been sitting in the chair, I should have made it to the bed last night, thinking to myself as I tried to move.
I put some more wood on the fire while it was still glowing to get myself warm again.

"I hate these winter months, it's too cold and too dark", I said out loud as if someone was listening.
I got up but my leg was still asleep as I shook it to get some life back in it as I looked for something to eat as I was hungry, the rabbit soup, the night before was good but now I needed something to start the day.
I cut a piece of bread that I bought from the village and a slice of dried beef, just to get me going and remove the night's sleep from my mouth. There wasn't much food in this old house of mine, never had a wife to help prepare anything for me, I do grow some vegetables when I get time, but as autumn was fast approaching, and me wishing I'd planted more earlier in the year, I must dig up the rest of them before it gets much colder. With the onset of autumn, I knew it was only going to get colder and darker earlier too. My food supplies were running low I would have to go to the village to get more food.
I kept thinking about what Arthur said in the Inn the night before about going into business with Thomas, what could they be up to I thought, and what were they going to do to this other gang once they find them?
I placed more logs on the fire in the hope it would keep the house warm during the day and still be alight by the time I got home later.
The sun was high in the sky by the time I got to village after making sure my horse was fed and watered, there were the usual faces of the traders whom I normally bought my supplies from, familiar faces bidding me a good day as they were trying to keep on my good side for my business, there were a lot of people going about their daily lives, children trying to steal what they could from the traders, hoping not to get caught as the punishment would be harsh, I just laughed to myself as I watched them.
I knew what supplies I needed and with not much money on my person I had to watch what I bought.

Being the only carpenter in the village one would think that I was rich but far from it, most people can hammer a nail in, so most people do things for themselves, it's only the larger jobs that I get, and those jobs take time so money, what there is of it is slow to come my way.

I took my meagre, purchases, and headed back to my house. On the way out of the village I saw George Chapman, he is a friend of Arthur and Thomas.

"Hello George", I said

He was dressed in a long coat tied up in the middle with a piece of string, trying to keep the wind and cold out and had a pair of what looked like rough leather gloves without any fingers so he could hold the reins of his horse.

"We don't get to see much of you around these parts". I said eyeing him up and down.

From the way he was dressed I'd have said his way through life hadn't treated him much better in the way of wealth either.

"Hello William", he said, in his country accent.

"I hope you are well"? I said.

"Oh yes, I am well as can be expected in this cold", Said George trying to hold his horse still.

What are you doing here, I haven't seen you for a while"? I asked.

"I'm here because Arthur sent a message and told me to come to Hawkhurst", he said not giving too much away.

"Did he say why"? I hesitated, thinking about Arthur's words of secrecy.

"He just said, come to Hawkhurst and be at the Oak an Ivy later", he said pulling his collar closer around his neck.

"Did you ask why"? I said, asking the same question a different way to try and get a response.

"Yes, he said something about a meeting, but he didn't say what for", he was more carefree of talking about it than I was.

"There is going to be a meeting there with a few others, are you going to be to be there too"? asked George.

I looked at him and could see him start to shiver as the cold was biting into him, his long coat didn't look to be doing much in the way of keeping out the cold.

"I should imagine you are as you always seem to be close to Arthur", he said.

"Do you have any idea as to why they have called this meeting"? I asked with anticipation and picking for information, looking about me to see if the coast was clear before gaining any knowledge.

"I have no idea why, I can't tell you any more than that, I was asked to make sure I was here and that's all, we shall just have to wait and see. But as far as I can tell from what I've heard it'll be good for everyone involved, but hearsay can always be distorted, so we will just have to wait until we are told". said George, leaning forward towards me before imparting me with that information.

"Yes, news will not be the same as it was intended, I will be there and await the news first-hand", I said.

With that he bid me farewell, "till later then", he said, and he carried along on his way to the village.

I bid him farewell and carried on with my journey, now my mind was racing, what could this news that Arthur was talking about this has got me wondering, I haven't seen George in a while, and how many others were going to be there?

I reached home with my stomach aching for some more food and my mind buzzing with questions.

The embers were still glowing nicely on the fire, so I was able to get some food cooking.

I will just have to wait, the questions slowly disappearing from my mind as I concentrated on my stomach. I put some mutton in a pan with some vegetables, I closed my eyes thinking about the day's events, the heat of my now roaring fire was beginning to send me to sleep again, happy to be back in the warm, I thought to myself, I took my boots off to warm my frozen wet feet.

I felt satisfied that I'd eaten, warmed my bones, I placed a few more logs on the fire in the hope it would still be alight when I returned, now I was ready to set out again to the Oak and Ivy for the meeting.

The food I cooked went well with a little drop of rum that I had in the house to help wash it down but now looking forward to a tankard of ale by a raging log fire with the company of good friends and to find out the news.

I saddled my horse again, he seemed reluctant to leave his warm, albeit small barn and mix of straw and oats that he was eating. The roads were soddened as it had been raining during the previous night, leaves covered the puddles and deep depressions, so I had to be careful where to lead my horse, the lamp I had with me wasn't giving off much light either, so it was slow going.

After a long and uncomfortable ride on my horse, back in the cold. I reached the Oak and Ivy to see a lot of horses tied up outside I was glad to finally reach the inn.

I tied my horse up next to the others, thinking he'll be happy now he has company, picked up some hay and a small bag of oats that was left in a small shelter kept next to the inn that John keeps, and placed it on the floor and emptied the bag of oats over the hay by the water trough, what a simple life a horses leads I thought to myself, I walked to the front of the inn and opened the large oak door to hear a rabble of noise coming from inside, a stark difference from the previous night, not quiet at all. I removed my hat and undid my coat, again my eyes getting used to the light that was inside the inn, I could make out Arthur, Thomas, George, who I'd met earlier in the village, John Diamond, John Mills **alias** Smoker**, Poole**, Richard Mills, James Stanford and George Kingsmill, Thomas's brother, all sitting in the corner drinking ale laughing and talking between themselves, above them a cloud of smoke now disbursing from the wind through the open door.

Anyone else in the inn had given them plenty of room and kept themselves to themselves.

"Hello William, come over, sit here", Arthur calling to me in an excited voice, as he was happy to see this gathering of old friends.

"Bar Keep", he paused as if to catch his breath," John", he called,

"Bring us more ale over here, Will has just arrived", he said with excitement in his voice.

I looked to see Thomas sitting next to Arthur to his left, smiling as he saw me.

I extinguished my lantern and placed it with the others by the fire and made my way over to where they were sitting.

"Move over everyone, make way so Will can sit down", Arthur shouted at the others.

I moved next to Arthur away from Thomas, I've always had a distrust for Thomas although we get on alright together, but there's something about him that I distrust, probably nothing, just me perhaps.

"Nice to see you all again", I said hiding my distrust.

"Yes, good to see you here", came the voices all talking at once.

John brought over the ales as requested and took some of the coins that were gathered in the center of the table.

"Have you had a good day William"? Thomas asked. "I heard that you met up with George earlier", he said.

"Well, I've had a busy day getting a few provisions from the village stores when I met George, it was good to see you again, George", I said, looking down at him whilst adjusting the stool on the uneven floor.

The door opened again and entered another figure, he came straight over and sat down near Thomas, a man with striking features, William Fairall.

This man I have heard about, seen him many times before, normally with Thomas, nasty to everyone except his friends and even then, you'd have to be careful.

Welcome Shepherd said Arthur and Thomas together.
I found out later from Smoker that William Fairall likes to be called Shepherd, doesn't like to incriminate himself by using his own name.
"I'm glad that we are all here", Arthur said, "shows loyalty, I like my friends to stay loyal it shows trust".
There were cheers as we raised our tankards to old and loyal friends.
Arthur wiped the ale from his lips and proceeded to fill his pipe with tobacco, Richard pulled a burning ember from the fire for Arthur to light his pipe.
"Listen", he said, taking puffs on his pipe, his pipe smoke was mixing with Smoker's who had filled and lit his as well.
There was silence as John came around to give us more candles for the table, there wasn't that many people in the Inn tonight, must have realised that Arthur and Thomas were going to be there, and stayed clear from their comments, or decided to leave earlier than normal.
"Come closer, I don't want to be overheard", said Arthur.
We all sat closer, not a good idea as Smoker stank plus his pipe tobacco didn't help, I think he hadn't bathed in months, come to think of it neither had any of us, it was far too cold for that.
Smoker was a funny sort of character, a comical chap, been known around Hawkhurst since he was a boy, he lost his parents while in his teens, and we think that's what changed him, having to fend for himself, he never learned how to read and write he was someone who would always help out, always willing to run errands for people, just to make a bit of money to support himself, some saw him as the village idiot, simple in the way he behaved, others saw him as a friend and he was always very loyal to his friends, and here he was sitting next to me puffing his smoke out and choking everyone in the process.

"We've have had an idea Thomas and I, we are fed up with living life at the lowest end while the rich get the best life, we have struggled through life just to make those in a richer position richer, and others at the lower end of society, including ourselves poorer, so we are going to changed things around". Said Arthur, looking at us all.

"I take it that all that is said tonight at this table will go no further"? with that he screwed his eyes up, looked around the room, paused then reached inside his coat and pulled a pistol out and placed it on the table.

There was a shocked surprise as we looked at the pistol.

"Yes, you have our word", could be heard through the startled rabble, looking at the pistol that just got our attention.

"Good, loyalty and friendship go a long way, I knew I could trust you all", Arthur laughed as he removed the pistol from the table to back under his coat.

"We need to sort out the gang of men that keep coming to our Village and taking the goods and money from us, we have an idea who they are but can't really be sure and now there's enough of us to put a stop to it, we are on the lookout for these men and have put the word out, so we now have many ears and eyes, we want to be in charge now, this is our village and that's the way that we want it to stay. Thomas, his brother George and I, have got our heads together and while we are making this village our own, we need to make money for ourselves, look at us all, we don't have a huge amount of money between all of us", said Arthur, looking around the table,

"I'm running a butcher's shop, Will is the local carpenter, Smoker is struggling to survive, we can do better, look at you George, when I saw you earlier, I felt sorry for you, your coat is done up only with string", he said.

"Aye, lost the buttons long time ago", said George, looking down at his coat then around at the others to see how they were dressed.

"We all look like we are the poorest in the village, it's time to change, it's our turn to make money and make a better life for ourselves, all of us, and that's what we are going to do, we have to be careful, we could lose it just as quick as we can make it, and with dire consequences from the customs men if they ever found out, I for one don't want to wear a noose, so we need your trust in this. What I'm about to tell you, you will keep to yourself, there is no going back, if you decide to leave the gang after there will be consequences from the rest of us, we couldn't have you going to the customs men, is that understood, if there's a problem with that then you can leave now before we go any further, it's going to be that simple". Said Arthur.
There was a pause as everyone looked at each other to see who was going to move or say something first.
"With that silence I take it I have your word that this will go no further", Arthur said looking round at all of us.
Thomas picked up his tankard of ale and held it over the center of the table.
"To us and the future", he said in a proud voice.
We all picked up our tankards to cheer on the toast that had been made.
"To us and the future", was said by everyone, not realising the full consequences of what the future held for them.
"From now on we begin", said Thomas, there was a pause we all took another mouthful of ale.
"In five days', time we will be getting some goods in from Guernsey, it's our first real shipment and it's our start to something big, our chance to change", said Arthur.
"A boat is coming in just off the coast at Fairlight full of goods, we'll go and meet it at Fairlight cove early on that morning, once we signal the coast is clear they will offload the goods into smaller boats and come ashore, then we'll load up our carts, and hide them somewhere where they can't be found by prying eyes". Said Arthur, being more open now.
"I take it you've organised that as well"? asked James.

"Aye, that we have, we are going to use a farm and farmhouse, friend of Smoker actually", said Thomas, with this Smoker removed his pipe from his mouth and tipped his head, as a way of acknowledgment, not saying a word, simply happy to listen and return the pipe to his mouth.
"So far, so good then, everything has been organised, we'll meet up before first light in five days' time, by the old windmill next to Gibbet's Marsh in Rye, all is set, and nothing should go wrong, at least we hope it doesn't, so don't be drinking too much in the Mermaid the night before". Continued Arthur.
"I take it everyone knows where that is"? asked Thomas, again looking around at everyone.
"Aye", came the response from around the table.
"Let's hope everything goes alright and we have no trouble", said Thomas, watching Arthur puffing on his pipe.
 "Any trouble from anyone and we will let them know who they are up against", Thomas continued, Arthur patted where his pistol was hiding, and smiling.
At that Thomas reached inside his coat and pulled out a pistol, placing it on the table. Thomas smiled, bearing his brown teeth. Arthur gave out a loud laugh as he saw the pistol.
"We have more where these came from for each of you", Thomas said, still grinning.
Thomas quickly replaced the pistol inside his coat.
"Shhh", John the barkeep came over again with more ale for all of them, and again taking the coins from the table, he turns and walks over to the fire to place more wood on the dying embers.
"So, what are the details of the plans", I said, taking a mouthful of ale, and what must have looked like excitement on my face.
"What goods will be coming from Guernsey and how much of it is there"? asked George.
"I wondered when someone would ask that", said Arthur.
"Got your interest now, have we"? Said Thomas.

"Keep your voice down, this place has ears", said Arthur, with this his face scoured and looked around the room, the fire now burning a bit brighter making the room flicker a bright yellow.

"It's not a huge amount, we will have Tea, some of this will be wrapped in bails and wrapped in oilskin to keep them watertight and easy to carry, spirits, gin and brandy, caramel a few silks", said Arthur.

"What's that caramel for, are we bringing food in as well"? said James, looking up with surprise.

"The way the French have made the brandy, it's as it was when it came out of the still, so don't go drinking it, its colourless and over proof, we wanted it that way as its cheaper for us, we can add water and the caramel to make it drinkable and give it some colour, plus we can water it down a little bit more, if need be, to make more profit, no one will know", said George Kingsmill.

"We've done a bit of looking around and asking the right questions to some people to see how things are done, we are not doing this totally ignorant,". Said Thomas in a sterner voice than his brother.

"We are going to meet before first light by the old Mill in Rye, so get there early", Said Arthur.

"That's a long way from here and getting there before first light I'll be travelling through the night", I said.

"Then you'll just have to organise yourself to get there earlier or spend the night at an Inn so that you can get there early, and that goes for the rest of you, if you are with us, you make the effort, no one lets us down or we all suffer", said Thomas.

"Let's get things straight, if we are all going to be in this then we all need to pull together to make this work, and if that means living rough, or having to spend a few shillings for the trouble then so be it, think of the rewards that will come later for a small inconvenience", said Arthur, reiterating what Thomas had just said.

"Thomas and I will be at the Mermaid, you lot can make your own plans", said Arthur, looking at me as if the comment was for me alone.

"I don't want anyone to be late. When we are set, we shall head off towards Fairlight, when we arrive, we will check to make sure the coast is clear and wait there on the beach, we will give off a signal for the boats to come in and get the goods off loaded.

We sent Richard Perin and Richard Glover over to Guernsey where, with the money that we gave them, should have bought a lot of goods, just enough to make a start, something small, we are hoping, about five carts full, rum, whiskey, brandy, tea and tobacco", with that Thomas burst out laughing!

"I don't suppose any of you have seen that much on one cart let alone five", said Thomas.

Arthur continued, looking at Thomas, hoping he hadn't drawn attention to us.

"We will meet Perin and the others down there, they will be waiting offshore waiting for our signal, if all is clear then they'll fill the rowing boats and bring them ashore, we'll load up the carts and take them back through Rye and onto the marshes to John's farm. We'll need about six carts just in case they've added some extras, to our cause", Arthur said with a smile.

"So, Smoker and George should have organised carts to help get the goods off the beach.

I take it this has already been taken care of this time"? Arthur said looking at Smoker and George.

"Aye that we have", said George, "I've managed to get two carts and six people bringing them, Smoker will bring two more carts, and I've organised a few lads to meet us with two more carts along the way, they will be stopping overnight at the ruins of Camber castle, just outside Rye".

"Good", said Arthur.

This time, I thought, "You've done this before"? I said, with a look of surprise.

"Yes, a few times", said Arthur, with excitement in his voice, "nothing for you to worry yourself about, nothing big", a big smile on his face.

"I take it John is still in agreement about using his barn Smoker"? said Thomas.

"He is, but not sure about his wife", Joked Smoker.

"Don't worry about her", Thomas said raising his voice and changing the expression on his face.

 "Shush," Arthur, looking at him as though he had forgetting where he was.

"She will do all right out of what we give her, no need to be moaning at us like she was family, she'll be fine, Thomas said, touching the area of his coat where he had his pistol.

"Don't worry, John will be waiting for us as planned, if he knows what's good for him". Said Arthur now patting his pistol again, with a glint in his eye.

I've never seen Arthur like this, I never knew he would relish using a pistol, if he had to use it, I was thinking to myself, would he?

This is a different side to Arthur I have never seen before; I know that he and Thomas have their way when they get together and have been spending quite a bit of time together recently, I would never have known they would get into something like this, I think Thomas would use it, no question, he seems to have a mean streak, good to stay on his good side.

"If all goes well, we should have tea, whisky, brandy, rum and anything else they bring over, we will celebrate here at the inn ". Said Arthur to cheers from the men.

"The brandy and whiskey are in casks", Arthur carried on before I interrupted him.

"casks"? I said.

"Yes", came the response, "half-anchors they call them, not a big cask like you're thinking lad, not like John's got at the back of the Inn, they are half the size, they are easier to handle, there'll be tea in oil skin bags, whiskey, brandy in half-anchors and whatever else Perin and Richard can bring over". Said Arthur, reaching into his pocket for his pouch of tobacco.

"Easier to transport and keep the sea from spoiling. They are made in such a way and got just the right amount inside them that if they were to be thrown overboard, we can pick them up later and they'll be just below the surface hidden from customs men. We are using Fairlight because that's where they are being dropped off plus we know the area and escape routes, and its quiet and want to keep it that way just in case customs come poking their noses into our affairs, don't you lot worry, everything has been sorted, should be easy, all you lot need to worry about is getting there". said Thomas.

"The boats will leave Guernsey at night from a secluded spot called Petit Bot Bay on the south side of the island, to avoid being seen, it'll be a big enough haul enough for us to sell, and keep some for ourselves, it'll keep us happy till the next time", Said Arthur.

Next time, I thought, let's see how this goes first before we get too excited about getting more goods in, I was beginning to feel a little nervous about what I was hearing, goods in from Guernsey, pistols, customs men, nooses, this didn't bear to well with my way of life.

I looked around at the others as they were taking this all in, listening without realising what they were getting themselves into, not thinking of the outcome should this go wrong, the consequences of getting involved with the customs men. I've seen others hung for stealing goods from shops, this is not our way of life, but as I've said I would join In and help anyway I could, there was the thought of having the others set about me now if I didn't.

"There will be many more and with bigger loads as and when we can afford, this is just the start, there's no turning back now, we sold the last lot of goods that we bought for more money than I can make in a month, do you think I'm not going to continue doing that, go back to a meagre money for being a butcher, get up early and work late for the rest of my life with nothing to show for it", said Arthur, getting red in the face as he thought about his past life

There was a pause as everyone let Arthur calm down.

"Life as a smuggler ha, smuggling or infamous traffic as I heard people call it" said Smoker, breaking the silence, a grin came to his lips bearing his black teeth, as his mind started to race with thoughts.

I stared blankly as I took another mouthful of ale.

"The rich steals from us with all their taxes so we just steals a little for ourselves, it's only fair, it will keep us on our toes and makes a bit of money for us to live the ways we want to". Said George. "I might even be able to afford a new coat", he laughed.

I looked across to Arthur, who seemed to be mesmerized by the embers of the fire.

"We likes to make it clear that we won't have anyone against us, anyone who get in our way will find trouble, we show gratitude to those that help us, of course this being only fair, and we like it done that way, and in a way, It's like we are adding members to our gang as they get some of the spoils, they won't go running to the customs for fear of revenge and reprisals, fear is a good friend to have in this line of work, it gives us control, and that's what we likes to have". Said Arthur looking at Thomas who gave an agreeable nod, confirming what was said.

Arthur taking another mouthful of ale and wiping the froth from his top lip, and now filling his pipe again.

"I take it we are all in agreement as to what we want from you lot, which is silence"? he said looking around at all of us.

A mumbled yes went around the table,

"You have our word", said George.

"In that case I think a round of rum to seal our accord and to the future", said George Kingsmill, calling over to John to bring a bottle of rum to the table.

"Well, I think we all know what is expected of you, don't let us down or you'll find us not so agreeable, we shall see you in five days' time at the old mill in Rye, early, after sunup, any questions? I should imagine I've covered everything, just don't be late down there, if there's any change to the plans, I'll let you know at the old mill, you'll find me here if you have anything to add, in the meantime I'm off, I'll leave you lot here to enjoy yourselves, something wrong with the ale in here tonight, not up to the usual standard, you lot enjoy yourselves, but again, keep all this to yourselves, don't let the drink talk", said Arthur

"And maybe we should get him some proper ale for next time?" said George, to a burst of laughter from around the table.

"Aye and throw in a few casks of brandy to for good measure". Said Smoker

Arthur smiled, as he stood up, raising the mug to his lips for the last time, getting his last mouthful of ale. He moved over to the fire to pick up a piece of wood to light his pipe and a lantern, pulled up his coat as if to brace for the cold night air, looking around at the others sitting nearby, to see if any of them had taken an interest in what was being said, then came past us.

"See you in five days' time, and don't be late", he said in a low voice as he picked up a tankard and banged it on the table, making Smoker jump in the process.

"Don't worry, we will be there", said Smoker.

Then Arthur made his way to the large wooden door.

"Don't be late William", Arthur looked my way as if I were going to let the side down.

"Don't worry, I'll be there", I said.

He opened the door, letting in the cold night air and leaves in as he went through, a loud bang as he shut the door, stopping the leaves dead in their tracks.

We were left just finishing our ale, he was right, it didn't taste as good as it did the previous night.

But then John brought over the bottle of rum and rest of us sat around drinking and talking about what we were going to do with the money and how things were going to change for the better.

The sparks began to fly from the dying embers as John the inn keeper threw on another log.

We drank the rest of the rum, feeling a bit better now and warmer to face the cold so we all decided as the bottle was finished the meeting was over now Arthur had gone and no one wanted to stay. Thomas got up and left with his brother and the others followed.

I stood up and moved to the fire, just to get the last bit of heat before facing the night air again, my back aching from the position I was sitting in, leaning back to get some feeling back in it, I'm not that old, but I feel a lot older probably because of the cold, colder this year than most I've known, and if old wife's tales are anything to go by will only get colder,

I picked up a lantern and lit it with one of the embers, watching the flame get stronger. John's dog looking as the light got brighter, I looked at him and his tail started to wag, I patted him on the head and made my way the door, the door was solid oak and kept the weather at bay. I ruffled my collar around my neck to keep the cold out, I looked back at John with a puzzled look on my face, "John", I said, "I've been coming here for many years now, you've had this mutt now for a few years, why have I never known its name", John laughed out loud, as he was cleaning a few tankards that were left on the bar, he still didn't answer my question as he was chuckling to himself, I left him to his work, I bid John a good night, then closed the oak door behind me, again with another unanswered question I thought to myself, I don't even know if it's a dog or a bitch. I stood outside again with a lantern to guide my way, nice feeling in there I thought to myself as I made my way over to my horse, oh well.

The night was cold, the sky was clear, stars were going to light my way, I could feel the cold cut deep to my bones, I mounted my horse, tilted my hat, braced myself towards the wind and headed home.

Hard to sleep with all the anticipation of the days to come, I lay still for a while trying to keep warm, my thoughts turning to the evenings events and those yet to come.

Chapter 2
First light (1730)

The coming days were cold and short, and darker in the evenings, I had lots of things to do, get my vegetables up out of the ground before winter set in, get provisions from the village stores, fixing a hole that had appeared in the stable roof because of all the wind, autumn and winter is not a pleasant time for anyone in my position, no money, not much work coming in, I wondered if being a carpenter in this small Village was worth the effort, there was more money to be had being a butcher either, even Arthur said he was struggling with money, still life must carry on or end up in the church yard with no more worries. I'm not that old, still got a few years to go so I shouldn't be thinking such things, life is what you make it no matter what comes your way, I should embrace the chance that's been given to me and make the best of it, I should do it not just for me or Arthur but the whole gang so that we all can get a better life.
The day before we were set to meet, I was woken up by the sound of the cockerel from my neighbour's farm,
"Maybe I'll use the pistol on that cockerel, when I get it" I said aloud, laughing to myself.
The sun was not up yet but leaving a red glow where it would appear just enough to cast a warm red glow through my window, I'm sure that bird was getting earlier, I mumbled to myself.
I managed to find my way in the dimly lit room and light a candle from the dying embers of the fire. I stoked the fire and threw some more wood on it to get it started again, cold in the mornings and cold in the evenings, no good for old bones, still one must survive, that's why we are taking this course of action so that we can get more pleasures out of life.

A quick mouthful of stale bread and a mouthful of mead after a warmup by the fire, then outside to ready the horse. I fed the horse some hay and oats. A smile came to my lips, how funny life is, I thought to myself, the horse gets more for breakfast than I do.

I placed the saddle on the horses back and struggled with the buckles and braces, my fingers now becoming numb with the cold. I was glad that I only had one horse to saddle and not worry about the carts that the others were bringing. Saddle on, I pulled a cover over my head to make sure I was warm, wrapping my coat up, and tucking a scarf inside; my fingerless gloves and scarf that my mother had made for me years ago, although threadbare, were still a blessing in the cold. I mounted my horse that at first seemed to protest but soon settled. I turned to see the sun almost breaking on the horizon and made off towards Rye and the adventures that lay ahead.

I knew it would take me a few hours at a steady trot, and wanted to get there before it got dark, I took with me some bread and a portion of ham and a small bottle of ale, this would see me see me well till I found somewhere to stay in Rye.

I reached Rye, there were lots of people rushing around as it was the day the farmers brought their sheep and cattle to town to be sold and were now rounding up the sheep and cattle that they didn't sell and were heading back out of the town, causing a commotion with the riders and their horses. A few small sailing ships were in the harbour loading up goods, with sailors stitching up a few torn sails, making ready to depart. I could see in the distance the masts of the larger ships that were tied up further out closer to the sea, Rye had silted up so the bigger ships couldn't get close to the town, this meant that there were a lot of people ferrying goods to and from the stores in the town to supply those ships, it was late afternoon and I was now feeling tired, I tied my horse up outside the Olde Bell Inn, as Thomas and Arthur said they were staying at the Mermaid, I thought this might be a lot quieter so that I could get to bed early.

I made my way to the main door of the stone-built Inn and looked up at the bell slightly swinging in the breeze, making me feel cold as the bell was quite heavy, I opened the door to be greeted by a warm fire and a friendly face ushering me in, "
"Hurry and close the door, the wind blows right off the marsh" a woman said from behind the bar.

The Inn looked warm and inviting, a warm light bathed the interior, darker than the Oak and Ivy as the windows were smaller, stale tobacco smoke and the smell of ale filled the air. Behind the bar was a pretty looking woman with long blonde hair wearing a pale blue dress with a scarf around her neck as if trying to keep warm, a man was sweeping up around the fire after placing more wood on it and stoking it with a poker making the embers fly up the chimney.

I walked towards the woman; she was wearing fingerless gloves like mine; these have become popular I thought to myself.

"Do you have any cheap rooms", I asked.

"All our rooms are cheap if you have money", came a sarcastic voice from behind the broom.

I looked round at him then to see he hadn't even looked up from what he was doing.
"Is it just yourself deary", said the woman, with a friendlier voice, as I turned back to face her to see her smiling face.
"yes" I said, "I only want it for the night, and I'll be gone early in the morning ".
"We have a few rooms now, you're lucky, if you'd have come earlier, we wouldn't have had any, because of the people coming to stay so they could buy the animals from the farmers and what with the sailors coming to town and wanting a warm bed after spending the night drinking at the inns.
It's my lucky day I thought to myself.
"that'll be tuppence for the night", She said, "You look frozen, I've got some stew cooking in a pot in the kitchen, would you like some? her voice was soft and comforting.
"How could I refuse from one so lovely as you", I said.
She giggled coyly and I watched as her cheeks turned red at my comment, I saw the man finally look up at me and give me a strange look.
"Go sit down my dear and I'll bring some over to you with a tankard of ale".
"I'll need to bed my horse down for the night first", I said, pointing towards the door,
"That's fine, he will look after your horse and feed him for you, smiling at me, the stable is only next door, Stuart!", She raised her voice at the man with the broom,
"Go and put this nice man's horse in the stable and give him some feed". She raised her voice in a command he knew he shouldn't argue with.
"He rested the broom against the wall as if to continue sweeping up on his return and mumbled to himself whilst putting on his coat and making his way towards the door.
I watch as her slim figure walked into the kitchen to prepare my meal.

I sat down for an extremely hot hearty meal, I must have made an impression on the woman as there was a lot to be eaten and she gave me two tankards of ale as well.
I thanked her for a lovely hot meal and bid her good night then went upstairs to my room.
"You're welcome deary", she said as she watched me climb the stairs.
I woke up very early the following morning, worried that I was going to be late, feeling a little excited, as this was something new, no one else was up at that time so I helped myself to some bread and cheese from the inn's kitchen.
I made my way to the old mill passing the harbour along the way, walking along side my horse, giving him chance to wake up, mist was rolling off the fields and inlet obscuring anything in the distance, I could hear the water lapping up against the boats as I neared the edge, trying to make out anything that resembled humans or horses in the mist. My horse and my own breath were only adding to the mire that was in front of me. The sails were silent at this time of morning and as there was no wind about.
As I continued walking the old mill rose out of the gloom and looked incredibly decrepit with more detail becoming clearer the closer, I got, it's a wonder it ever worked in the condition it was in, most of it being covered in vines. I could hear voices just beyond the mill, and could make out the figure of Arthur as I got closer, Thomas was behind him along with George on a large cart,
"Morning", said Arthur,
"Not a pleasant one", Came a voice from a grey figure sitting on the cart.
"Don't worry; you'll be warm enough once we get started," said Thomas.
"Where's Smoker?" I asked.
Just then a figure on another horse and cart appeared out the mist behind them, followed by two more carts just behind him.

"Me and James have been here for a while", the fog was thicker earlier, the fog might be a problem which we hadn't bargained for, especially when looking for signals on the beach". said Smoker.
"I'm glad we could all make it, there's loyalty", said Thomas looking over at Arthur.
"We've got to meet the others first, let's hope they are at the castle", said Smoker.
"Smoker; pass me that sacking off your cart will you"? said Arthur.
Smoker reached under his seat and passed the sacking to Arthur.
Arthur reached inside the sack and pulled out a pistol and handed it to George.
"I take it you know how to use this"? he said as he passed a pistol to me.
"Yes", I said, as he reached inside the sacking for some leather bags.
"Keeps these dry", he said, "gunpowder, wadding and some shot, everything you need to convince someone you mean business", said Arthur laughing out loud, Thomas and the others joining in.
"Oh, and be careful, they are both loaded, be very careful who you point them at", Thomas said changing the tone.
"Let's head off", we want to be there before the others get there, they won't want to be kept waiting offshore, not in this weather", Arthur said.
We made our way towards Winchelsea and Arthur sent me off towards Camber castle to get the others who had stayed the night there.
Two more members were waiting with George and the carts at the old castle just as Smoker had said.
"Good morning hope you enjoyed your stay", I said.
"Not likely, uncomfortable, dark and scary being here, who chose this place for us to stay", one said as he stomped on the fire that they made to stay warm during the night.

"This was my idea", quipped George, laughing to himself. "Come on, we can't hang about, we've got to catch up with the others.

We set off across the fields towards Winchelsea then along the coastal road towards Fairlight, we managed to pick up some speed as the road was a bit smoother in places and catch up with the others.

Arthur led the way, always showing leadership in the smallest of things, he was someone you could rely on, true to his friends and would help in any way he could, never run in a fight, unheard of, he would be at the front, the first to strike a blow, we could all rely on him especially me being his good friend, he was more like a brother to me, he was always the strongest out of the two of us, always there when I needed him, and when my father died, through his own fault I might add, always drunk, fell off his horse one night coming back from the inn, fell off his horse and hit his head on a rock, no one was sure how long he had been laying there, but when he was found he was stone cold, Arthur said he was always drinking and served him right, he said he died the way he lived, drunk. Arthur just seemed to take to being the head, strong in character, like it was the natural thing to do. He helped me from time to time in looking after my mum now that my father wasn't around. Then one fateful day, my mum wasn't there anymore, she died in her sleep, bless her, never a bad word was said to anyone, she just got on with her daily chores and kept herself to herself. They were buried in the local church next to each other, not sure she would have like that, and in life I'm sure she was unhappy with her relationship with my dad as he was always at the inn. Life goes on and I did what was needed to survive, but it was hard, work was hard to find, and with little money coming to us life was a struggle.

Arthur met me one night in the Mermaid Inn, a few months after my mums passing, he said he had something he wanted to tell me, he had a secret and I should never tell a living soul,

"I've managed to get some money", he said.
"And with it we can buy food to eat", "and maybe, just maybe things will start to look better, we won't have to suffer any longer".

After that Arthur gave me some money to help me buy tools to start a carpentry business and that's what I've been doing ever since, I suppose that will change now.

Maybe this was the start of it all, without me asking questions as to how he came by the money, maybe now he was in with Thomas is how this plans all came about.

Arthur was working as a butcher in Hawkhurst, he's good at it too, having spent several years as an apprentice in Marden, he said it was good to find a proper trade, and learning the skills of a butcher was something he liked doing.

After his apprentice ended, he sold his shop there and returned to Hawkhurst to continue his trade. He did this for a while but confided in me that some men kept coming to the shop in Marden and wanted goods for free and threatening him if he refused. This went on for some time, taking more and more from him, what with high taxes, rent and these people robbing him of his stock. He said the gang, would go around and threaten other storekeepers as well for money and goods, not just Arthur. They took it upon themselves to get things for free, so to speak, maybe that's why he came to Hawkhurst to get away from them and start anew.

They just managed to take what they wanted from the farmers and other people, "they only took what they needed and a little bit extra to sell", he said, "just enough so that we could carry on, not enough to break us ", it made things more difficult than they already were.

I'd forgotten what he told me about the gangs and wondered why he was feeling low about the shop and his trade, they are still doing it to him now in Hawkhurst, now it all begins to make sense, from what Arthur was saying, things could be about to change, for us all.

Time passed quickly, and we were soon nearing our destination, the ground had turned from a muddy dirt track to pebbles, we could hear the waves breaking against the shoreline in the distance. The fog was so thick on the coast, thicker than inland, which was good as our work would go unnoticed, but a problem to see any signals.

"Right Smoker, you wait here with the horses, can't bring them across the pebbles, keep lookout in case anyone comes by", said Thomas.

"Give the horses a little feed to keep them quiet", I said to Smoker.

"Good idea to keep them calm", said Thomas.

We dismounted and left Smoker to tend the horses and keep look out. As Smoker reached for a bag of straw, we trudged across the pebbles, this soon had us warm.

"Wait here", said Arthur, "go and have a look William", he said.

I carried on walking a bit further, the breaking sea getting louder as I approached the shoreline, in the distance I could hear voices, and I could just make out four faint small rowing boats offshore, I looked around to make sure the coast was clear then went back to get the others.

"They are here, and close to the shoreline", I said, "just a little way off, four boats I can just make out. as you said there would be". I said.

Arthur's face lit up with a big grin,

"Good, they have not let us down and managed to not get caught by the customs men", said Arthur.

"George, Will, quick, wade out a bit and get their attention, lighting a fire won't do any good in this fog, bring them in so we can offload the goods", said Thomas.

We all moved further out to meet them and pull the boats closer.

"Any trouble Mr. Glover", Arthur said,

"None at all Mr. Grey", came the reply,

"The sea is like a mill pond due to this fog, ideal for getting from France under cover, lack of a breeze made it slow going though, only problem was just the cold getting into my bones", said Richard.

"No problems in France", said Thomas.

"None, everything is fine", said Benjamin, climbing out of a boat to start unloading.

"Good to see you again Benjamin, glad you could make it, how was Romsey when you left"?

"Romsey is still as quiet as normal, nothing much happens there", said Benjamin, climbing out of the boat.

"Have you two got time to talk? let's get these boats unloaded then we will talk, try and keep the goods out of the water, don't want to spoil anything after all the trouble we have gone through, I want everything off including the rope, be extra careful not to get the ropes wet". Said Thomas in a stern voice.

Arthur turned and called to us to give a hand in unloading. Just then one of the crew members in the boats from the clipper started to shout,

" Come on you lot you are taking too long".

With that Arthur and Thomas drew their pistols and pointed right at him.

"We'll have you quite", said Thomas, as he grabbed him by the hair and pulled him out of the boat.

"you'll do as you are told by us, we bought these goods with good money and you will keep your noise down so as not to attract attention to us", said Thomas, shoving the pistol under the man's chin.

"William, make sure they are not carrying pistols, and get them off them", said Arthur.

I reached inside my coat and pulled out my pistol, walking towards the others in the boat,

Wasn't sure I'd be using it, but they all seemed to open their coats and let me search and take any weapons that they had on them.

"What is your name"? said Thomas, looking at the man he had by the scruff.

"Jenkins", he said, gulping as the pistol pushed further into his flesh.

"Ah, you must be a new crew member working on this ship for your captain", said Arthur.

"Your captain is a good friend of ours, he's a man of trust, loyal, I hope we are not going to have any problems with his crew upsetting things for everyone now, are we"? asked Thomas

"No", said Jenkins,

Arthur looked at Thomas and then the others in the boat.

"Same goes for us too" came voices from the men in the boat.

"I know the rest of you, seen you before, you lot we can trust, this one being new we don't trust yet, I'll be looking to you lot to teach this one the ways of the rest of you", said Thomas not breaking eye contact Jenkins.

Arthur ushered Thomas to lower his pistol.

"If there is any trouble from any of you, then you'll have your captain and us to answer to, do you understand"? said Arthur.

With that Thomas released his grip on Jenkins, he rearranged his coat that Thomas had hold of and stood up, Jenkins held out his hand to Thomas, "you'll have no trouble from me, or any of us, you have my word".

With an unsure look in his eye Thomas took his hand and shook it, still untrusting as he still had his pistol trained at Jenkins.

"Right, you lot," Said Arthur", let's get these boats unloaded, this fog could lift at any time".

The four boats weren't exactly that small and looking at all the barrels, sacking and bales of whatever was in them, that was on board each boat, there didn't look like there was a lot of room to sit comfortably, just enough room to row with not much leg room.

The barrels being small were easy to handle but there was a lot of them, brandy and rum was in most of them, I heard Arthur saying.
We unloaded the goods onto the beach, and now looking at it all, was a pretty pile.
"James, take these pistols and go with Richard Glover to the ship, just for backup, so that we don't get any problems out there with the crew of the ship, oh and explain to the captain as to why we took his crews weapons, I'm sure he'd like to know, we will see you back at the Ivy in a few days' time", said Arthur.
Arthur reached into his inside pocket, pulled out a cloth bag and placed it into James's hands, patted him on the right arm, mumbled something to him, with that he turned, pushed the boats out and jumped in, with a few strokes they were heading away from the shore.
The fog was starting to lift and now I could see moored further out to sea, a small ship that had brought the goods across from Guernsey.
"I told them to head for Ramsgate, they should be there by night fall", said Arthur.
Everything was taken care of, not one detail left out, the ship would head for Ramsgate, do some fishing on the way just to keep the customs quiet in case any questions were asked.
"Come on you lot, let's not stand idly by, we've now got to get this lot onto the carts before this fog lifts, so let's hurry". Said Arthur,
"George, help William lift those half-anchors, its best to put one on each shoulder, helps to carry them better, and don't drop them", said Thomas.
Then we watched Thomas lift two and place one on each shoulder,
"that's how you do it, he makes it looks easy, come on I'll show you", said George,

It took a few attempts to get them balanced on my shoulder, considering there was either rum or brandy moving about inside did make it a bit awkward.

"No problem, ", I said, trying to lift the second one like Thomas.

"When they make these half barrels, they make them, so they can be carried, good job these are only half-anchors, you would be struggling with a full anchors", Thomas laughed.

"Come on you lot, hurry up and load this lot up on the carts", Arthur said looking impatient.

We took several journeys to load the carts, with Smoker, George and Benjamin distributing the loads evenly on the carts, we covered the goods with old sacks and placing the ropes on top, don't know why as there was a lot, couldn't really hide what was on the carts.

"This is a nice haul", I said.

"it's only a small amount", said Arthur.

"No, not that load, this lot", I said as I showed him three swords, three pistols and six knives that I took off the other members of the crew.

"They'll all come in handy", said Smoker, looking at the extras we collected, they all laughed.

"Come on, let's get and hide this lot away", Said Smoker getting impatient.

We finally made our way off the beach, remounted our horses, and disappeared back into the fog that was only patchy now with the sun coming up and casting a warm glow.

"That was the easy part, now we have to get this lot inland without being seen," said George.

"it's good that we have some fog on our side then", said Arthur.

"Yes, don't want anyone seeing what we are doing, but we are ready for them" Thomas said, laughing out loud, patting the side where his pistol was resting.

We started out with a gentle trot heading inland, I pulled alongside Arthur, I asked him why we got so much rope when we could bring our own.
He gave out a belly laugh then started coughing like he was choking.
"That's not rope lad", he said still trying to catch his breath, "that's tobacco, wound to make it look like rope, so as not to raise suspicion, had you fooled too", he said chuckling to himself.
I thought how everything had been thought out down to the last details, it made me wonder just how long they had been doing this without me knowing, I was close to Arthur and even I didn't suspect what he was doing.
After a while we stopped at what looked like a farm somewhere close to Northiam, a remote farmhouse through a small, wooded area, away from prying eyes, nice and secluded. Smoker led the horses with the carts behind a large barn where they were kept quiet with some more hay.
"This is John's farm" Arthur said, "he's an old friend of Smoker and George, he knows we are coming, it's just his wife that doesn't know anything and we'd like to keep it that way".
"Smoker, go and have a look to see if the coast is clear, make sure it is before you come back here, try and get John on his own rather than with his wife", said Arthur.
With that Smoker got off his horse and walked towards the farmhouse.
 The farmhouse looked quite enough, but you could never tell, not from where we were hiding anyway.
Smoker disappeared round the other side of the barn and headed off towards the farmhouse while we kept the horses quiet, Smoker, was an old friend of John's would not raise John's wife's suspicions.
"This is where we are going to store this lot", said Thomas.

John's wife was none too keen on John mixing with Thomas and Arthur, and always showed them a discerning look at them when they were with John, she would have wanted John to turn them away on many occasions, I'm sure if she knew what we were up to she would disapprove.

After a short wait, we heard footsteps approaching, not one but two.

"Good day Arthur", said John.

"Hello John, it's been a while", said Arthur.

"Yes, it has, I can see you have a lot of goods, will you be putting it all in the barn and the outbuildings?" said John, scratching his head, wondering where it would all fit.

"No not all of it, we want to keep some", said Arthur.

John didn't even ask what was in the casks or bags, all he did was what he was asked, that's how Arthur liked things, don't like people being nosey, friends or not.

"We might have some more for you to store for us in a few days' time if that's all right" said Thomas with a grin.

"This lot won't be here long either, we will come along soon to get rid of it for you, that'll stop your wife from moaning," said Thomas with a laugh.

"Well, you are welcome to store whatever you need, and you know me, everything will be kept secret".

"I'm sure it will", said Thomas staring at him with a glare.

"How's you good lady wife, well I hope?", Asked Arthur, quickly changing the subject.

"Yes, she is, but out at present, had to go to Arundel, visiting her sisters who is feeling ill, so she gone to care for her for a few weeks till she is well again".

Thomas, George, Smoker Benjamin had already begun to unload and store some of the goods in the barn and other buildings, "hide it well lads, don't want anyone snooping around and finding anything", "will do Arthur", came the reply.

"We have a little something for you John for helping us, I know your lady wife likes tea, and for you we have some good brandy and rum to help keep out the cold" said Arthur handing him a large leather bag. "You'll also find some tobacco in there too that you ask for".
"Thank you, Arthur, I appreciate that, it's always good doing business with you, will you be needing any payment towards this"? He asked as he tipped his hat to thank him.
"You know that won't be necessary if we are using your barn, you look after us, we look after you, that's the way it will be", said Arthur.
By now the sun was fully up and the fog had cleared, "it's turned out nice now", said George,
"It's about time, I was frozen this morning by the sea", I said, sending a shiver through my bones thinking about it.
"You should feel what it's like out at sea then ", said Benjamin.
"No thanks" said George rubbing his hands together.
 "It's one of those days where you just can't seem to get warm", "I'm better now unloading these spoils", said George,
"Hurry up you lot", said Arthur,
"We still have to get back; we are meeting the others tonight for a little celebration at the Mermaid".
"A celebration for what"? asked Smoker.
"For a successful haul, this is just the start, the loads will be bigger, and we will have to be more cunning so as not to get caught, so we are celebrating tonight and I want a few others in on this, as we get bigger loads then we will need more people to help us, a lot more people", grinned Arthur,
"I take it we will have the pleasure of your company tonight Benjamin, as a matter of fact, you can stay with me for a few days before you go back to Romsey", enquired Arthur.
Benjamin had been friends with Arthur and Thomas for many years, but as he lived in Romsey didn't get to see each other much.

"That's kind of you, of course I'll be there, wouldn't miss a good drink with good company, and thanks for the offer, I was wondering where I was going to be sleeping", said Benjamin.

All the goods had been stored in John's farm buildings, they had done a good job in concealing it, even John would have had trouble finding it and it was his farm.

"If your wife won't be coming home for a while you are welcome to come to the Mermaid tonight John, we would like your company", said Arthur.

"I might just do that, maybe after finishing the farm chores that I have to do, I could do with a drink and maybe a hot meal from the Inn, that'll save me cooking anything".

John bid us all a farewell and turned and walked back to his farmhouse.

Arthur climbed back on his horse.

"This is to all of you, make sure you are there tonight at the Mermaid, I've got some plans that I want to go over with you all for another job that's coming up, and I think this one will give us a bigger haul", said Arthur, with his authoritarian voice.

"We will be there", was the murmur from the others.

"A celebration is called for after today, a good job done by you all, it would be good to celebrate, this job had gone well, kind of keeping our new gang happy and trying some of the spoils as well", Said Thomas.

With that we parted company and headed off in different directions to not arouse suspicions now the sun was up, my mind was now in thought for the evening's celebrations.

The afternoon sun was slowly beginning to lose the little warmth that it had as I made off towards Peasmarsh so I could pick up a few supplies then onto Rye.

I finally I made my way back to Rye, the wind had picked up and I could taste the salt in the air as I neared the town, my clothes already covered in salt from being in the sea this morning and still felt damp and rubbing against my legs as I rode. I could see the lanterns tied to the masts of ships that were in the harbour. The road was dusty and long and all I could think about was getting some ale down inside me to rid me of the dust, dirt, and salt. After what seemed like hours and saddle sore from riding all day it was good to be back in Rye again, I could pay a visit to the Olde Bell Inn and see that bar maid, I thought to myself, then thought it might cause trouble between her and her husband, she did look nice though, maybe, I laughed to myself. The church on the hill was a sight for sore eyes, things were quiet in the town as I made my way through the cobbled streets, just the odd sailor going about his business, less boats in the harbour and the few shops that were there had closed and most of the townsfolk had gone to the warmth of their homes. The suns heat had now gone and its was setting behind the harbour, creating silhouettes of the masts, a cool breeze was blowing in from the sea and the cold was now digging into my hands, making it hard to keep hold on the reins. The houses that I passed with their candle lit windows were my only source of heat, thinking how nice it would be to be in front of an open fire right now, and not out here in the crisp evening air. I knew that the Inn was close to the church, not long now, I thought to myself as I started to climb the cobbled street towards the Mermaid Inn the road narrowed as I neared the inn. I could still hear in the distance the blacksmith toiling away on his anvil, finishing off his days' work from the last of the dying embers of his furnace, I think my horse was stepping in time to his hammering. For me, my day was done, I was saddle sore and couldn't wait to have a drink. Parched, tired, a drink and a rest would keep me in good stead, if I were lucky there might still be some food left. The inn keeper always had something on the go knowing one or more of us would turn up. This was one of our favourite inns, we always get a good gathering of friends. It is the one Inn that Thomas liked best, probably because of its location, right close to the sea, he could easily make some money selling goods that the sailors were keen to buy. As I drew into the courtyard, I could see Arthur's, Smoker's, and George's horse and a few more already tethered, and from what I could hear celebrations were already under way.

I tied my horse up against a hook on the wall, untied the saddle with my cold fingers fighting with the buckles and straps, and removed it and placed it in a storeroom at the back of the inn, kept for regulars.

I made sure my horse was given a good feed with plenty of water to drink before heading on inside.

I climbed the small steps leading up to the inn door, my cold hands trying to move the latch and get it to open. The door was heavy and made of solid oak, it creaked open to a welcoming scene.

It seems that in my absence celebration were well under way, I couldn't wait to get close to the fire before I did anything else, I needed warming up before I too could enjoy myself. All the gang were here, none were missing, except for the poor souls heading out at sea towards Ramsgate, I'm sure anyone else would have regretted it if they had, or at least Arthur would have made his feelings about it known. "A friend is a friend and should be treated as such, and enemy is exactly that and has no place with us, no place at all". I heard Arthur say.

I was starting to warm up, mostly because of the atmosphere in the inn, it was great to see everyone, although there were a few faces that I didn't recognise. I managed to find a stool to sit on and get a bowl of stew at a table close to Arthur, just what I needed I thought, I sat eating it with a large lump of bread and very tasty too and a nice tankard of ale. A young boy kept looking towards where we were all sitting and at Arthur, he moved across the floor to where Smoker was and started talking to Smoker, a young lad by the look of him no more than a teenager, hardly got to the age of shaving.
This didn't go unnoticed, as I could see Thomas was watching him.
"I think I've seen him taking an interest in us when we were here before, not sure what he is up to, I think we should keep an eye on him, never can trust people when they start to ask questions", said Thomas.
"Benjamin, come here", Shouted Thomas above the noise Benjamin came over to Thomas and he whispered into Benjamin's ear, then Benjamin turned, looked around then walked over to where Smoker was standing.
"You worry too much Thomas, relax and enjoy your ale, enjoy yourself and make merry, we've all earned it", said Arthur, his heavy hand slapping me on the back then dinging his big fingers into my shoulder, catching me off-guard, as I started to choke on the mouthful of bread I'd just eaten.
The night worn on with everyone drinking and singing, eventually, things began to quieten down, and the locals and sailors left, leaving the Inn to ourselves.
Thomas called everyone over and after filling our tankards again we gathered around where Arthur and Thomas were sitting.
"I'm glad we are all here, and I'm glad to see you could make it as well John". Said Arthur.
John lifting his tankard as a way of acknowledgement.

"We've had a good day and we've found buyers for all the goods; Thomas and George Kingsmill are going to London with a few carts loaded of goods from John's farm to be sold so we will all be getting some well-earned money", this was met with cheers and laughter from everyone.
"It doesn't stop there", he said.
"We've got another job lined up", he said, taking a large mouthful of ale,
"Ale better this time", I said, remembering the other day.
"Much better, not that I can taste it much as this is my sixth one", Arthur said laughing out loud.
"This time I'm putting William here in charge, it's about time you branched out, showed us what you can do." he said, with a grin on his face.
"I'm putting my trust in you", he said looking down at me.
"I know I can trust you in this matter and that you'll take care of it, and I want everyone to follow Will's orders, is that clear"?
A murmur came from the crowd, "We are with you Will", said George from the back.
"All of you gather round closer and listen carefully, we have another ship coming in with goods from France arriving at Dungeness two days from now. Arthur said filling his pipe with tobacco, probably from the goods we brought in this morning I thought smiling to myself.
I have already organised as to who's going with you, there's around Ten of you,
"Ten", I said,
 "Yes, there will be four carts, and this should be enough to carry all the goods, and I want them all to be brought back to John's farm again, as before, with his wife still away at her sisters, we can divide the goods in his barn, away from prying eyes and move it to different locations later, we also got buyers for what's coming in and I can't let them down, I take it this is still fine John", said Arthur, trying to find John in the crowd.

"Yes, all is good, never been better, she's still away and as Thomas is taking goods out this will make room for more to come in", said John.

"You've all got pistols so if you get any trouble, you'll know what to do", said Thomas, staring down to me as if he didn't need to say anymore.

"I can trust you William, you've always been a loyal friend, so don't let us down on this. We would be there to help you, but we have got to be elsewhere organising other shipments that we want brought over from Jersey and Guernsey, so will be away for a few days, and with Thomas taking the other goods to London for sale that'll mean someone stepping up and being in charge, that's why we are choosing you". Said Arthur.

"I was going to ask why you are putting me in charge, but now I know", I said looking at the others fooling around and getting louder as they made merry.

"The drink is getting to them, more drink for everyone", Arthur shouted to the inn keeper, hoping he would hear him above the noise.

"Come on lad, he said, drink up and get some more ales in", Arthur and Thomas laughing loudly now.

The night wore on and we all drank till the early of the morning. The inn keeper said we could sleep in the spare rooms that they had upstairs; this was far more comfortable than what I was used to. In my little house, I can't find comfort, the rain comes in through the roof when it rains, the wind howls through the cracks in the doors, windows broken and need fixing, when I can find the time.

The evening wore on and I managed to escape the din that was going on downstairs, it's been a long day and I finally got to my room, my head spinning from the ale, I took off my shoes and fell onto the bed, I could still hear the voices of the others as they sat talking and laughing downstairs. The warmth of the bed clothes soon had me drifting off to sleep, with thoughts of what Arthur had been telling me.

The next morning, I awoke feeling hungry, and realising that with all the excitement the night before, I hadn't eaten much just a small amount of stew.
I put my shoes on and run some water through my hair to make me look a bit more respectable.
I went downstairs to find that Arthur and Thomas were already up and eating what looked like ham and eggs by the big log fire, watching them made me even more hungry.
"Would you like some food"? came a voice from behind the bar, my wife is cooking in the back if you want some", he said.
"Yes please, I'm starving", feeling my mouth was dry as well, "and a mug of tea if you have any please", knowing Thomas would have already given some to the Innkeeper, as this was his regular.
"How are you William, did you enjoy yourself last night"? asked Arthur.
"Yes, I enjoyed it a lot, it's good to catch up with old friends", I said looking at them.
"Aye, that it is lad", Arthur said running a lump of bread through his egg.
"You two look like you haven't been drinking at all, you were drinking ale last night, I'm sure of it", I said, looking at them as if the alcohol the night before hadn't affected them.
"We are used to it", said Thomas, laughing.
"When you've drunk as much as we have, you'd be used to it too", laughed Arthur, finishing off his mouthful of bread. "I'll chat with you later with more details as to what we spoke of last night after you've eaten something, as you look a bit pale", he said, continuing to laugh.
I left them to carry on eating as the bar keeper brought a large helping for me from the kitchen, two eggs, a thick slice of ham and bread, a mug a tea made from our stock of tea, I thought to myself.
I felt satisfied and fully refreshed and with a full belly and sat down next to Arthur.

"You wanted to fill me in with more details about Dungeness", I said

"Yes, William I do", he reached into his pocket and handing me a scrap of paper.

"Don't lose this, here is a list of all that we expect from the shipment in Dungeness tomorrow. Take Smoker, George, James, and Perrin, he's arrived here from Fordingbridge, he's going along to help while he's over here with us, take them and the others that Smoker has organised. They all know what to do anyway, just be careful and bring our goods back to John's farm as instructed", said Arthur.

"Arthur, you can trust me, I won't let you down", I said.

"I know I can lad, I know I can", Arthur said putting his big hand on my shoulder as a mark of acknowledgement.

Just then a woman came into the Inn and asked about her son, she was looking distraught, she was speaking to the inn keeper, I heard her say his name Simon James, she hasn't seen him since last night and he hasn't been home from what in could hear from their conversation.

"Isn't that the fellow that was talking with Smoker last night", I said to Thomas.

He just raised a finger to his lips so that I made not another sound.

She rushed out the door in tears, unable to get any information about her son.

The day was peaceful after that as I watched our friends slowly wake up from wherever they lay and meet again at the bar.

"Get yourself sorted and organised, we want you to be prepared for Dungeness, chat with Smoker and George to work out where you're going to meet up", said Arthur.

"Just make sure they are not drunk, I want them turning up fresh as well", I said.

"Don't worry you'll be fine", said Arthur. he must have seen me looking anxious.

"Here and take this with you", he said handing me a leather pouch of coins.

"Thanks Arthur, I could do with some as my purse is near empty", I said holding the pouch in my hands.

"This is a small payment to be handed to James Sutherland who you'll be meeting tomorrow, he'll be one of the sailors on the boat, give it to no one else, and a little something for yourselves along the way", Arthur said placing another small pouch in my hands wrapping his big hands around mine.

I spoke to Smoker to work out the finer details together, to meet at Lydd in a days' time with the carts at the ready, we would make sure that the goods would be delivered safely.

We stayed for a few more ales in the Mermaid before we all started to go our own way and drift our way home.

George, James, and Perrin and the others had already saddled up, and had left.

Now was my turn, I looked at Thomas and Arthur who were deep in conversation, probably planning what they both had to do, I said goodbye to them, but they couldn't have heard me. I had other things to worry about, the fact of putting me in charge of the next job rather than one of the others, but as he said, he can trust me, I hope that trust is not misplaced, and I can get the goods delivered safely back to john's farm. The first job yesterday had gone smoothly and I for one wanted the same with the Dungeness job under my charge.

I got outside, there was a heavy frost, the pathways were white, another cold ride home I thought, oh well, better get going.

The day went slowly, but tried to keep myself busy, I thought I'd have a go at fixing the hole in my roof, but on closer inspection it required more items than I had lying about, another trip to Hawkhurst would have to wait till after we had this Dungeness job was out of the way, plus I wouldn't be able to concentrate on making the job as good as I'd have like with my thoughts being elsewhere, I decided to go back in the house, relax by a warm fire and think of the coming events.

I got up early the following day and made my way towards Lydd to the arranged meeting point with Smoker, nothing to eat, just water to drink, I couldn't eat, I was far too worried. What if we got caught, what if they didn't turn up, everything was racing through my mind?

I must have been keen as I was the first to arrive, I made myself comfortable while I waited. I checked to make sure my pistol was loaded with the gunpowder and wadding in place, I checked my bag of wadding and the shot several times just to make sure, never can be too careful, and always be prepared I thought to myself.

I wondered if I could ever use it against another person or just use it as a threat, I'd never really handled a pistol before so wasn't so sure, although it worked fine without firing it at Fairlight.

Just then I heard Smokers and Perrins voice coming along the road and behind them the others.

"Morning, I can see we are all here", I said".

"Morning" said all the others.

"Let's be off, we want to get there before the boats arrive", I said mounting up on my horse.

"Just before we leave, make sure your pistols are loaded, you never know what to expect, the last time at Fairlight I thought the crew members were going to turn on us, so never trust anyone where there's money to be gained", I said, sounding like a voice of authority.

It was a short time before we arrived at Dungeness, looking out to sea we could see four boats heading inland.

"They must be for us", said James, pointing out to sea.

"Let's get down there and meet them, and get the goods loaded up onto the carts", said James.

This was a pebble beach making the way across to the boats with the horses and carts hard work, so we left them with Perrin to look after and to use him as a lookout, as there was no fog to hide us from anyone, but Dungeness is so secluded no one will see us anyway, probably why Arthur chose this spot to bring the goods ashore, I thought to myself.
"This is going to be hard work across these pebbles, so let's put your backs into it and get those carts loaded, and let's be quick about it, I don't want this to take all day", I said.
Smoker looked at me, "You're doing good, you'll be fine handling this lot", he laughed.
After several journeys back and forth all the goods were loaded on to the carts, one of the men came over to me.
"I take it you must be Will? you seem to be the one in charge here", he said.
"And you must be James Sutherland", I said holding out my hand, as a greeting.
"You have something for me", he said looking me up and down while shaking my hand, not knowing what to expect.
I reached inside my coat to find the leather pouch that Arthur had given me and handed it to him,
"It's nice doing business with you", I said not letting go of the pouch.
"Any messages for Arthur or Thomas", I said, before letting him have the pouch.
"No", he said, all is good, he said, touching his hat and tipping his head.
"Till next time", he said with a smile, then turned and made his way cross the beach to the waiting boats.
We made our way off the beach and headed again towards Northiam with another successful haul. All seemed to go smoothly, Arthur for one would be pleased with the way that was handled, I'm sure he'd be happy to put me in charge again, all that worrying I was doing, and it was that easy I thought to myself.

This was very much the way things went for a while, a few years had passed, and what turned out to be a small part time enterprise has turned into a big business, just as Arthur had predicted. More goods were brought in from France and wherever he could purchase goods and sell it on for a profit, the gang had grown now to more members than I could name and from all over the south and according to Arthur we even had contacts as far down as Dorset.

We sold wool from the farmers here on the marsh and got a good price for the wool over in France and Belgium, even that was heavily taxed by the government, so we did the farmers a favour and kept a lot of the proceeds for ourselves, well we weren't going to work for nothing. We had buyers in London and all around and as far north as Norfolk and beyond, places I'd never heard of all wanting to pay our prices for our goods to avoid paying the kings taxes.

We were all doing well now, and we also sorted out the lot that kept threatening Arthur in his shop and the people of the village, they were rogue members of the Hastings gang, trying to go it alone, let's just say that Arthur Thomas, Dimond, Smoker, James and a few others had lain in wait one day when these men came round demanding money, seems a really nice time was had setting about them and from what I heard and few broken bones in the process, possibly one person seemed to lose his life in the process, to be honest that did serve them right, I'm sure they got the message and won't be bothering us again. I was happy to see George in some better clothes for a change, no string tied round his stomach, you now had to look twice just to make sure it was him. My larder was better stocked, and I'd got someone to in to retile my barn as the roof was beyond repair, money seems to roll in from all quarters. Villagers were now on our side too, as they were reaping the rewards from the goods that we were bringing in and selling to them, they were enjoying lower prices that we were charging, no tax to pay so everyone was happy, and people said they would help us wherever they could, which made the Hawkhurst gang as we became known and its members something you'd want to keep secret. This life was much better just as Arthur had said, but it wasn't all easy, we still had to be wary. Difficult I know from the size that we'd grown to, but we had to take care so as not to draw the attraction of the customs men that were in the area. Word had got around that they were interested in a large gang residing in Kent and would have liked to have caught anyone who would have information to catch us in the act of smuggling, but we always seemed to be one step ahead of them, had to be, with the threat of a noose tightening around your neck made us tougher and more careful than ever. And one person kept getting too close and causing us more problems than we needed, that person is our old friend, riding officer Thomas Carswell. He had successfully caught a few of our members and members from the Hastings gang and were now spending time in gaol, to make it worse he's also stolen from us on several occasions our goods that we had bought and paid for, so now we were after him just as much as he was after us, basically he had to go.

Chapter 3
Etchingham (**1740**)

We got a message from a rider that Arthur wanted to see us at the Ivy as soon as we could.
I saddled up my horse and made my way over to Hawkhurst. "Come in Will", said Arthur from his favorite place in the inn, "come in have some ale".
Arthur was sitting with Thomas, Smoker, James, George Stamford, Diamond, Benjamin Tapner and Barnett Woolett.
"We've got another job for you lot, Thomas and I are going to busy, we've got to go to London to sell some goods to a new buyer there he's got a lot of money and a lot more connections so we are both going to seal a deal that could make us more money than ever, so listen carefully, but you don't need to worry yourself about that", he said puffing on his pipe.
"We have some goods stored in a barn in Etchingham, there's quite a lot, enough to make us a lot of money, I want you lot and a few others to go down there and bring it back to the Ivy and Oak as we've got another buyer in London for all of it, take whoever you need, I reckon about fifteen of you need to go, make sure you are all armed with pistols and a few blunderbusses and sharpen your swords just in case of trouble, again I want you to be in charge Will, I hope you can handle that many"? said Arthur
"That's no problem, with Smoker, Diamond, George and James there with me we should be fine in handling it all", I said.
I've known James Stanford for about four years now, we get on well together, a trusted friend of Arthur and Thomas, someone you could rely on in a fight, strong, and has proved himself many times within the gang.

"Smoker and Benjamin, I want you to round up a few others to go with you, you'll need a few carts, about five should be enough for the goods we've got down there with a few hands loading it up to bring it back here, the items have been there for a few days now, it's time to move it and get it back here before it's found, wouldn't want that would we", said Arthur.

"No, that would be the last thing we want, why has it taken so long to get it back here"? I asked.

"We've engaged the services of Captain Clay who with his cutter, he has arrived with goods along the coast and the goods have already been transported to Etchingham it's taken a lot of organising for me with the help of Thomas and the Hastings gang". Arthur said, looking straight at me.

"They could have brought it straight to here, I said looking at them puzzled.

"That was the plan, but customs men were seen along the road, so they diverted over to Etchingham and stored it there instead so we could pick it up.

"One of our fellow members from Etchingham said that that more customs men were also seen in the surrounding area, so we just laid low till now, but our contact in London said that they want it as soon as we can get it there, so we have got to get it moved, transported to London and sold, It's taken a lot of organising and money to get these goods in the country, so at first light in the morning I want you to be in Etchingham to collect it and get it here as quick as you can, got to meet up with my brother George and get it to him, he is going to London in two days to get it sold, so, you will be in charge, make sure you get it all, I don't want anyone else getting their hands on it". Said Thomas, taking over where Arthur left off.

"We have joined forces with a few members of the Hastings gang now, getting more members all the time, they are with us now, we don't expect any trouble from them, between us and them we have managed to get more tea, whiskey, brandy, silks, tobacco, and a few kegs of rum and from France and Guernsey. As I said, we've put everything into this, so we don't want things to go wrong", said Arthur, looking sternly.
"Can that lot from Hastings be trusted? I know the problems you had with them in the past, I for one don't want anything to do with them, I don't like them and certainly don't trust them", I said.
"After the rouge ones were sorted out the rest of the members thought better of going against us, our reputation has grown bigger than they could ever be so some have decided to come with us, and as a result the Hastings gang are practically no more.
"Here", said Arthur, placing a crumpled piece of paper into my hand, "
don't worry too much about the Hastings gang, they are fine with us now, this is a list of what we have and where to find it, it was hidden safely in and around the village, but we've had to move some of it to different location and that list shows where they were and where they are now, most is stored in one barn, that couldn't be helped, just too many nosey people prying into our affairs so it was moved to make it safer, just go around to the other locations and make sure we got it all".
Said Arthur.
"A cutter can carry a lot…was it full", I asked.
"It was enough", he said laughing out loud.
"That's not funny, leaving most of it in one barn, that's taking a big risk, and you're saying about customs men in the area, our necks are on the line on this one, we've also got to get it back here without being seem, this is too much of a risk", I said, I couldn't believe my ears, here I was raising my voice to Arthur and Thomas.

"We have been doing a lot of business lately with our friends from France and while the opportunity is there, we are going to take it, there's only about five cart loads worth of goods stored down there, so it shouldn't be a problem for you all, get that lot loaded, gather the rest from around the village and get it back here for George to take to London, should be an easy task for you lot. The Hastings gang have done their bit, they offloaded the goods from the cutter and got it as far to Etchingham, where they hid it all, so you might meet a few of them while you are there, now it's up to you, to finish what was started, they don't have the contacts in London like we do, so we've struck an accord with them over this one, this time, they helped pay for the goods, they helped offload, we do the rest, business is business, we have to expand plus it limits the risk if the goods are found, we only lose half".
Arthur said not raising his voice in response to mine.
"I take it the word has already gone out to the other members from Etchingham to keep a look out for any customs men and report back"? I said.
"Yes, all been taken care of, there's a few members keeping guard over it and in and around the village right now till you get there tomorrow.
All you have to worry about is getting the goods back here and we'll do the rest", said Arthur, his voice a little calmer.
"Right, let me have a look at the list and go through it with me", I said, with this Arthur pulled out his pipe to fill it with tobacco and handed me the list to look at.
I glanced over the list to see what goods we should be expecting.
"Someone is bound to see us with this amount of goods", I said looking at the list.
"Not many people saw us hiding it", said Thomas with a laugh.
"Don't worry no one will talk if they know what's good for them", said Arthur, now drawing smoke through his pipe.

"I think we are well known enough now that no one's going to say a word, if they know what's good for them", said Thomas taking over while Arthur was puffing on his pipe.
"Yes, Smoker laughed, "should do by now, he said playing with Arthur's smoke with his fingers.
"All we have to do is threaten them", said Smoker.
"Yes, but someone was poking their nose into our affairs in the first place to make you move it into that barn so obviously the threats are not working". I said.
"threaten" said Arthur, removing the pipe from his lips halfway through sucking on it.
"We will make no idle threats with these people, we will burn down their house with their families still in it, farmers will get their barns burnt down to if they go against us, I want people to get the message that we are in business, and we mean business, they will not go against us or refuse us again", said Arthur his voice louder and his face turning red, and then puffing faster on his pipe.
"Whoever it is that's been sniffing around our business, we will find them, and wo betide what will happen to them, they will regret the day they heard the name Hawkhurst gang. If they do or attempt to go to the magistrate or customs, they won't see their family members again, that's for sure, they will learn the hard way, so while you are there ask around to see if you can come up with a name, we will make them pay", Thomas said finishing off the sentence for Arthur, so he could compose himself again.
"Go and get me another ale William, get that lazy bartender working his arm pouring me another ale, get yourself one as well, as a matter of fact get us all an ale, lets cheer ourselves up, we deserve it, a big day tomorrow, more goods to be had, more money", said Arthur.

I suppose we had to be ruthless, it's us or them and we were not going to let people get away with refusing us or looking into our business, besides, we gave them a little something if they keep our goods hidden and say nothing, we looked after them, a little payment for their help, we get more than enough to share it around, we were getting more people on
our side, so they didn't talk, it is better to have them as friends rather than enemies, and they really wouldn't want to make enemies of us that's for sure, but, I thought, there's always going to be someone that will think he knows better, and whoever it is, is going to suffer the consequences.
The door opened and I saw some more friendly faces coming in. Arthur got up and went to talk to them, I could hear them laughing as the barkeeper served them their ale, reliving old tales I expect. There were a few new faces in the group, only heard about them from Arthur and Thomas, and I think if I'm right, these were the other part of the gang from Hastings as I heard one of the names as they came in, Jeremiah, they must have been the extra men that Arthur was talking about.
Arthur came over to me. "This is Jeremiah, he's going with you tomorrow so he can see how we handle things, he's from the Hastings gang, so he won't know any of you lot, but after a day with you all he'll get to know you all better, so you do as William says tomorrow, they'll look after you Jeremiah", Said Arthur.
Jeremiah didn't look too much from what I saw, a little bit skinny perhaps, looks like he could do with a good feed, but we would look after him and make sure he didn't get into any trouble.
Everything was going well; I could see that everyone was enjoying the atmosphere with the celebrations going on long into the night.
The barkeeper said that we could sleep in the stables behind the inn rather than get home in the dark, which has happened many times before and was always welcomed.

Finding a place to sleep in such a small stable with about 30 drunken men wasn't going to be easy, but the night wore on and the drink took its toll and sleep finally got the better of us. We were up early the following day, as we were ordered to do. James had already saddled his horse and was eating what looked like some left-over bread and a leg of chicken he found in the kitchen from the night before. He had already got five other men together from what I could see in the dark, they were just waiting for me.

"Did you manage to sleep last night James after the celebrations", I asked.

"I did, but slept in the barn behind the Inn, we couldn't all fit in that small stable, beside all that snoring would have kept us awake from what we could hear, it was shall we say, more comfortable, mostly because the girl who works in the bar came in as well", James said with a grin, showing his black teeth in the dim light.

" Well done James for getting with the bar maid". A cheer went up from all the others.

I could just make out, George, Poison from the Hastings gang and Smoker and a lot of other familiar faces in the gloom, hunched over the saddles on their horses as if to extend their rest time.

"I thought there were going to be more members coming", I said.

"There are, we will meet them in Hurst Green at the start of the ridgeway track, on the way, it's all been organised", said George.

I'm in charge and seem to be the last to know, would be nice to get all the information before any events, I thought to myself.

I could see a dim glow on the horizon, a glow from the sun trying to make its way up and push the night away.

"Come on, we have to be in Etchingham, so we need to get going", said James, as I was just finding my foot in the stirrups.

"Don't worry, we'll get there in good time". I said, getting myself comfortable in the saddle.

"Did Arthur tell you where we need to go"? I asked James, as he seemed to know more than me.

"Don't worry, he gave me a list as well and told me everything before he got drunk, he said he'd tell me as well just in case anything happened to you, he wants to make sure nothing happens and we get the goods back here no matter what, you still have your list"? asked James.

I patted my chest to where I put the list.

We both started laughing about Arthur getting drunk as we made our way into the gloom.

"Jeremiah, I called out, "stick close to me"!

Just as we left the village a rider came towards us at full gallop, stopping in time to just catch his breath.

"It's about time you got here, as Carswell and his men are in the village, asking questions", said the rider, trying to keep his horse under control.

This was not what I wanted to hear, my first thought was, we've lost the goods, the others won't be happy, then the thought of the noose around our necks if we went any further and tried to get it back, my mind was racing.

"We should go back and get Arthur or Thomas to help", said Smoker.

"No! We are too far now, we can still go there, they don't know us, if they find any goods, they won't know it's ours", said James.

"You're right James, and they may not find anything", I said, still with my mind thinking of how we can get out of this.

"All depends on who's been talking", said Jeremiah.

They could see the worried look on my face, if someone has been talking then we would have to deal with them too.

"Good, we will ride in Etchingham and see what's happening then we can formulate a plan when we find out more". I said.

We carried on along the Ridgeway track to join with the other members and who had extra carts then peeled off across the fields leaving the carts to take the road into Etchingham to reduce the number of us and not raise suspicions.

We stopped in a field overlooking the village by a small clump of trees, the sun was breaking through and giving off a little heat, not many people were up or about at this time of the morning, just the shopkeepers going about their business and preparing their shops. I pulled out the list to find out where the barn was located, we heard the carts arrive and enter the village, and stop at a trough so they could give water to the horses. I studied the list and map trying to get our bearings from where we were, we couldn't see any of Carswell's men so we made our way into the village and onto Oxenbridge lane junction as directed on the map, we could see in the distance the farm where the barn was where Arthur said most of the goods would be stored. Just then we saw some figures moving around in red jackets along the road by the farm.

"Dragoons! quick get off your horses, Poison said, "We don't want to be seen".

"They are looking in the barn, the goods have been found by the dragoons", said James, trying to keep his voice low.

"What is Arthur going to say", came a voice from behind.

"It doesn't matter what Arthur says, if they have found it then we need to get it back", I said, thinking of what action to take, seems I was more fearful of Arthur and Thomas than I was of a few dragoons.

"We can't take on the dragoons, there are too many of them for us to take on, and you've never fired your pistol yet, do you think you will", said James.

"I'm hoping not to find out, but to get the goods back might leave us with no choice", I said with a worried look on my face that I didn't want the others to see.

"let's wait and watch to see what happens", then we can decide what to do, it's too far to get help from Arthur so we are on our own", I said.

"Poison, come here, I want you to get closer and see if they find anything, keep low and don't get seen, make a note of how many red coats there are, I take it you can count", I said, taking command of the situation.

"Oh, I can count", said Poison, staring through the bushes, trying to make a rough count from his position.

We hid the horses in a small wood so that we didn't get noticed, Poison moved off on foot to get a closer look.

"Arthur is not going to be happy if we don't get those goods", said James worryingly.

"I know, our only hope is that it's not found, or they decide to leave it there and go to get more men to collect later, leaving a smaller guard that we can tackle, that's what I'm hoping for, he'll be more annoyed if one of us are caught, I would like to find out who it was who told the dragoons", said Smoker, pulling out a knife.

"Let's not rush to conclusions, let's see what Poison has to say, they might only be a few or just using it to rest, or just passing through, we can worry about revenge later, if it comes to that", I said.

With my words came Poison, now out of breath.

"They've got it, they have found what we've come for, they could have found the other stash too as it's been loaded on to four carts and fifteen dragoons from what I could see" He exclaimed.

"And", he said catching his breath.

"It's our old friend riding officer Thomas Carswell". Said Poison, we all listened intently wanting Poison to hurry and explain.

"I've heard of him, but never seen him", I said.

He's not a person to be messed with, good with a pistol and very good with a sword, we're no match for him or fifteen dragoons, we've had a lot of encounters with him in the past with us from Hastings, he could get us hanged if we ever got caught by him and his dragoons, always sniffing around where he is not wanted, he's a nasty piece of work, if your guilty or not you'll get hanged, he loves his job", said Poison, shuffling around anxiously.

"it's not good, this is not good at all", Poison went on mumbling to himself.

We looked at each other, thinking what to do next, almost lost for words, torn between taking on the dragoons or telling Arthur the goods have been taken.

"I'm sure they'll be heading back to Hastings with the goods as Carswell has an office there", said Poison.

"Quick James go back to Hurst Green and round a few more gang members, you know their whereabouts around there so you're the best one, get them and we'll meet up outside Hurst Green, if they are headed towards Hastings, we could head them off, but keep out of sight, follow them to see where they go and we will meet up along the way", I said.

"Are you thinking of taking on the dragoons? that's not a good idea, let's just follow keeping them in our sights at a distance while we wait for you, south of Hurst Green", said James looking worried.

"I don't know what I'm going to do yet, what Poison says about this man that he shouldn't be messed with, plus he's got those dragoons with him so doesn't look good does it? but we do have the advantage that we know where they are going, hopefully, and they don't know we are here, so we have an advantage and the element of surprise, it's just whether we have the courage to take them on and get our goods back", I said trying to summon my own courage.

With that James run into the woods where the horses were being kept, after a few moments was galloping across the fields towards Hurst Green.

"Poison, take two others go check for the rest of the goods in the village, here's the list of where everything is hidden, take three carts, load them up and we'll meet you back in Hawkhurst, oh and if you can ask around to see if anyone knows anything, you might get someone to offer information with a little persuasion, to find out if anyone's been talking, Carswell wasn't here through luck". I said, looking through the bushes at the dragoons.

If James comes back with more members, he knows better than anyone to where the other gang members live in the village, if he could round up a enough of them we might stand a chance, this was risky to say the least, I was thinking to myself, we could lose men, dragoons are armed with swords and pistols, we all have pistols and many of us carry knives and swords and thankfully Arthur said to take a few blunderbuss's with us, but could we really take on dragoons, are the men up to it, there's not a lot of us, but are we ready to fight against trained dragoons?

The sun was now fully up, and we could see in the distance that the dragoons were now riding off with three carts and what we could make out they were fully loaded and covered in sacking.

We moved to get our horses, as we were running, I asked Poison how many dragoons there were,

"About twelve, fifteen, maybe more couldn't really see them all, some were still in the barn when I came away", said Poison, becoming out of breath.

"Get going and look for the rest of the goods", I said to Poison.

"Good Will, you'll be fine, you are definitely outnumbered if you try to get the goods back", he said, then he headed in the other direction keeping low as he went.

Our hearts were beating faster as we now kept the dragoons in sight but at a good distance.

We entered Hurst Green, and we could still see Carswell's party in the distance, moving at a steady pace heading towards Hastings as Poison suspected.

I was getting worried that James wouldn't be able to get many of the gang to help us, we needed them now, I would be more comfortable if we had more on our side if we did decide to take them on.

With Hurst Green behind us we wondered how long it would be before they spotted us.

"If we can't take them on and get our goods back, we can see where they will store the goods and maybe get more of us to get them back at a later date", I said to Smoker.

"That's one option, but Arthur said he's got to get them back so George Kingsmill can get it to London for the buyer, George, Arthur and Thomas won't be too pleased if we lose a buyer", said Smoker.

"We need James back here, I shouldn't have sent them to Hurst Green to round up more of the gang, we are now down on numbers, it'll be foolish to take on Carswell", I said to Smoker.

"And you sent Poison with two others to round up the other goods", said Smoker.

He looked at me with a worried look, not wanting to be in my position, but willing to help with ideas, whatever I decided this wasn't going to end well for us, would we ever see our goods again, would James help us somehow, I knew that some of us would be killed if we confronted them head on, it was at this thought I wished someone else was in charge, to make the decisions.

I wondered where James had got to, if he managed to get anyone else or just decided to run off and not bother, surely not, I thought, hundreds of things went through my mind, not wanting to believe any of them, Smoker could see I was deep in thought.

Just then we heard pistol shots and see smoke from a small, wooded area in the distance, left of where the dragoons were, from our high vantage point we could see the dragoons were being shot at and jumped over a hedge on the opposite side leaving the carts where they were and started firing back towards the trees on the left.

"Quick, into this field", I shouted.

We moved into a field on the right and galloped towards Carswell's men, we took up positions behind the dragoons in another wooded area and started firing our pistols towards Carswell and his men, they were firing back in both directions faster than we could reload but they were now outnumbered by us and whoever it was firing from the other side of the road. Gunpowder smoke filled the air, it was hard to see who we were firing at. The red tunics of the dragoons made them stand out just behind the hedge. This was a bit of luck I thought to myself, this could be our chance to overpower the dragoons and get our goods back, let's hope the ones they were firing at would give up our goods easily otherwise we'd be fighting them as well. Before long there was an eerie silence from where the dragoons were, we waited for the smoke to clear before moving forward. We advanced forward slowly managing to use the trees for cover drawing our swords as we did so. We stopped close to where the dragoons were, looking for signs of life but could see no movement, maybe just a ploy I thought, a trap, to entice us in then overpower us with swords.

"Let's move forward slowly", I whispered to the men.

We crept up slowly to where the dragoons were, it wasn't a pleasant site, men in red dragoon suits were scattered around everywhere, red tunics soaking up blood everywhere, I could see two dragoons sitting on the ground throwing their swords on the ground away from them then put their hands on their heads.

We waited for a while as the gun smoke cleared, till we could see no other signs of movement from the other dragoons, I looked at Jeremiah, Smoker, and the others.
"That was over so quickly, it's hard to tell what happened", said Poison.
"Could we have really beaten the dragoons, and who were they shooting at on the other side of the road", I said.
"let's keep our heads down till we find out who the others are, quick reload before they show themselves", I said.
"There's James", Smoker shouted, as the smoke cleared, we saw James appear with his pistol pointing at the two remaining dragoons.
"And look who he has with him", I said.
We all moved closer to where the dragoons lay.
James came across the road, with an excited look on his face followed with a large group of men, some with swords in one hand and large knives in the other.
"I managed to round up about thirty men from the area and managed to get ourselves in front of the dragoons without being seen, then positioned ourselves in this little wood and waited for them to come down the hill, we could see you lot behind them higher up the hill, we decided to ambush the dragoons as they rode past and hoped you would see what was happening and catch up, and I'm glad you did, they reloaded a lot quicker than we could and without you bringing up the rear they would have certainly got the better of us despite our numbers. My heart was pounding but when I saw you lot firing back from behind them, I knew we had the advantage of numbers on our side, I'm only glad some of your shot didn't find its way towards us". Said James.
We looked around and taking the pistols, muskets, swords off the dead dragoons that littered the area, with Carswell being one of the victims.
"He won't be any problems to us now", said Jeremiah, standing over the body of Carswell.

"We decided this small, wooded area was our best chance to take them William, we knew you were behind them and would back us up when you realised what was happening, so we decided it was the best time to attack and get it over without you" James said laughing.

"We saw what was happening, but we didn't know it was you, I thought we'd be fighting you afterwards for our goods", I said laughing as if a big pressure had been lifted. this will teach them a lesson and anyone else, taking what's ours", I said.

"We should kill the other dragoons", Said Smoker.

"No, we will take them back with us and decide what to do with them later, after we have beaten them for a while". I said looking at him, smiling.

"Oh, yes", I'll look forward to that", said James.

There wasn't many of the dragoons to worry about now anyway.

"Smoker can you collect all the weapons off the dragoons, and any money you find on the bodies as well, share anything you find between yourselves, at least we haven't got to load the carts", I said laughing out loud.

"Yes sir", said Smoker standing to attention and saluting me, as if to mock the now dead dragoons.

All the men were praising themselves and reliving the moment of the battle.

James and the others were thanking all those that were involved.

"I'm glad that's over I was worried sick as to what to do, no doubt Arthur and Thomas will reward all of you for your efforts, from what I've seen of your loyalty today I certainly would, this is one for the Hawkhurst gang", I said, with cheers coming from the men.

We turned the horses and carts around, making sure our goods were secured to the carts we made our way back into Hurst green, leaving the bodies of Carswell and the dragoons behind for others to find and worry about.

"We can leave them here as a reminder to others not to cross us", said Jeremiah, stamping on Carswell's head and spitting at his dead body as he came past it, he quickly grabbed a blunderbuss from one of the other men and aimed it at Carswell corpse.

"Hope you rot in hell", he said wiping the spittle from his mouth, then pulled the trigger, sending bits of Carswell in all directions.

"James take a few men and a couple of carts back over to Etchingham to make sure there are no more goods stored in any of the barns or hiding places, you have your list, you'll find Poison somewhere in the village. While you are at it, ask around to find out why Carswell was there, and I don't mind if certain barns were to burn if you don't get or like the answers", I said.

With that he smiled and shouted for a few men to follow him.

Chapter 4
A large haul (1740)

We headed back towards Hawkhurst across the fields leaving the carts to follow the road, making the two dragoons walk on foot, their blood soaking into their red tunics.

"So, what have you got planned for these two", Jeremiah asked almost like he couldn't wait for a response, eager to get his hands on them.

"I haven't decided yet, we shall teach them a lesson before the day is out, you really have had a bad run in with these dragoons haven't you". I said looking across at him.

"Yes, Carswell and his dragoons caught three of our men in the past and strung them up for having been caught with goods on them, plus he's taken a lot of our goods in the past, so yes, I happy now he's gone, let him rot where he lays", said Jeremiah.

"The way that blunderbuss went off he's laying scattered everywhere", I said, that made Jerimiah laugh out loud.

"I'm happy that you are now on our side", I said smiling to him.

This got a worried look from both dragoons, being tied up and not knowing your fate can be unimaginable especially in the position that they were in, seeing their leader recently killed, for me this seemed punishment enough, but for the rest they had other ideas, they all wanted to kill them on the spot, especially Jeremiah who seemed to hate all dragoons.

We entered into a wooded area and then a clearing somewhere between Hurst Green and Hawkhurst so decided to stop and rest.

"All right, tie them up, bind them tight, hands and feet, beat them up all you like, but don't kill them just yet" I said, just to get the dragoons more worried.

With that the others dismounted from their horses and set about tieing them up to a tree and beating them, kicking, even getting a strong branch and a rock to beat them with, they slumped over, blood dripping from their wounds, they picked them both up again, re-tieing the ropes and continued to beat them some more, when Smoker and the others became tired, they left the dragoons where they collapsed still tied to the tree. Jeremiah pulled out a large knife and put it to the throat of one of the dragoon's, drawing blood with the sharp point, pouring water over the man's head to wake him up, the man came round to see the knife at his throat.
"Think of all the trouble you caused, you and Carswell", said Jeremiah, looking at the man with disgust.
"You really don't like dragoons do you Jeremiah"? said George.
"No, I don't, a few close friends have died because of Dragoons, I just wish this was Carswell instead of him", again putting the point of the knife to the dragoon's throat, then before anyone could stop him, he slowly pushed the knife deep into the dragoon's throat, he gurgled for a bit and covering Jeremiah in blood. The man just looked at him as the life drained from his face, Jeremiah not breaking eye contact so he could watch him die.
Smoker ran off to the edge of the clearing to be sick at the sight of so much blood and the gurgling that came from the dragoon as we watched him die.
"I wanted them to go free and tell what's happened here as a warning to others". I said.
"Can someone get me a large rock", George called out as he looked at the other unconscious dragoon.
"Here's a large rock", Jeremiah said, dropping it at George's feet.
"What do you want that for"? he asked.
"Well, if we don't kill this one then what's to stop them from coming back and shooting at us again", said George,

He untied the dragoon from the tree and placed the soldier's hand on a large tree root and bought the rock down onto it several times, you could hear the bones crunch as the rock hit home, then calmly did the other hand.

"That sounded bad, gave me the shivers", said Smoker.

He won't be firing back now, shouldn't think he could hold a pistol with those hands", said George as he brought the rock down again on the dragoons shin bones hearing them both snap under the rock before throwing the blood-stained rock into the bushes.

"That should do it, he'll survive", laughed Jeremiah, stamping on the face of the dragon as he lay there.

"Come on, we are done here, as we all mounted up". Said George.

"We need to get back and help out with the goods",

Just as we mounted up, Jeremiah, looked at us then walked over to the other dragoon who was still unconscious, grabbed the man, lifting him up by the hair, put the knife to his throat and slit it, the knife going so deep he nearly cut his head off.

"No! Why did you do that"? I shouted at him.

"He would only tell and get others back in the area to hunt us down, better that there are no witnesses, they won't know who to blame for killing Carswell or the dragoons", Said Jeremiah, wiping the blood off his knife on the dragoon tunic.

"I suppose that a good point, better to have no witnesses at all, I'm glad you were here then, I didn't think of that". I said, feeling sorry for the poor dragoons,

"Arthur said you might be soft and need toughening up a bit", said Jeremiah getting on his horses laughing.

~~Yes~~, I thought, I was a bit soft, I don't want to kill anyone in cold blood, firing at someone in the distance is different as you don't really know if you've hit anyone, but taking a knife and sticking it in their throat, that's not me.

I sent Smoker on ahead to catch up with the carts and make sure they got to the Inn safely.

"We shall have to meet George Kingsmill in the morning so he can take the goods to London", I said, knowing that Arthur wanted George Kingsmill to take it all to London to be sold, I wasn't sure we had it all until Poison and James returned to the Oak and Ivy.

We covered the two dead dragoons with leaves, then made our way back onto the road to Hawkhurst.

We couldn't have hoped for a better outcome, getting the goods back off the dragoons, doing away with Thomas Carswell, getting a bigger, better stock of weapons, things would be better off now for us and the gang in Hastings, Arthur would be pleased too, and adding another notch of trust in me for leading this gang to a small but worthy victory, and this is all thanks to James and the others.

We got close to the Ivy and Oak inn; we could see that the carts we sent on ahead with the goods on had already arrived. Arthur was checking them over with George Kingsmill by his side, he saw us coming and was grinning from ear to ear.

"Well Lad", said Arthur, with a huge grin on his face.

"You've done well, you've all done very well, Smoker was telling me all about it just now, I'm glad that you got our goods back, and to get rid of Carswell as well, that will go down well, I can't tell you how happy I am at this good news, that was some good thinking too, to round up the other members and ambush them," said Arthur.

"Well, you've got James to thank for that, moving on ahead and getting ready to ambush Carswell, it was a stroke of luck that James rounded up so many gang members, we were able to ambush them", I said.

We got around behind them, so Carswell didn't have a chance, James on one side while we were on the other", said Jeremiah.

"I also understand from Smoker that you let the men have some fun with the dragoons you captured", I don't mind that, I don't mind that at all, I'm glad Jeremiah was there to finish them off for you, we don't want any loose ends or anyone to recognise us", Said Arthur.
"Yes, he was right not to leave any evidence behind leading towards us, Jeremiah dispatched, those dragoons without flinching", I said.
"Keep on his good side", said Arthur.
"who's side"?
"Jeremiah, he is a killer and has got a nasty reputation and a quick temper", said Arthur, quietly.
"I'll take heed of your words Arthur, having seen what he can do, I'm glad he's on our side, you should have seen what he did to those dragoons".
"No need to repeat it Will, I just heard it all from Smoker, and yes would turn anyone's stomach, but remember William, it's us or them, remember that", Arthur said looking round at the carts. "Now we need to get this lot taken round to George's place as he's got to take it to London early in the morning with a few men to guard it, unload it all and stack it neatly and try and get it on fewer carts and get it covered properly, don't want people to see what we have".
"We have to see if it's all here first, I sent James and Poison back to Etchingham to check the barns and find out any information as to why Carswell was there with our goods", I said.
"Yes, well done, I hadn't thought of that, we will check it later when the others arrive back, make a start on it anyway, and well done, well done everyone,", said Arthur.
"I'm glad you said George wasn't going on his own, you never know what might happen", I said.
"Do you really think that anyone would try to rob us"? Arthur said with a smile of confidence".

"Of course, he's not going alone, there's too much at stake to send our goods with one man", Arthur said, "but don't let that concern you, I've got a few more jobs for you worry yourself over, don't worry these are only minor jobs, we have a few barns that we need to get our stock from, and now you've proved yourself I'd rather you do it", he said placing his big hand on my shoulder.

"Get those carts moving" he announced with a booming voice.

"The rest of you, let's go and get a drink and celebrate our victory", Arthur said, feeling proud that he's got the right men for the right job.

We headed off into the Oak and Ivy for a well-earned drink, and some hot food.

It was a short time later that James, Poison and the others returned, with full carts and smelling of smoke.

"You lot smell of smoke, what have you been up to", asked Thomas.

"Well William asked us to go round Etchingham and collect the rest of the goods that got left behind, while we were there we asked a few questions to the locals, most people said nothing and hurried away, more from recognising us more than anything, but there was this one man who looked very nervous when confronted by us, and on asking questions about Carswell the man broke down and confessed that Carswell had in fact beaten him into telling him who the goods belonged to, and because of that they wouldn't take him to the magistrate for giving evidence. Unfortunately for the man, me and James are not so forgiving, we ransacked his house removing his belongings, and there's a lot of good stuff on the cart, we then tied the man up to the stairs and set fire to the house, we watched from outside as his house burnt to the ground, no one came out and no one came out to help almost like they knew it was him that told Carswell and decided helping was not a good idea", said Poison

In the years that followed we grew stronger and more confident and took more chances with bigger shipments, from France, Germany, Guernsey, and silks and spices all the way from India our reign stretched from all around Kent's coast all the way to down to Dorset, we had bigger and bigger hauls and a lot more hiding places than we could remember, we even organised teams of men to dig tunnels in and around Hawkhurst, Rye, Etchingham, Goudhurst, Cranbrook, everywhere where there was enterprise we would be hiding goods.

We had some losses though, one of the gang members that James had rounded up at Hurst Green to ambush Carswell and his men. George Chapman was recognised by one the villagers. He was drinking in a tavern where, he was recognised and arrested, word has it that he put up a fight first before they took him.

Arthur was none too happy that he was recognised by one of the villagers, none too happy at all in fact, and sent a few gang members to find the name of the one had a loose tongue and kill all his family and burn the house down, from what I heard a few villagers were tortured till they gave up the names. There were few people that were involved in giving up information to the customs and those families are no more.

"We will have no one go against us", I could hear Arthur say. Putting fear into people will keep us safe.

George was put on trial and was found guilty of having a hand in the murder of Thomas Carswell, and he paid the price for keeping quiet about the Hawkhurst gang as we were now known as. He was hanged at Hurst Green for his crimes. We know he didn't kill Carswell, but the magistrate thought it would be a good idea to make an example of him in the hope that some might change our way, that didn't work as it only made us stronger.

For the most we kept everyone happy from the spoils that we managed to bring in and were happy that we weren't paying such huge taxes that were levied on it. We enjoyed what we did and became popular with everyone, after all, people were like us, they just wanted to pay for the goods a lot cheaper than they could get them in the stores that they have in their towns or villages, which kept them happy and quiet about what we did, oh yes, we became extremely popular.

We kept the flow of goods coming in from France, Holland, Guernsey and Spain, and our contacts would stretch as far down as India getting goods cheaply for us, but there was always a problem, and a big one at that, and it was the English Channel, if there was a place to get caught that would be it, most of the goods came in at night or during rough weather to avoid detection, always dangerous, but the rewards were just, we risked everything so why would we want to give the King money for doing nothing while we risked our lives, no, it was all ours, ours to sell to whoever, we were making money and happy to help our fellow villages in what we could get.

Our strength was now in numbers and reputation, no one would be stupid enough to go to the authorities and report us, most would just plead ignorance or turn a blind eye whenever we passed, ask no questions, tell no lies. We were such that we could call up about five hundred men in an hour if we needed, I didn't believe it was possible, but there was just such a time when this was put to the test.

Chapter 5
Richard Hawkins (1740)

We had established ourselves as the largest most dangerous gang around, probably not the best title to have but it did keep the competition at bay as there were other established gangs in and around Kent and they knew better to keep out of our way, but even though we had this reputation there was still the odd gang who would try and take us on. We were enjoying the lifestyle that we had created for ourselves, but like everything not everything goes according to plan.

A small group in the gang, still under the watchful eyes of Arthur and Thomas, went off to hijack a few carriages that carried goods, money, and jewels to and from London and made money from that too, this was a way of keeping the men busy in between the goods coming in from the coast, we don't quite know how much the members gained from it, if the gang got a percentage from what they were doing then everyone was happy.

Arthur made so much money from what he did he decided to buy a bigger house for himself. He looked everywhere but no house was big enough or grand enough that was now fitting for the status that he made for himself. He told me he could always see himself as a gentleman, but with his background this was never going to happen, but now he had a chance to make something of it, although getting it with blood on his hands, and being a smuggler, thief, wasn't going to get him in high society, but if it changed him for the better then let him try, he deserved his moment of glory.

We met up one afternoon, just a few gang members in the Oak and Ivy, Arthur was with Thomas and George along with Poison. I came in with James, Jeremiah, Diamond, and Smoker, just having a little get together while things were calm, basically we were waiting for another load of contraband to come in from the Channel Islands.

"I want to buy a bigger house, somewhere that's big enough to enjoy the comforts of home", said Arthur, out of the blue.

"You already own several properties in the area", said Thomas.

"I know, we own, Highgate house, which is not much of a house, it's large enough I agree but we use that to store our contraband, not much use to live in", said Arthur.

"Yes, lots or rooms but no space", Thomas laughed.

"Hawkhurst Place", said Jeremiah.

"Too small", besides, I'll have you lot coming and going getting items dumped in the pond its linked to, plus it's a very cold house", Arthur said reaching into the fire for some wood to light his pipe.

"We have Tudor Hall that you could use as your house", Diamond said sipping on his ale.

"Those won't do, I need something a lot bigger, I'll be looking around for something else around the area, something large and dare I say opulent", Arthur said, his eyes staring at the fire as he pondered.

"If you don't need it right away, you could always build it, that way you'll have it just the way you want", said Thomas, jokingly.

That's a really good idea, I hadn't thought of that", said Arthur.

"Hmm", he mumbled, now further deep in thought.

"I could build lots of hiding places in it so contraband won't be found, plus a purpose-built tunnel, and escape routes as well, unlike the one the lads built from Hawkhurst place to tubs ponds, that still needs to be widened by the way as part of it collapsed", said Arthur looking towards Thomas, as a command to get it done.

"That's being taken care of, we are still waiting for wood", said Thomas poking my arm because I'm supposed to be suppling it.

"I need to find some land to build this house on, I don't want to travel far, I still want to be in Hawkhurst, so the next time you are all in Hawkhurst have a look round for me and let me know, we either build it as new or convert something else, either way we need to have a lot of land around it to keep prying eyes out of our business.

Just then the door opened and in came Edward Savage.

"We haven't seen him round here for a while, I wonder what brings him here. Hello Edward, how are you and what brings us this honour of your company"? asked Thomas.

"I was doing some business of my own over this way buying some hops from Marden and thought I'd pay you all a visit, seeing as I haven't been here for a while", Said Edward.

"Well, it's always good to see you, "said Arthur, finally taking his tankard from his lips.

"John, bring our old friend Ed an ale, and a brandy from your good stock", called Thomas.

"Aye, will do", came the voice behind the bar.

"Yes, I was just over this way getting some nice hops, that had been stored for me and thought it's about time I came and got it, plus I was getting low, and I thought why not come down and see you lot", said Edward.

"Glad to have you here", said Arthur.

"I can't stay long though I do have to get back, an inn won't run itself", said Edward.

"true", said Thomas.

"Are you alright for stock; do you need anything"? Arthur said taking another mouthful of ale.

"I'm alright for ale, now I have the hops", said Edward, now lifting the glass of brandy to his lips, cheers, gentlemen", he said as he swallowed the brandy in one go, then we watched as his face scrunched up.

"Wow this is strong", he said.

"Seems you're lacking the good stuff over your way", said George.

"If you let me have fifty bottles of that Brandy, and fifty bottles of rum, fifty sacks of tea to take with me, that should do me for a while. The tea you sent me before was short by one bag, at least I think it was", said Edward.

"The last lot of stock I sent you was accurate, I put it together myself", said Thomas, sounding a bit stern, at the thought.

"I'm not going to argue that fact with you, but the order for twenty bags that I asked for when I counted it was only eighteen after I had used one", said Edward, looking a bit concerned, trying not to get into an argument with Thomas.

"Well, seems you've got a thief in your mitts", said Arthur not taking it too seriously at first.

"Who has access to you stock then Edward, you need to think hard as it was all there when it left here", said Thomas.

"Well, there is a lad that helps around the alehouse when it gets busy, he's the only one who could have taken it, but I'm sure it wasn't him, my wife said that when she went to get another bag she could have sworn that one was missing and wasn't sure if I had moved any, I never followed it up or thought anything of it, running an Inn gets very busy so I must have been preoccupied to notice, I suppose that Richard Hawkins could have taken it, I don't know why, I give him enough while he's working for me, he seems honest enough, but if you say you sent all twenty then he would be the only one who could have taken them.

Now Arthur's face had changed.

"No one steals from us or our friends, no one! Seems this chap, whoever he is, if it is him that's taken it should be taught a lesson, a lesson he won't forget.", said Arthur, called over to John to bring him a large brandy.

"Right, when you go back to your alehouse Ed, take Smoker with you and Jeremiah round up a few others and find out if this Richard Hawkins did take the tea", said Arthur, drinking the brandy down in one gulp, his face unchanging as it hit his throat.

Smoker and Jeremiah finished their ale and went out to round up a few others to go with them.

Edward and Thomas finished their ale as well and went to get the stock that Edward had asked for, which left Arthur, James, Diamond, and myself in the inn.

"You've heard of Jeremiah's reputation", asked Arthur.

"I've seen him in action with those two dragoons, he seems to enjoy what he does, what have you heard about him"? I asked.

"He has a very violent streak, he's very loyal and won't have a bad thing said, especially about his friends, he took on three sailors when he was living in Hastings, so I heard, he broke the arm of one, gouged out the eyes of another and threw the third out through the window, not satisfied that he'd done enough he went outside to hit the sailor some more with a bottle of rum over the head several times till the bottle smashed then he sliced open the sailors tunic and carved a skull and crossbones on the man's chest while he lay unconscious, in front of men, women and children, not sure how it all started but that's how it finished, he's not one to messed with, so don't ever cross him, because you never know what he's going to do. It's good that he's on our side, if this Hawkins has stolen from us then I'm sure Jeremiah will find out, and if he does, I'm sure Jeremiah will make him pay for it." Said Arthur, with us listening intently.

Just then Thomas and Edward appeared with a small bag of money that Thomas handed to Arthur.

"I'm ready to leave now, be on my way, it was good to see you all again, maybe I'll stay a little longer next time, Smoker and Jeremiah are waiting outside with a few others, so I'll be off", said Edward.

"You go with them William, make sure they see it through and find out the truth from this fellow, get the tea back if you can, if he's still got it, or make him pay".

"Alright, but I'm not prepared to go to….", I paused…

"Where is it that you live"? I said looking at Edward.

"Slindon, just west of Arundel, said Edward.
"that's a long way", I said, as a complaint and trying to get out of it.
"Stop complaining, it won't take you long, you can stay at Edwards Alehouse, he'll look after you all, don't worry, now get going, and remember we'll have no one stealing from us, make sure you have your pistols and knives ready as you might meet some unsavoury characters along the way", said Thomas.
With that we all burst out laughing.
We got on our horses and Edward checking to make sure his goods were firmly secured on his cart before we set off. The afternoon sun was a welcome sight, but we knew it wouldn't last long, the sunlight in January doesn't last long, the snow had long melted but still left pools of stagnant water in the ruts where the carts had been. It hadn't been a cold winter, not as bad as some, but still it was cold outside. We made our way into the night travelling as best we could on our horses. Stopping for the night at an inn somewhere close to Brighthelmston.
The following day just as they were about to mount up, we saw Thomas Winter,
"Hello Tom, this makes a change, nice to see you, how are you", Said Edward.
"How are you Edward", said Thomas looking at us all in a curious manner.
"What are you doing this way," continued Edward.
"Oh, I was doing some business in Brighthelmston and stayed here overnight, I'm now on my way back to Arundel to visit my family. He said checking the bridle on his horse.
"Oh, this is Will, Smoker, Diamond and Jeremiah, by the way", he said as he introduced us all to Thomas Winter.
Thomas touched his brow as he bid us all a good morning.
"We are all on our way to meet someone, someone who Arthur Gray thinks has stolen from us".

It turns out that Edward is also friends of Arthur, Thomas, and George Kingsmill, there are so many members of the Hawkhurst gang that you have to beware just who you talk to and what you say, even this far away from Hawkhurst.
"If you don't mind, may I join you on your journey, you can tell me all about it on the way", said Thomas trying to get his foot into the stirrup.
"We don't mind at all, more company the better", said Edward, rechecking the load on his cart before jumping up in the seat.
We continued our journey to Slindon, with Edward and Thomas talking between themselves for the rest of the journey, reliving old times and stopped for another short stop at Arundel, which to my mind was the best place I've seen, the castle and cathedral mingled with the surrounding forests.
We didn't have time to admire the scenery, as our journey was nearly at an end.
"Well, you lot, Thomas is going to come with us and find this Hawkins, he thinks this boy needs to be taught a lesson as well, likes to get his hands dirty, if you know what I mean", he said laughing out loud.
"He lives in Yapton and works in Slindon doing different jobs to get by, last I heard he was working as a labourer, during the day, somewhere in the village", Edward said.
"We'll look around and ask a few people, take Edward and Thomas over to the Dog and Partridge and wait for us there", Said Jeremiah.
"No good us splitting up as you lot don't know what he looks like", said Edward.
"We don't need everyone to get him, he'll come along", said Jeremiah, patting his side where his pistol was.
Slindon wasn't a large village, and it didn't take long to find the whereabouts of Richard Hawkins.
"There he is on the roof of the barn", Edward pointed to two workers on the roof of a barn that was having its roof repaired.

We galloped over to the barn and Jeremiah leapt off his horse just as a young lad was just coming down the ladder, Jeremiah leapt over a wall and grabbed the boy by his hair, pulling him down, he landed with a crunch along with the pile of tiles that was on the ground.

"Oi", what are you doing down there", shouted a voice from the roof, the roofer made his way to the ladder is if to come down and help the lad.

"Mind your business", Jeremiah called out, bringing his pistol that was tucked into his belt.

"This don't concern the likes of you", said Jeremiah now pointing the pistol at the roofer, he stopped in his tracks halfway down the ladder, watching to see what was happening, frozen in fear.

I also pulled my pistol out pointed it at the roofer on the ladder and looking around to make sure no one else wanted to get involved.

"Get up, is your name Richard Hawkins"? said Jeremiah.

"What have I done, what do you want me for, there's been a mistake"? Hawkins cried, claiming his innocence.

"Answer the question", said Jeremiah, as he now trained his pistol on Hawkins.

"Yes, my name is Richard Hawkins, he could have told you that", said Hawkins pointing towards Edward.

Edward threw a rope to Jeremiah, who quickly bound Hawkins hands and tied the other end to the cart.

Thomas followed behind so as to keep an eye on him in case he made an escape from his bindings.

"Let's be off", said Diamond.

I kept my pistol trained on the roofer, as the others got on their horses.

"Be about your business, this doesn't concern you, we only want to ask him a few questions, he'll be back soon enough", I said, ushering my horse to back up away from the barn, I put my pistol back into my coat and made to follow the others.

We made our way through the village to the Dog and Partridge.

We pulled up behind the rear of the Inn and loosened the rope from the cart Hawkins was tied to, he tried to break free as the rope was freed from the cart, but Jeremiah was quick and tripped him up, so he fell onto the ground, hitting his head with a thump.

"You'll save us the trouble with you hitting your head like that", said Jeremiah, smiling.

"I'm innocent, I haven't done anything", said Hawkins getting back on his feet. With that Jeremiah, punched him in the stomach then the face.

"We shall see"", said Jerimiah, as Hawkins fell to the floor again, his teeth filling with blood.

Jeremiah pulled on the rope and dragged him across the ground where he lay and through the door of the inn to where the others were waiting, Hawkins could see them carrying whips and feared the worst.

"You've got the wrong man, I have done nothing to you", said Hawkins, again pleading his innocence, and not knowing what it was all about.

He was tied to the rafters of the roof in the back room on the inn by his hands, with his feet tied together so he was left hanging there.

"I'm going to enjoy this", said Jeremiah, finding some axle grease and rubbing it into the whip, his hand running down his whip massaging the grease into it to make it more supple as Hawkins watched.

We all stood back as Jeremiah unleashed the whip, hitting Hawkins about eight times around his body.

"Open his shirt, let him feel it against his skin", said Thomas.

I pulled out my knife and run it up Hawkins back, slicing through his shirt, his back showing cuts as the whip sliced through his skin, then I turned the blade over and ran it down his back scoring a line of blood all the way down.

Hawkins was crying in pain as the knife ran across the cuts, still pleading his innocence.

"Stop your pleading and take your punishment like a real man", said Smoker enjoying the occasion and filling his pipe with tobacco.

A few more lashes were delivered across Hawkins face and body, causing him to scream in agony.

"Please stop, I'm innocent, why are you doing this to me, I haven't done anything to you, I'm only a labourer", he said spitting blood from his mouth.

Jeremiah stopped whipping the boy, and walked over to him, and punched him five times in the stomach, Hawkins writhing in pain.

Smoker had filled his pipe with tobacco and pulled a piece of burning wood from the fire to light it, still with the wood flaming he put it against Hawkins cheek, Hawkins moving his head back to avoid the flames, I moved forward to hold his head still as the burning wood made contact, Thomas delivered a few punches to his stomach, then to his face right where he'd just been burnt. Hawkins fell unconscious from the pain and just hung there for a while. Water was thrown over Hawkins and he came to and looked at Edward.

Smoker went outside and grabbed a handful of dirt and gravel, came in and rubbed it into Hawkins back, only to hear Hawkins scream again.

"You were working for me at the Inn and helping at the bar, you had access to the store, is that correct", said Edward.

Hawkins looked around at the men who were doing this to him for a moment, taking everything in, trying to ignore the pain he was in, his mind not knowing why.

"I was working for you, and I helped you a lot, I did everything for you", his voice not sounding like his own, his lips had swollen and his mouth full of blood, moving his tongue around he could feel something in his mouth, he spat it out to realise it was a few of his teeth.

"Then it could only have been you", said Edward.

"Only be me, what"? he cried.

"There was a bag of tea missing from my store, the bag of tea that was supplied by Arthur Gray, and bought and paid for from him with my own money, I don't suppose you know who he is do you"? Said Edward.

"No, I don't, said Hawkins, his tongue, searching his mouth for any more broken teeth.

"He's a man you don't mess with, as a matter of fact so are we", said Jeremiah.

"I only took a bag of tea, I didn't think you'd mind, and I was going to give you the money for it when I got it", said Hawkins.

"Well, we did mind, and so did Arthur Gray, and as far as we are concerned that's stealing and you are a thief, and thieves have to be punished", said Jeremiah.

Jeremiah was cleaning his whip and rubbing more axle grease into it while staring Hawkins in the face, a big smile on his face as he started to whip Hawkins again, Hawkins body slumped again as he fell unconscious through the pain.

Smoker pulled out a small knife and slowly pushed it into Hawkins side, to see if he was unconscious.

"That went right up to the hilt so he must be out cold", said Smoker.

"Let me try", said Jeremiah, with a grin on his face.

With that he ran the knife over Hawkins back to see him flinching slightly, then across his chest and stomach, then across the boy's cheeks and forehead.

"Yes, his is unconscious", said Jeremiah, laughing.

We watched him hanging there for a while, cleaning our blades and whips on Hawkins clothes.

Hawkins came to again, unable to open one of his eyes and blood filled the other.

"He looks in a bit of a mess now, not sure anyone will recognise him, not such a pretty boy now are you", Jeremiah laughed right in his face as he delivered another punch to his stomach.

"Not sure your roofer friend will want you now, no good for anything anymore", I said kicking in the groin then watched him wince with pain

"Cut him down, let's get rid of him, I hate thieves", Said Smoker.

With that Jeremiah cut the ropes that went round the rafters, and Hawkins fell to the blood-soaked floor.

Edward and Thomas grabbed the rope and dragged Hawkins through the dirt outside to the cart, they picked him up and threw him on the cart to hear him groan.

"He's making some strange noises, he's must still alive then", said Jeremiah, as he left the inn, making his way to his horse.

"What shall we do with him now", I said, getting back on my horse.

"I think I know where we can leave him, I know a nice quiet spot", said Edward, climbing up on the cart.

Together we followed Edward on the cart, watching to see if Hawkins would get up, but he just lay there rocking with the motion of the cart.

We rode till we were outside Slindon and into a park, where Edward said there was a small lake.

We dragged Hawkins off the cart by his feet, his head hitting the floor with a bang.

"We can't just leave him here, the first thing he's going to do is tell everyone what happened if he survives", I said.

With that Jeremiah pulled out his knife and stabbed Hawkins a few times in the chest and stomach.

"I'm not sure he's going to survive that", said Jeremiah, wiping the bade on Hawkins clothes again.

"See if he's got any money on him to pay for the tea that he stole then tie a few rocks to his body and let's dump him in the lake, dead men will tell no lies", I said.

We found a few rocks and tied them to Hawkins, and a few more stuffed into his trousers just for good measure, and we threw his body as far as we could and hoping the lake was deep enough.

This was done and very soon Hawkins body was at the bottom of the lake and soon forgotten, we made our way back to Hawkhurst, Edward went back to Slindon and carried on as if nothing happed.

"Shame no one will know it was us as a deterrent for others to not cross us", I said.

"I'm sure questions will be asked, and they'll have to find someone else to accuse of his demise, he's only a labourer so he won't be missed", said Smoker, laughing out loud.

Life carried on as normal and the likes of Hawkins were soon forgotten.

The odd villager who thought they were doing good by their actions by thinking of going to the customs men were soon dealt with and again life returned to normal. Goods were coming in from afar, as well as going out, villagers would benefit for our goods as well, so we soon had a lot of people on our side taking advantage of our lower prices. A few more years had passed without too many problems, none that we couldn't handle anyway, and life seemed good.

Arthur finally got his house built and he was pleased with the results. We came to visit him just after it was finished, not furnished as yet though and while he was showing us around the empty rooms he suddenly disappeared, then reappeared a short time later. He was laughing when he said he'd gone down a trap door escape route without any of us knowing, one of many he had built into his new house. Trap doors and secret passageways plus two tunnels leading to various parts of the garden, it was set back from the road, large bushes shield it from being seen. With the extra outbuildings that he's also having built he should be able to store more, but he said he's not storing much, and the outbuildings are for his horses.

Chapter 6
Shoreham by sea (1744)

I went to Hawkhurst one morning, I got my horse ready and made off to village to stock up on a few items, money was no problem anymore Arthur had seen to that, and now with all the money I was getting it was my turn to start looking for a new house.

As I arrived in Village, I could see Arthur getting off a cart, strange I haven't seen him on a cart for a while, probably stocking up with items as well.

As I neared his cart, I could see a young boy lurking near the back of his cart, I got off my horse to find him with his hand under the sacking, helping himself to a few items, taking advantage of Arthur going inside a shop.

I pulled out my knife and came up behind the boy.

"What have we here then"? I said, he froze on the spot as he felt the cold steel of my blade touch his neck.

"We hate thieves, do you know what we do with thieves"? I said holding his arm and pushing the blade against his windpipe, feeling him gulp against it.

Just then Arthur came out of the shop, with a surprised look as I was holding this young boy with a knife to his throat, wondering what was going on.

Arthur threw his goods to the back of the cart and drew his knife out, and held it against the boy stomach, before asking any questions.

"I caught him helping himself to what's on your cart Arthur", I said, tightening my grip, even though I had Arthur there and was blocking any escape route he might have had.

A tear come to the boy's eyes.

"How old are you boy"? Arthur's voice was deep and menacing.

"I'm, I'm fifteen sir", said the boy, too frightened to even speak.

"What's you name boy, and what were you thinking of doing with the things on my cart", came the next question from Arthur.
"I'm sorry sir, I didn't mean to.
"Didn't mean to what"? his voice becoming impatient for not answering his last question, Arthur started to pick at the boy's buttons on his jacket with his knife.
"I'm still waiting for you to tell me your name, are you deaf or dumb"? I could see no matter how young this boy was Arthur was on the verge of losing his temper with him, and that would be bad for the boy.
"it's Mark sir", said the boy, trembling as he watched Arthur's face turn red.
"Mark Who", said Arthur, losing his patients as he punched the boy in the face, making blood stream from his nose.
"Mark Hammond" said the boy now with his teeth covered in blood.
"Do you live around here", I said, a little calmer than Arthur.
"I live with my mum and dad at The Moor, close to the green, by the church", said the boy, trying to wipe the blood from his mouth.
"We know where the Moor is, do you know who we are", I asked.
"I think I have heard of you, but never seen your faces", said the boy still trembling.
"Well now you have, and I suggest you have a good look at Arthur Grey, so you know not to cross my path in future, and if you have any friends who also think they can help themselves to other people's things then I suggest you tell them as well, we hate thieves and we deal with them severely", said Arthur, now picking at the boys last button and opening his jacket so his knife wouldn't feel much resistance.
Arthur held the boy at arm's length and whispered in my ear. Then he let go of the boy and put his knife away, went to his cart and got some rope.

"Hold your hands out boy and put your legs together", said Arthur firmly.
The boy did as he was told and soon his hands and legs were bound.
I mounted my horse and Arthur picked up the boy and threw him over my horse behind me as if he weighed nothing, then we trotted out of the Village towards Sandhurst. Arthur got on his cart and made off in the other direction as if nothing had happened.
Just outside Sandhurst we left the road and into a small, wooded area. I dismounted and threw the boy to the ground. I kicked him while he lay there, then set about punching him as hard as I could while he was still tied up.
"I told you we don't like thieves", I said as my foot found his mouth splitting his lip open.
As he lay there covered in blood, I sat astride his chest making it hard for him to breathe and pulled out my knife again. His eyes wide as he saw the blade in front of his face.
"I like this knife, out of all the weapons I carry this one I like the most, I take my time to get this knife the sharpest, a blunt knife is no good at all. It's good for gutting pigs, sheep, and scum like you who want to help their selves to other people goods", I said looking down at the boy, his face covered in blood, tears and leaves.
"I don't ever want to see you again in Hawkhurst or anywhere else for that matter, you keep out of our way or else, you will feel it slicing your throat from ear to ear, you know you will have to pay just for trying to steal from us", I said, I could see his eyes widen.
"Please sir, have a heart, I've learned my lesson, I won't do it again", said the boy trying to plead with my good nature, which seemed to have left me.

"I would normally, but today I feel you caught me in a bad mood, and I caught you trying to steal from a good friend of mine, in future you'll know the name Arthur Gray and the Hawkhurst gang and think twice about helping yourself, we have many friends in the Village and all of them have eyes. With that I took hold of his hands and held them close his face, and moved my knife to cut the rope and run the blade gently across his fingers, he looked at me, his eyes wider as he looked at his hand and closed his eyes, I stood up over him as he lay there, then I stood on his hand, still exposing his fingers, pinning his arm to the ground, then my knife selected a finger and dug into his skin, blood was everywhere as I got off him, I cut the ropes to his feet, I threw an old rag for him to wrap his hand in, he picked up his finger stood up and looked at me.

"You got off lightly, let that be a lesson to you, now go, before I change my mind and take off the rest of your fingers", I said.

With that he turned and ran off into the woods, silently.

I never got any items from Hawkhurst because of him, I cleaned most of the blood off my hands with some wet leaves and made my way back to the village to get the food that I needed.

Arthur was still there going from shop to shop.

We walked together over to the horse trough so I could wash all the blood off my hands.

"Thanks for looking out for me Will, he would have made off with all the goods I bought if you hadn't stopped him, I take it you sorted him out", said Arthur.

"No problem Arthur, that's what friends are for, we look out for each other, I don't think we'll see him again around here, if you did, you'll recognise him as he now has one finger missing, he was a brave lad, he didn't even make a noise when my knife found his bone", I said.

"Oh well, lessoned learnt", said Arthur.

"Before you go off about your business, I've been meaning to come and see you, we are going to Shoreham by sea on business in the next few days", said Arthur.

"Who is we"? I said.

"As many as we can get together, the more I can get then the more that will help out, I need help in bringing back some more goods that have come in from the Channel Islands and I need to see someone about getting more goods in, business is looking up, we can all go and help and make a few days of it, visit a few inns, catch up with old friends, you know how it is", said Arthur.

"Sounds good to me, we could do with more stock coming in, I've been selling quite a bit around my way to the locals, I'll bring you the money for that next time we go the Oak and Ivy.

"That's fine, we'll meet up there on Friday two days' time, around noon, should give us time to prepare before we set off for Shoreham by sea by sea", Said Arthur.

"Good, I will see you at the Inn", I said

"And Will, thanks again for what you did".

My hands clean again I made off to get my goods while Arthur again made his way back to towards Ticehurst.

The day arrived with a lot of us gathering outside the Oak and Ivy inn, and having prepared for the journey with horses and carts enough to carry our goods back, made our way down to Shoreham by sea, stopping overnight at an inn in Lewes, we knew that the Inn was frequented by the customs men, and they would hold goods that were brought in through Rye, we were hoping they would be there so we could help ourselves to what they had with them, it would only add to our tally, but there was no customs men to be seen, so we settled down to a night of drinking and continued our journey the following morning.

We headed for Brighthelmston along the coast, it was the first time that I had been there, seemed to be so many people rushing around, just looked like chaos, not like Hawkhurst at all, Arthur, Thomas, and everyone else seem to take it all in their stride, happy to be there with all the shops and people, the horses and horse drawn carriages creating a lot of the noise, I suppose in their mind all they could see was more trade, more profit, where's there's people there's going to money. They've been here before I thought to myself, must have done if they've got contacts this way. There were lots of shops, butchers with meat hanging outside, the smell of freshly made bread wafted through the air, traders calling out to anyone wanting to buy from them, and the fishermen bringing in fish from the boats just offshore just added to the pace, I had only grown up in a small village, so this was a sight to behold and the largest busies place I have ever seen. We carried on through Brighthelmston along the coast road the crowds becoming less the further we went, I could see many ships out to sea, the sea breeze hitting my face, fresh but with the same smell of salt as was Hastings, but Hastings the beach area was more alive with the fishing boats, pulled up on shore and fishermen repairing their nets in and drying huts. Everyone seems to take heed by the amount of us that were travelling, keeping their distance even though there were many crowds, they all gave us clearance when we passed. We left Brighthelmston and travelled through Hove and onto Shoreham by sea. This place was nothing like Brighthelmston, smaller, quiet, still had a harbour where the fishing boats gathered but nothing as fast paste with the hustle and bustle of Brighthelmston.

We followed Arthur as he seemed to know where he was going, just left it up to him, till we stopped at a place close to the river.

"Gather round, we will head off to the Beehive Inn, we won't all fit in there but there's a cottage next door to that and they said anytime we come this way they'll gladly let us stay, so make yourselves comfortable as you'll be there for a couple of days while we get things sorted, if you won't fit in here then look elsewhere but at the Beehive inn is where we will meet up at", Said Thomas looking round at everyone.

"Oh, and try and keep out of trouble, if you can", said Arthur, with a knowing look that he knows that won't happen.

"We'll do our best", came voices from the rear.

There was about 20 of us, no idea if all of us would be able to fit in, but the cottage next to the Inn looked a lot bigger, so I decided that this was where I would be sleeping, no point trying to sleep, in an inn with this lot drinking all night, I thought to myself.

Arthur and Thomas had the same idea and gave their horses to a stable hand to look after their horses. We ate hot food and drank into the night, and it seemed the locals kept away on hearing the noise that was going on from inside the Inn, a few members decided to go outside and try other inns that were spread around the town, I'm sure by the way they looked in the morning they had been trying to fight the locals, the fisherman and locals must have been tougher than our lot by the look of it, listening to them talking it sounds like they enjoyed themselves either way.

Thomas took a few men to go back to Shoreham by sea to see a friend, after he had breakfast, "going to try and get some more business our way", he said, and Arthur went to see his contact in Shoreham by sea further along the coast with a few others leaving us behind to look after the inn while they were away.

Later, in the day Thomas came riding back to the Inn in a flustered state and shouting that they had been set up by the customs men.

"Where's Arthur", Thomas shouted as the door of the inn swung open.

"He's not back yet, he said he wouldn't be that long", said Smoker.

"We need to find him and get him back now", said Thomas looking even more agitated.

"What's wrong", came a few voices from the inn, sounding concerned.

"We were drinking with my friend at his house with a few others, when suddenly customs man burst in with swords drawn. There was a scuffle and a few of us managed to get free and go out through the back door.

We ran back to the front of the building again and mingled in the crowd to see them coming out, there were four customs men and they took my friend and three others, all four were bound together, I'm sure they would have taken them to the local gaol, not sure why they came, but come they did and now they've got our men, so not sure what to do now, that's why I need to speak with Arthur", Thomas sitting down now, staring into space trying to replay everything that happened.

"I'm not sure where Arthur is so will just have to wait for his return". I said handing Thomas a brandy trying to calm him down.

"That could have been me going off to gaol", said Thomas drinking the brandy in one gulp then wiping his mouth with his sleeve.

"Does anyone here know where the gaol is in this town, the customs office"? asked Smoker.

"I do", said the inn keeper.

"It's on the quayside, white building blue windows, normally got a flag flapping about on the roof, you can't miss it". He said, wiping down the ale off the bar, carrying on with his business trying not to show any concern.

"I'm going there to have a look and see what I can find out", said Smoker, finishing off his ale.

"Anyone wants to come with me", he asked looking around.

"I'll come", said John, gulping down his brandy.

"From what I could see they took at least four of us so the others must have got away, if you can check out who they have got in the gaol, whoever it is I'm sure Arthur will not be too pleased that they have been caught", said Thomas looking a little calmer now.

With that Smoker and John left to see what they could find out.

It was the following day that Arthur appeared and having heard the news from what Smoker had found out he was not pleased at all.

"Thomas, you've seen these customs men so you should recognise them, find out where they are, where they drink or live, find out anything you can about these men, I want them, they will pay for what they have done", said Arthur.

"Smoker, you've seen the building, is there any way that you can think of that we can get the men out of that gaol"? said Arthur now turning to Smoker.

This was Arthur doing what he does best, taking control of the situation even though there was no possible way to rescue our men he was going to give it a good try.

"I went to the gaol and saw about eight customs men inside, the gaol where the men were kept was at the rear of the building the walls looked solid, with bars at the windows, I managed to speak to one of our men through the bars who said four of them were captured and would go before the magistrate on Tuesday, for smuggling goods in from Jersey, seems the customs men were very happy they had been caught and laughing all the way to the gaol, they said they would be swinging from a rope by the end of the week, I didn't have time to ask their names, as one of the customs men saw me", said Smoker

"That's not going to happen, we shall get them out, they won't hang, we come down here on good terms, all friendly, no friends of ours are going to hang, not now, not if we can help it", said Arthur, getting red in the face with anger and punching the pillar that was holding up the ceiling causing the room to shake.

"We shall come up with a plan to get them out, we can't just go barging in there with pistols drawn", I said.

"We shall deal with those customs men too", said Arthur now with his knife drawn and stabbing the pillar, taking his anger out on it.

"let's all calm down, have a drink and work this out, we will find a way somehow", I said going to the bar to geta bottle of brandy from the bar keep.

"Go on Thomas, take Smoker, John and Jeremiah with you and try and find information about these customs men, someone must know them, know where they live, I want them found, don't come back till you find them", said Arthur, running the blade across his hand drawing blood.

We sat for a few hours going over a few plans and drinking in the bar, but without knowing all the information that Thomas, Smoker and John had found out all we could do was drink till they come back. Arthur was now digging a hole in the table with his knife, still agitated by the situation.

We drank into the night till sleep got the better of us, the others had not returned so we decided the best thing would be to go to bed and decide what we would do in the morning on the others return.

Sun came up bright and early and everyone was buzzing as Thomas and the others had returned with the news about the customs men.

"We know where one of the customs men live, we'll get him and he can show us where the others live, check your firearms, make sure they are all loaded, sharpen those swords and knives, we are going to get these customs men, take them and trade them for the others in gaol", said Thomas.

We checked over our pistols and make sure the flints were in place and the gunpowder was dry, Arthur gave his knife a quick sharpen having used it to take out his anger on the furniture the night before.

We all mounted up and went into the town, Smoker, John and Jeremiah were at the front leading the way as they knew where to find the customs men, we all had our pistols and blunderbusses ready as we went through the streets, rage must have got the better of us as we opened fire on the town, shooting windows and signs making sure everyone knew we were there, people running and screaming everywhere to get out of our way, one man tried to run past Jeremiah but he got too close to him, Jeremiah's foot caught him square on the jaw laying him unconscious then his horse trample across his legs as he lay there. Shortly afterwards we came upon a house where Smoker said one of the customs men lived, we got off our horses and reloaded our pistols quietly out of sight.

"Thomas, take Smoker and Diamond round the back, make sure no one comes out, the rest of us are going in the front, grab everyone in there, his wife, his kids, we want them all". Said Arthur, reaching inside his coat for his gunpowder bag.

"Are we all loaded? John, Jeremiah, together, go and kick the door down it looks strong door". Said Arthur tamping down the wadding in his pistol.

Together the two of them moved to the front door with their pistols drawn, synchronising their movements they kicked the door down with the first kick, sending it flying off its hinges We followed them in and there was a big fight, one of the men quickly stood up and held his hands up as if to give up straight away, the others took a little more persuading before they finally gave up seeing that they were vastly outnumbered, there were only four of them, the others at the rear of the house kicked down the back door and came rushing in shouting, only to see it was all over.

We looked at the men to find out who it was lived there and see if Thomas could recognised anyone who took his friends.

"This is the man", said Thomas pointing his pistol in the man face.

"Wait…. these are the other three that were with him yesterday, these are the other customs men, I didn't recognise them out of uniform", said Thomas looking at all four of them. As we were talking amongst ourselves and happy, we had all four of them, things calmed down, then one of the men seeing a chance to escape broke free and fought his way out through the back door, Jeremiah quickly drawing his pistol fired at him, hitting the door frame sending splinters flying everywhere then gave chase, but he lost him down an alleyways somewhere.

With the other three we bound their arms together and tied them to each other so they couldn't run off then we placed a noose around their necks pulling it tight, took them out the front and tied them all to a horse so they couldn't escape.

We then proceeded to go out of the town to work out the next part of the plan of how to exchange these for our men in gaol. We came to a clearing in a small wood just outside Shoreham by sea.

"Who is in charge out of you lot", said Thomas getting off his horse.

"No one's in charge", came a frightened voice of one of the customs men.

"Ah, must be you then", said Arthur, getting off his horse and pulling out a knife.

"He who speaks first must be the bravest", said Thomas.

"Why did you break into my friend's house", said Thomas, running a stone down his knife, sharpening the edge in front of the customs men.

"We were given a warrant by the magistrates office to go and get them, because we had information that they had been smuggling", said the man.

"What's your names", said Thomas.

"Only so we can write it on your tombstones", chipped in Smoker.

"That's Bolton, he's James and I'm Jones", said Jones.
"Who was that who managed to run off", asked Jeremiah.
"That was Quaff", said Jones.
"We shall remember that name for next time we come here, we'll be looking for him, cheating us", said Thomas.
"You have our men in your gaol, are they still there, are they being looked after? We are going to trade you for them, we shall see if your magistrate will put a price on your heads to get you back", said Arthur.
"Well,", said Jones swallowing hard.
"Well, what", said Thomas, moving nearer, staring at him intensely for what he was about to hear.
"They are not there anymore, not at the gaol", said Jones, now looking worried.
"What"! Shouted Thomas, as if he hadn't heard the first time.
"They were moved last night, more customs men came and took them off somewhere", said Jones.
"Took them off, off where"? said Thomas, now pulling out his pistol and pointing it at the man.
"I don't know, all I know is they are no longer at the gaol, they were moved in the night, apparently someone was seen trying to talk to them, so they were moved in case someone tried to rescue them, and we have no idea where they were taken, and as far as we know they are no longer in Shoreham by sea", said Jones.
"Dam" said Arthur again inflicting some damage to a tree with his knife.
Thomas punched Bolton in the face with all his anger thrown into one punch sending him flying backwards hitting his head on the tree behind him, then and hit the other two in the stomach and all three slumped to the ground.
"Which one of you put their hands up when we broke down your door"? said Arthur.
"I did", said Jones.
"Why did you do that". Said Thomas.

"I had my suspicions as to who we were going to arrest, and when you lot came through the door, I knew we'd have no chance of fighting and winning against you, I know who you are and your reputation, but we were just following orders", said Jones, blood streaming from his nose where Thomas hit him.

"Our Reputation has come this far? Brave, wise and stupid at the same time, stupid for being in the customs, it seems, but good that you took heed of our reputation, this has gone in your favour, I'm going to let you go", said Arthur, you seem to have an honest disposition.

He couldn't believe his ears and tears began to roll down his cheeks, we couldn't believe our ears either, Jeremiah kicked the grass up, feeling like he's missed out on putting his knife to good use.

"I will tell you now, no harm will come to you or your brethren if you keep your mouth shut, else you will suffer the same fate as your two friends here, we know who you are and where to find you, and we will find you have no fear, your family will also suffer, that's just going to be the way it is, that way if we come back to these parts again, you will turn away and walk in the other direction, you had best warm this Quaff to do the same or you and your family will do the suffering", is this clear enough for you to understand?

Jones, wiping the tears from his eyes with relief answered "yes", in a broken voice that could barely be heard.

"Cut him free Jeremiah", said Arthur.

Jeremiah walked over to Jones with a snarled look of disbelief, almost growling as he cut the ropes away, but still managed to dig the knife into his flesh and draw blood.

"Your free, now go", said Arthur, he pulled out his pistol and fired it at the ground where Jones was standing causing Jones to jump back, he turned, and run into the woods.

"Pick these two up and tie them to the horses, we will go back to Hawkhurst, nothing we can do will save our friends, not now, we don't even know where they are, all we can hope for is they find some way of escaping wherever they may be", said Arthur.
"Maybe they'll get off lightly", said Smoker trying to make everyone feel better.
"No way, not with this lot, if they've been taken elsewhere to avoid escape, I don't hold out much hope for them, taking these customs men away will make me feel better", said Thomas, as he took out his whip.
Jeremiah bent down to pick the men up but not before he gave them both a hard kick to the face.
The two men walked behind the horses and every now and then we would take it in turn to beat them with the whip watching them squeal in pain as each time would open a new wound, this carried on for several hours till we come to another clearing just outside Ticehurst.
"We stop here", said Arthur.
We got off our horses again and Arthur looked at the men.
"you two are scared aren't you", said Smoker, grinning.
"Yes", came a weak reply.
"And so, you should be, you are going to pay for what you've done and suffer the pain of our friends", said Thomas.
"Please don't hurt us anymore, we won't tell, we won't say a word, we will give up the customs, we can join you", pleaded Bolton.
"One thing you are going to understand, we hate custom men and their officers, once a custom man always a custom man, how could you possibly join us, why would we want you", said Jeremiah, grabbing the man by his balls and twisting them hard, he winced with pain, again collapsing to the ground.

"Strip them off naked, and tie them to those trees facing each over, and get a fire started, we don't want them to get cold, let's have a bit of fun". Said Arthur climbing down from his horse.

The men were tied naked to the trees facing each other towards the fire, we commenced whipping their bodies till they were running with blood.

"Put some more wood on that fire, they still look cold", Thomas laughed.

With that more wood was gathered and thrown on to make a large fire, this went on for some time with the men being half burnt to death, their bodies blistered from the heat, their hair had gone from the front and a smell of burning flesh was in the air, the two men begging us to kill them, we carried on whipping them more and more till they both slumped unconscious from the pain they had endured, their skin peeling from them in strips.

"That's enough cut them down and throw them in their rags and on the back of a cart", said Arthur.

"Smoker, George and James, take these two worthless carcasses down to Rye, what's left of them and put them on a boat, I don't care where it's going just make sure they don't come back here, we will meet you back at the Ivy, they will remember this day and what they've done for the rest of their miserable lives, you'll live to regret you had dealings with the Hawkhurst Gang.

With that we put their clothes on, their skin was peeling where the fire was so hot and now their clothes were rubbing against their wounds, we threw them both on the back of the cart and Jermiah jumped on the cart and punched and kicked both men, probably out of spite for letting the other one go, when Jeremiah had enough, we made their way off to Rye as we carried on our journey back to Hawkhurst.

Chapter 7
Choose your friends wisely. (1744)

Things quietened down for a while. Business was up, more and more goods coming across the channel, customs men visiting Rye, which was normal, it was a port after all, Arthur looked like he was beginning to mellow, he seemed happier in himself, maybe trying to shake off his violent streak which he had, and turning himself into the gentleman figure he seemed to yearn for now he had the wealth to go with it, I'm sure he thought he could fit in to high society in London if he wanted to, he did like to wear the clothes of a gentleman and strut around the village sometimes, with shop keepers calling him Mister, he even had a cane and decided to buy a nice plush carriage so he could go places in comfort. He showed us the inside of the carriage once, looked nice with stitched leather and red cloth higher up the inside and up around the roof, I saw him going around the village a few times in it, with a driver on top, getting used to the high life.

Now here he was back in the Oak and Ivy dressed back in what I would call his working clothes, not as posh as the others but these he didn't mind getting a little dirt on them. A few of us were sitting round drinking at the Oak and Ivy and reliving a few memories that we had amassed together on our journey to fortune and Thomas Winter was there paying us another visit from Lewes to get more good no doubt.

Smoker was telling us how he woke up one morning and tried to light his fire, he tried everything, his lamps were empty of oil, he couldn't find his fire steel at first, when he did he lost the flint that he had, couldn't rub two length of wood together as it was damp, the more he told us of the situation the more we fell about laughing, eventually he had to go to his neighbours in the pouring rain which was across a muddy field to get a flint, a fire steel and some oil just so he could get his fire lit, he was covered in mud and freezing cold when he got back home with his hands so cold he couldn't use the fire steel anyway.

I relived the day we took on Carswell, and was laughing at Poison because I had to ask if he could count,

"Well, I didn't know if he could or couldn't", I said laughing into my ale.

Thomas Winter spoke up, "I remember the time I was with Arthur and travelling back from Tonebridge where we met that fellow who was selling laces, do you remember him Arthur"? said Thomas.

"Yes, I remember him, that was ages ago", said Arthur taking another mouthful of ale.

"He'd been traveling around the country with those fancy samples of lace, carried them everywhere, trying to sell them, worth about fifty pounds if memory serves me well", said Thomas, finishing his tenth ale.

I looked at him and he could barely sit up straight as he told his story.

"Well, it seems that although Arthur likes to make money, he doesn't like to spend it and should an opportunity arise, and here was an opportunity that good old Arthur here couldn't resist", said Thomas, his words beginning to slur.

Everyone was smiling at this because we knew that Arthur wouldn't miss that opportunity especially if the lace was worth fifty pounds, we were eager to hear the rest of the story.

"Well, the poor man didn't know what to do when Arthur took his beloved lace from him, well what could you do, look at the size of him", said Thomas.

We all burst out laughing at this as Arthur was no small man by any means.

"Well, Arthur took it and went on his merry way back here to Hawkhurst thinking he had done good by taking the lace, but little did we know the man followed you back here, found out who you were and who your friends were and got one of your friends who I remember it was George Kingsmill, who in turn came to see you to appeal to your better nature to get it back from you", said Thomas.

"Yes, he was persistence, I'll give him that", laughed Arthur.

"Well, here we are again with another opportunity, well Arthur wasn't going to just give it up like that was he? So, Arthur said yes, you can have it back at a cost of ten guineas, to which the man joyfully accepted and gladly paid up", said Thomas.

Again, everyone burst out laughing at the outcome of the story.

"You should have been hanged for doing that" said Thomas reaching down to see if his tankard had a few drops left.

Immediately Arthur drew out his knife and pushed it into Thomas face slicing deep into Thomas's jaw down to the bone, blood covered the table.

The look of shock on Thomas Winters face as his hand went to cover the wound.

"You ever mention that affair again you will surely meet your death", said Arthur, wiping his knife on Thomas's sleeve.

Thomas rose from his stool and with blood gushing from the wound as he staggered through the door and out of the Inn.

"Well, I'm not sure we will be seeing the likes of Thomas Winter again, said Smoker trying to make light of it.

"No one tells me I should hang for the things I do, no one", said Arthur, returning to his ale.

And there was I thinking Arthur was changing, seems we were stuck with him being the way he was.

Chapter 8
Montivilliers (1744)

I was called to a meeting along with the others as it turned out at the Oak and Ivy. There were a lot of gang members there, the place was crowded, after the initial greetings from everyone I saw Arthur, Thomas and George sitting at the usual table looking flustered, Arthur banging his fist on the table, from what I could see through the crowd they were arguing about something, I needed to get closer.
"Good morning everyone", I said as I neared their table and trying to put light on anything that was going on.
"Come and sit-down Will, we are trying to sort out a problem", said George.
I listened to the conversation trying to piece together what was going on without them having to repeat anything to me.
"The cutters have been organised, the goods will be coming in, that part has been taken care of, I don't see any problems with the French side, Pascal and his friends should have taken care of any problems in France, Richard and Shepherd are sorting out the last of the goods on the last cutter, it's what happens once it reaches our shores, we still need to organise it over here. We've got to get everyone organised, this is an exceptionally large shipment and its arriving in Pevensey in two days' time. Everyone needs to play their part, we've got to get as many packhorses with carts as we can find, this so far will be our biggest haul, a lot of money has been spent on this and we don't want any problems.
We need to round up as many people as we can, I want all those that are with us to play their part in helping, they like us having cheaper goods to buy so let them help, storekeepers, street traders, anyone who can help, and I don't want to hear anyone saying no, this is for them as much as it is for us, they enjoy the spoils so make them help", said Arthur trying to resolve the problem.

"What if they don't want to help"? said Thomas.
"If they don't then just write down their name and where they live or work and that person will be paying double for their goods in future from us, they can't have it both ways, that'll make them think twice about refusing", said Arthur, getting calmer now, convincing himself that this has now been taken care of.
"William, make sure that we have plenty of shot, wadding and gunpowder, and if you can find some more pistols, I think we may need a lot more", said Thomas, looking at me.
"When we round up the rest of the gang, I want to make sure their pistols are loaded and they've got plenty of shot just in case, we don't want any trouble, we must protect what is ours at any cost, so make sure each member gets one. We are going to meet everyone at sunset just outside Pevensey, organise people, horses, and carts, we can load up everything and get it through Kent and hidden, that is going to be the biggest challenge. We are expecting those three cutters from Le Havre so we'll need all the horses, carts and people we can muster, borrow all you can from the villagers and get their help too, I need people to go to the outlying villagers and get as many as you can we are expecting a lot, don't take no for an answer from the villagers, remember they gain from our spoils too, so if they want goods, they had better help", said Arthur.

Meanwhile while Arthur and the others were organising from the English side, in busy little inn in the backstreets in the quiet town of Montivilliers in France, two man were eagerly awaiting the arrival of a man known only to them as Pascal.
"Do you have any idea what this Pascal looks like"? said Richard, taking another mouthful of ale, "this ale tastes a bit different to what we are used to", he said wiping his mouth, staring into the tankard.
"You are always fussing when we come to France, I know as much as you do, what Thomas told us before we left Rye", said Shepherd, trying to stay calm and relaxed.

"He's a Frenchman. he will be wearing a hat with a white band around it, and he will have a large moustache, and a cane, so I don't think that will be difficult to spot, not amongst this crowd", said Shepherd, looking around and laughing.
The Inn was full of workers that had finished their days work, a lot covered in mud from building and coal dust, spending the whole day shoveling coal to keep the furnaces stoked, and the usual number of sailors coming inland to seek a quiet drinking den as most inns on the sea front would be full.
"Let's hope he doesn't let us down", said Richard.
The smile left Shepherd's lips, "It's not us he'll be letting down, its Arthur and Thomas and the rest of the gang, with that I wouldn't want to be in his shoes if he did, Thomas said he will be here and that's that, all we need to do is wait here as instructed, try and enjoy your ale and try to look like you fit in". said Shepherd, looking Richard up and down.
"Fit in, what do you mean? said Richard.
"Well, you don't exactly look relaxed do you, you look nervous all the time and its beginning to show," said Shepherd.
"How can I relax? Do you know what they will do to us if we are caught"? Trying not to raise his voice, "I can't wait to be halfway across the channel and back to England, I don't like coming to France, neither of us can speak French which is never good, and we must both stand out in a crowd, just by the way we are dressed let alone if we dare speak", said Richard taking another mouthful of ale, screwing his face up at the taste,
"I don't know why we get chosen for these jobs, this is the third time we've come here, there are other members in the gang you know, why can't they come here instead, give them a chance to taste this ale". Said Richard nervously

"Well, we are here now so we must do the best we can in this situation, we've got to make sure that all the goods get on those ships, not sure how as two cutters have already been loaded and have set sail and waiting out in the channel, Thomas won't be too pleased if we let him down, he doesn't like coming here himself, so we must do as he's asked, and we must do it right or face his wrath, if you don't like it you can always tell him when we get back to England". Said Shepherd sternly. "And keep your voice down you'll give us away by the way you are carrying on, so calm down, have a smoke on your pipe, that normally calms you down". Said Shepherd, peering around the room.
The inn was dark even though it was daylight outside, the windows were small and dirty, many years of grime and smoke built up on the windows inside and out, candles were lit on each table and the room filled with pipe smoke, there were a lot of people in there and noise with a small group playing a piano and singing songs in French.
The inn keeper was filling tankards with ale with what looked like his wife, the whole inn gave off an air of everyone enjoying themselves, with the odd drunkard trying to chat with the bar keeper's wife and getting nowhere.
"Seems like everyone has finished work and come here to get a drink before going home" said Richard, "with the amount of people in here we might not see this Pascal, let's hope he gets here soon",
"So, do I, you're making me nervous, and you're beginning to get on my nerves with your whining", said Shepherd.
Just then the door opened, Richard looked up and peered over the crowd of people, "it's about time", said Richard, nudging Shepherd and pointing to the door, "I think this must be our man", he said taking a larger gulp of beer in an excited way. Shepherd made his way through the crowd being closely followed by Richard over to the man who was wearing exactly as they've been told.
"I take it, you must be Pascal"?

"Oui monsieur, my name is Pascal, and you must be either Shepherd or Richard"? He said reaching out his hand.
"I'm Shepherd and he is Richard", Shaking him by the hand and turning around and pointing to Richard who was just finishing his ale and placing his tankard on a nearby table.
"We don't have long; we must hurry if we are to catch the tide". Pascal said In a French accent.
Richard and Shepherd picked up their coats and leather bags from the table they were sitting and followed Pascal through the door.
"Hurry, this way, everything has been organised, but not as we had planned, there have been more customs men seen in the harbour, so we've had to change our plans, but all is good, all is good", said Pascal in a whisper.
"It's difficult to speak in the inn as there are ears all about us, we have two carts full of goods that are waiting down a back street which we need to get the goods to Harfleur, there we will load four small boats and row under the cover of darkness to Le Havre, we will then load everything onto a waiting ship which will take you back to England."
"Wait a minute", said Shepherd,
"Thomas said there would be a lot more than two carts worth and we ourselves organised more, we can't go back with those meagre supplies, what have you done with the rest, we've been here for a few months buying and organising this trip, with the goods we have bought there should be a huge amount, we've organised and paid for three cutters to take our goods back to England Thomas won't be very happy without the rest that he has bought, and he's paid good money, now is not the time to short change us"? said Shepherd, turning to face Pascal

"I can see why monsieur Thomas put you in charge, he said with a smile, you are good, but don't worry Monsieur, as I've said there have been a lot of customs men in the area so we've had to be extra careful, there has been several loads delivered and stowed on the two ships already, there is more delivered and stowed on the last ship as we speak, so do not worry you will have your three ships full of goods, these two carts are the last of it, we couldn't take it all at once for fear of being caught"

"Good thinking, we don't want to be caught", said Richard, "But we will have to check to make sure everything is there", said Shepherd.

"it's not my intention to steal from monsieur Thomas, but if that is your wish then we won't stop you," said Pascal. "Everything will be in order, after all we want to be doing business with you again", he said with a grin, showing his blackened teeth.

Pascal was dressed considerably well for a smuggler, he must have been doing alright for himself with Thomas's and Arthur's money, he held himself quite well, coming across as a gentleman, good clothes, hair, and moustache trimmed, trying to be someone he's not, Shepherd thought to himself.

The back streets of Montivilliers were quiet now, the sun was setting, not many people were out, many of them had either gone home before the dark of night or ended up in the Inn's that were spread across the town, either way it would make it easy to transport the two carts down to Harfleur without too many eyes looking.

They turned a corner into a darkened alley to find two horse and carts fully loaded and covered with sacking.

"Avez-vous eu des problèmes pendant que j'étais parti"? Pascal said to two of his colleagues who were sitting waiting on the carts.

"Non Pascal, tout est calme", came the reply.

"All is good monsieur Shepherd", said Pascal, "all is good, let us be on our way".

With that Richard climbed up on one cart while Shepherd got on the other. Pascal got on his horse and led the way.
They travelled about 30 mins and a steady pace till they came to the village of Harfleur.
The dark of night was now upon them, no lanterns were lighting their way either, making it difficult to see their way, trying to keep quiet and low so as not to be seen, the dirt track road had made the going hard and shaking the loads about on the carts.
"We are heading for the river just outside the town where it's quite, we will be there very soon", Pascal said in a quiet voice.
They arrived at a narrow wooden bridge which went over the river.
"Wait here", said Pascal.
He carried on across the bridge, looking all around him as he did. Just then a figure appeared from the bushes and approached and spoke to him.
He turned and came back to where they were waiting, Richard looking tense as normal.
"Quickly, the coast is clear", said Pascal, getting off his horse.
A half-moon was rising just above the horizon, giving off a small amount of light, just enough to light the way.
They moved across the bridge to where some more friends of Pascal's were waiting by four rowing boats, Pascal went over and spoke to them in French, they came straight over to the carts and immediately started to unload the carts and fill up the rowing boats. Before long with all of them helping the boats were loaded. Pascal went over to the two men in the carts, and they watched as he shook hands with them, he handed one of the men the reins of his horse and what seemed like a small leather pouch, and in no time, they were gone.
Shepherd and Richard made their way down the bank, trying not to fall in the river, and clumsily entered a rowing boat each, Pascal soon followed getting into one of the other boats and all four boats proceeded to move quietly downstream.

Pascal called out and said, "we will soon be on the canal de Tancarville, it's a bit busy down there with many boats, sailors and customs men so we have to be careful and quite as we can, try not to make a noise, the moon rising is not going to help".

We let one boat go at a time and kept close to the shore, we proceeded very quietly making sure that we stopped rowing whenever we saw someone on the quayside and before long, we saw the lanterns hanging from the poop deck and quarter deck lighting our way on the waiting ship.

"Il est là notre beau bateau", said pascal, bringing his hands to his mouth to hide his excitement.

"She is a fine ship no, a fine example of a two masted ship"? said Pascal in a low voice.

"We didn't respond as we couldn't see much in the dim light and we didn't want to make any noise, but the look on Pascal's face was one of excitement, as if the end of the journey that he'd been through with his men were nearly done.

As we grew nearer to the ship it was just like Pascal had said, I'm sure that our hearts were making more noise than we made while rowing.

"That's only one ship", said Richard, obviously not hearing the conversation that was had earlier.

"The other two left earlier, they couldn't risk being here with all the goods on board, so they left earlier and are sitting outside the harbour about thirty miles out", said Pascal running his fingers down his moustache making sure it was still looking tidy.

We pulled along the far side of the ship to be hidden from the quayside, Pascal called up to the deck, and a deck hands promptly threw down some ropes and two rope ladders.

Soon men were coming down the ladders and the ropes and tieing them to the loads in the boats, one after the other, it was hot work and with the aid of the crew mates the boats were soon emptied, and the goods stored safely somewhere on the ship.

Again, Pascal said something to the four men in the boats and handed one a small bag.

The rope ladders were pulled up and another two ropes were sent down to the row boats, all four row boats were tied to the ship then they pushed off the side of the boat and headed out into the darkness.

The call to cast off was given and every one of the crew seemed to appear from nowhere, silently pulling on ropes and rushing up into the rigging.

I could feel us moving and a lookout was talking to the men in the boats something in French, from what Shepherd observed was the row boats were pulling the ship out of the harbour, moving the ship very slowly.

A cabin boy ushered us to follow him, the captain wanted to see you, he said in broken English.

"That's better let's get below deck out of the way", said Richard.

"I told you, you worry too much", Said Shepard.

"I know, but I have every right to be, remember the last time we were here, and that chap got caught for smuggling, he got hanged right in the middle of the town so that everyone could see, and I'm sure the hangman didn't do a good job as it took him a long time to stop kicking, and I don't want the same to happen to me. This is so risky for us, we are in a foreign country, we really don't know anyone, so no one will help us", said Richard.

"The gains outweigh the risks, as long as we are careful then all should be fine, Thomas and Arthur don't just send us over here with no planning, everything is carefully planned as much as they can do, but they have trusted people and they will look after us, think of the Hawkhurst gang as one big family that stretches far and wide", said Shepherd, looking at Richard still fidgeting.

Even so, I'd feel a lot better when we are further out to sea, all the time we are on this ship I will be worrying, I'll be happy when we reach the shores of England and not France", said Richard.

"You'll always be worrying, you're that sort of chap, you've worried all your life", said Shepherd, laughing to himself.

They followed the cabin boy towards the stern of the ship, and entered through a solid oak door, into the Great cabin, the captain was sitting behind a large table covered in what looked like maps of the sea and coastal routes, behind the captain was a large window and they could see the lanterns of the French port of Le Havre disappearing into the distance.

"Welcome aboard, said the captain, my name is captain Cribb", "You must be the fellows that Arthur Gray told me about".

"Have you seen him"? said Richard.

Just then a knock at the door and Pascal Entered and stood behind everyone, listening to what was being said.

"Welcome Pascal, I take it everything has gone according to plan, no trouble to be had", said Cribb.

Everything is perfect captain, just as we planned", said Pascal brushing down his clothes and stroking his moustache.

The cabin boy walked over to a large cupboard and took out a bottle of Rum and proceeded to fill glasses and hand them out to us all.

"A toast gentleman, a toast to a successful trip", said captain Cribb.

We all drank to the toast as the cabin boy disappeared through the oak door to leave us to talk.

"By now all the last stock that was brought aboard has been stored and hidden below", said the captain.

"We have to check it to make sure it's all here", said Richard.

"Do you not trust us"? the captain said looking at Richard in disbelief, with Pascal looking at him as if he couldn't believe his ears either.

"Well, it's just that Artur asked us to check to make sure it's all here". Said Richard trying to hide his embarrassment having drawn attention to himself.

"Your Mr. Gray sent me a letter with all the details, details were in fact, explicit, as to what he wants in the way of goods, he's particularly good at what he's does your Mr. Gray, he never leaves things out so everything is in order, but by all means we will give you the opportunity if you wish to go and check the goods, but I'll warn you, it won't be easy to find if my crew have done their job and I can assure you, they do it well. Your Mr. Gray is thorough in getting his goods, but he's not very good with paying out money, he's short-changed me with my money this time", he said pouring himself another glass of rum.

"Did he, I'm sure it wasn't intentional, there's a lot of goods there even on those two boats we came in on, not considering the others two cutters that have already set sail", said Shepherd.

"Such as that maybe, perhaps he did it, just to make sure he gets everything he asks for; but he's got to realise we are all working together, and besides some of the goods are paid for with my own money and if we get caught then that's my money lost once the customs men get hold of it". Said Cribb

"There's nothing we can do, while we are out at sea", said Shepherd.

"Yes, there is, you can tell him from me that in future, if he wants to carry on doing business with me, he'll have to pay the full amount of his half upfront, or he can find himself another ship and another captain to deliver his goods, and he won't find too many willing parties to be doing that". Said Cribb.

"I'm not going to get into any arguments with anyone, but I think you'll find there's plenty of ships that will take our goods across, you get rewarded plenty and the other two ships captains will too, Arthur knows the risks you have to take, we all do, I know he takes care of all that help him, so if you want to tell him you no longer want to help Arthur then you'll have to tell him yourself and face the consequences", said Shepherd, now feeling in charge

"Consequences, what consequences", said Cribb, looking sternly at the both of them standing there.

"That sound like a threat to me", said Cribb.

"I'm sorry Captain, it's been a long day, maybe that was the wrong use of words given the situation, I will let him know, that's all I can do, I will speak to him for you and tell him what you've told me, but remember I cannot speak for him, I've seen his temper, and if he's not getting his own way with someone going against his plans then that'll just make him worse, plus there's Thomas Kingsmill to worry about as well, It wouldn't pay you to go against them once they have got plans set in place", said Shepherd.

"That again sounds like another threat", the captain going behind his desk and opened the draw, reached in, and pulled out a pistol.

Shepherd, Richard, and Pascal looked shocked at seeing the pistol.

The captain laughed, "don't worry, I'm not going to use it, I just reminded myself that I need to clean and load it, so don't be alarmed".

There was a sigh of relief as the captain placed the pistol down on the desk.

"I never said I was going against them, I only said about getting paid to do the work beforehand so as I don't have to use my own money, that's not too much to ask in the circumstances, after all I have my own debts to pay as well as a crew". Said the captain.

We've come here on good faith and on Arthur's orders we don't need Arthur thinking we've done anything to annoy this captain and spoil things for him in the future, we want to keep captain Cribb on our side, so we will do our best to convince him of this way forward, thought Shepherd.

"Not to show any disrespect to you and your crew captain Cribb", Said Shepherd, trying to be as tactful as he could, "but I think Arthur has given you most of the payment for the goods, you could if you wanted sail anywhere in the world and sell the goods elsewhere and not worry about Arthur and Thomas ever again, so I can see his point for not paying fully upfront like you ask, if indeed it wasn't an error on his part". Said Shepherd.

Cribb looked at Shepherd with a glare in his eye,

"You mean to say that Arthur doesn't trust me after all the time that we've known each other"? Said the captain.

"To be honest with you, I'm not sure he trusts anyone, especially now he's in this business, I think he doesn't even trust us", said Shepherd, trying to find the next words so as not to annoy him further.

"Well, I can understand that", laughed Cribb, "but we are all in this together with me and my ship and crew taking the biggest risks". Said the captain.

"Arthur is not going to change the way he does business; he needs some guarantee that he's going to get his goods". Said Shepherd.

"Hmm", mumbled Cribb, I don't see that as being fair at all, and shows no trust in those around him", said the captain, turning his back on Shepherd, to ponder the point.

"I will speak to him personally for you when we land and the next time we come to France and use your services to ask if we can extra funds to pay you, not sure how that will be with him, but that's the best I can do, now he'll have to put his trust in us with extra money", said Shepherd.

"He's got to start trusting his own, while you are having this um, word with Arthur and Thomas, tell them I would like a bigger share for our work, we do take the extra risk, risk to lose everything if we are caught, especially with this ship and its crew, both are hard to find, that would be better, you tell them that, and yes, I do know what Arthur and Thomas both like, but business is business, shall we say sixty, forty", said Cribb.

"Now that is something you'll have to take up with Arthur, I'm not going to mention anything like that to him". Said Shepherd, shying away from another confrontation.

"But I wouldn't start being greedy with what you're asking if I were you, they are not people to be crossed at all, whatever arrangement you've got with them you had better see them in person", said Shepherd.

"Now, now gentlemen please, let's just enjoy the journey, have a drink and be put all this behind us, I'm sure things can get resolved amicably", said Pascal, reaching for a bottle of rum that was on the captain's table.

"I will compose a letter to Arthur, and word it such as to give him no ill, and hand it to you before you embark with the goods, and I hope that he will see things my way so that we can have a better partnership and trust in this matter for our future business together, and you can tell him personally, seeing as you show no trust to me either, I won't be doing any more runs for him until this is resolved. After I've unloaded the goods on board I am heading for Ramsgate for a few days, and I'll expect an answer from him there. In the meantime, please let my cabin boy show you where you can rest for the night, we have a long journey back to England," said Cribb.

"it's not that far", said Richard.

Cribb looked at Shepherd as if not to believe his ears on what Richard had just said.

"It is if we don't want to be seen by anyone, there is the English Navy and French navy out here that we have to avoid, so we can't go directly to England, plus we have to anchor offshore so as not to raise suspicions, we will be back in England by tomorrow evening and ready for Pevensey the following day, you do understand, don't you"? said Cribb, looking at Richard.

Richard just nodded in agreement.

"This is the part that your Arthur doesn't control, this is the part that I'm in control of, so we do as I say out here and I take no commands from anyone not even your Arthur Gray or Thomas Kingsmill when we are at sea, at first light someone will show you around the stored goods so that you can check what is on board, but I'm sure you won't need to as everything will be in order, unless of course your trust is of elsewhere too", said Cribb looking at everyone as if trust is now in question.

Shepherd raised his glass to the captain's good health and drank the rest of the rum that was in it.

"Until then, I suggest you enjoy our hospitality, my cabin boy will show you to the galley for some refreshments and put some food in your bellies and then your bunks". Said Cribb.

"Pascal, please call the cabin boy for him to show these gentlemen to the mess room and their cabins". Said Cribb picking up the pistol to inspect it.

"I'm sorry if there's been a misunderstanding between us, it's just that Arthur has put trust in us to take care of business while he's not here, and if there's been anything said to the contrary, then we apologies to you as captain of this ship", said Shepherd, backing down and trying to get the captains trust back and trying to make amends of the situation, for now it was he who would have to face Arthur and Thomas if this situation cannot be resolved.

The captain and Pascal bid them both a good night as they left the captain's cabin.
The cabin boy showed them where to get some food, some bread that smelt like it had been baked that day and a few slices of beef with a bottle of rum each.
"This is good", said Richard, taking a mouthful of rum "much better than we had in the Inn".
"I'm not thinking about that", said Shepherd,
"I've now got to tell Arthur that there'll be no more goods coming in from France from Captain Cribb until he gives an answer, and I expect I will have to go to Ramsgate and face the captain again with that answer, I know Arthur or Thomas will have something to say about Cribb going back on his word, or wanting more money for the journeys that he's doing, knowing those two like I do, a friend is a friend and someone who goes against the gang should watch out, it'll be a wonder captain Cribb will still be able to sail this ship once they've set fire to it, not good to go against them", said Shepherd, looking at Richard pulling up an old blanket to sleep under.
Shepherd look worried for once, as he undid the cork from his rum and proceeded to take a few mouthfuls from the bottle.
Shepherd was woken up early by the cabin boy, who looked bright and cheerful,
"This way sir", he said,
Shepherd kicked Richard who mumbled something as if still partly dreaming. Both rubbing the sleep from their eyes and rubbing their heads for the realisation that the rum was stronger than they thought.
They were led to the quarter deck where they met Pascal,
"Good morning to you both, ah I see you like the rum, and maybe just a bit too much for your heads this morning". said Pascal.
"We are fine", said Shepherd looking out to sea and wondering why they were up before the sun.

"We have work to do", said Pascal, "you wanted to check on all the goods before we got to England, there is a lot of it, and we thought you'd want to make an early start on doing it". With that Pascal called to two of the deck hands.
"Johnson and Barrows here will show you around to where the goods are stored, you can split up in pairs to get through it quickly before we make land, Lanterns are full of oil to help you in the dark, and best of luck, when you are done you can have something to eat in the galley, you'll have worked up an appetite by then, so I'll see you back up here when you are done, don't take too long monsieur, we are close to shore". Said Pascal in his French accent.
"After last night conversation with the captain about trust, I think we will leave checking over the goods for now, of course any irregularities will be sorted out later", said Shepherd rubbing his neck and blinking towards the sun light, as if that's a cure for heavy drinking.
"I thought we were not landing till nightfall", said Richard.
"Correct", said Pascal.
With that Pascal turned and went into a cabin and closed the door.
"Strange", said Richard.
"Not really", said Johnson, "Pascal doesn't like the cold while on deck, and the sea air doesn't always agree with him".
"So why did he come out here then"? said Richard.
"To look after you two I suppose", said Johnson, "besides, we have to get this done quickly, if we encountered any Navy ships out here then we will have to weigh anchor and run, you won't want to be below deck if that happens, the goods might not be tied down enough and you could get crushed down there, so let's get on and get it done, I'm starving as it is".
"Well, Mr. Johnson, I take it the goods are stowed away in places that are hard to find, is that correct"? said Shepherd.
"Aye, that's correct", said Johnson.

"I would like to take a quick look but for now we shall just have to take your word that it's all there, besides no one is checking the other two ships, so may as well get something to eat now that we are up, I'm starving", said Shepherd.
The sun was just showing an orange glow on the horizon as they made their way below deck carrying their only light from the lanterns into the gloom.
After a short time later the four of them arrived back on deck to a sun high in the sky.
"I'll take those", said Barrows, taking the lanterns from them.
Johnson knocked on the door of Pascal's cabin.
"Ah monsieur, all finished, all present and correct from what you have on your orders I take it"? said Pascal.
"No, we decided against that, from what the captain was saying about trust we did have a quick look and found it very hard to find anything that resembles anything smuggled at all, so we gave up and had something to eat instead", said Richard.
"Difficult", said Shepherd laughing.
"What is so funny monsieur", said Pascal.
"Without Johnson and Barrow, we would never have found any of it, we only saw a small portion, that was good enough for us as we passed through to get something to eat", said Shepherd, "they have certainly done a good job of concealing it".
"Of course, monsieur", we also know the penalty for smuggling, that is why we must take care where we put it, this is not a game, this is life, and we take every precaution no matter whose goods they are. You will only find the legitimate stock that the captain has purchased that needs to go to Ramsgate with the correct paperwork, not monsieur Arthur's goods". said Pascal.
Although Shepherd had done this trip a few times, he could now piece together just what a big operation this was to get goods to and from France, a lot bigger than he had imagined.

He looked out to sea, trying to take it all in, when Richard said, "Come on shepherd, stop daydreaming, let's go back to the cabin and get some rest before nightfall", said Richard, pulling him by the sleeve.

"Enjoy your rest, I will see you both later", said Pascal, as he disappeared back to his quarters.

Chapter 9
The Pevensey landing (1744)

The day before the landing at Pevensey was hectic, everyone rushing around, Arthur, Thomas, Smoker, and myself were shouting orders to everyone in the Village of Hawkhurst and surrounding villages.
"We need more horses and a lot more carts and tell them to bring ropes and sacking as well, here's a map showing the location that everyone needs to be at tomorrow, makes sure that people see it and know where it is". Said Thomas, handy me a parchment.
 I took ten men on a cart and paid a visit to Sissinghurst, Benenden, Rolvenden, Cranbrook, Flimwell and Ticehurst and at each village, we split up to ask around and managed to get more carts and extra people to take them, at Sissinghurst alone we found fifteen people that could provide us with horses along with riders that were willing to help, we told them to make their way to Norman's Bay near Pevensey by tomorrow night and wait for everyone there and don't let us down, we carried on our journey going from village to village and getting the same response all the villagers seemed willing to help, I lost count of how many, but I think in total we managed to get around thirty five carts and about ninety people and just as many horses. I kept thinking that I may have overdone it a bit and got far too many carts, but Arthur said he wanted all that we could get help with, and as the word went out that the Hawkhurst gang wanted them then everyone was happy to oblige, after all they are the ones who benefit from cheaper prices for their tea, brandy, and gin. We sold a lot of gin in Hawkhurst and Northiam, so much, so that when I was speaking to one of the shop keepers in the village, they had so much gin that they were using it to clean their windows with as well as their pots and pans for cooking, I was thinking we should raise the price of the stuff.

We got back to the Inn after a long day riding around Kent and surrounding areas.

"I hope you told them all to get down to Pevensey for tomorrow night and showed them all the map that Thomas gave you, we don't want anyone to go missing"? said Arthur, with all the others that are going there should be a lot, and we'll need them too, three cutters will be our biggest haul to date, so the more people and carts we have the better.

Other gang members went in different direction to do the same as us and gather as many people, horses, and carts as they could, and they too were given maps of where to go and stay. Surely, we had enough just from the people I got.

Smoker came back to the Ivy and said that he had rounded up at least twenty-five carts and one hundred and seventy-five people and horses from going to Peasmarsh, Northiam, Rye, Sandhurst and Newenden and surrounding areas.

John came back from where he had been and said he's got about eighty.

"I hope you all told them where to be", Said Arthur.

"Don't worry Arthur, they'll be there if they know what's good for them", came and voice from the rear.

"Make sure you've all got plenty of rope and any sacking you can find to cover the goods with", said Thomas looking round at everyone.

"Good, that's most things taken care of, we will leave and make our way to Normans Bay to catch the tide and get our goods on dry land". Said Arthur, heading into the Ivy.

"Anyone for a drink, I'm buying", said Arthur, in a happier mood.

We stayed in the Oak and Ivy till it was late, then Arthur announced, "We should get going, make sure your carts are ready, we are leaving.

We travelled through the night, just our lanterns lighting the way, I'm sure we looked suspicious if anyone saw us, there was a lot of us, but we didn't care, we were big enough now and our name made people turn the other way when we came through their village, we did what we want, now.
The sun still was just coming up by the time we reached Pevensey we could see the field close to Normans Bay filling up with people and carts waiting, there were loads of lanterns all lit up, showing just how many were in the field, there were more people in that field than there were residents living in Pevensey I reckon, laughing to myself.
Thomas got everyone's attention
"Put out any fires that you have lit for fear of attracting too much attention, we chose this spot as it in a hollow close to the beach away from the locals, and lighting fires will give us away, just be patient, we are just waiting for tonight then we can get back home".
There was a lot of people there and more kept turning up.
"Are you sure this field is big enough", I said Looking at Arthur and Thomas, who were also looking a bit worried at the amount of people that had gathered. As more and more people arrived, we sent a few of them off to the beach away from the field to wait.
As the day wore on there was a few stragglers that were turning up, the sun was starting to set, I looked out on the horizon.
"Look out there", I said to Arthur, pointing out to sea, "I can see two masts just on the horizon".
"That could well be one of our ships, if it is then two more will be close to it, they are getting close to shore ready for later tonight", said Arthur, as he rushed off to find Thomas and tell him what we've seen.

"No way would anyone stop us now, not with this many people here. I moved to where Arthur and Thomas were. This is it, it is happening, very soon we'll have more goods that we know what to do with", said Arthur, a big smile came on Arthur's and Thomas's face as they looked out to sea, just catching a glimpse of the masts.

Thomas went to speak to all the people gathered there to inform them what was expected of them all.

"There will be three large cutters loaded with goods, all three have come in from France and they are fully loaded, your job will be to offload the rowing boats as they come in and stack the goods onto carts and the saddle bags on your horses, we need to hurry to get this done as quickly and as quietly as possible", said Thomas.

"Three cutters are going to be a lot of goods, now I can see why you wanted a lot of carts, I thought we had too many", I said to Arthur, looking around the field and all those that had gathered along the beach.

"Ahh, you've been thinking too small again, the size of our gang now has grown from strength to strength so why not use it, customs men are not around, we no longer have Carswell on our back, so while things are good, we shall take advantage of it", said Arthur.

I could see the look of anticipation building on his face, eager to see if what he's organised has once again come to fruition, he's becoming more powerful leading this gang and happy to once again bring himself more and more money to keep him in the lifestyle he's become used to.

We arrived at the beach just as the warm glow of the sun could be seen on the horizon, the wind picking up as we went over the sand dunes, there in front of us were three cutters had moved closer inland and were waiting offshore just pulling their sails in and dropping anchors, boats were being lowered and already starting to offload our goods into them.

I looked at him, a big smile came on his face as the wind blew at his already unkempt hair, he went over to Thomas and patted him on the back with his big hand, not saying a word, just smiling together as they both ran across the beach.
"Come on you lot, get those goods onto the carts, everyone give them a hand when they come ashore, I don't want to be down here too long, let's get moving", Arthur shouted.
There was a burst of activity on the beach, bodies moving back and forth, wading out to bring the boats in closer, the rowers in the boats looking exhausted as they fought against the waves, again and again rowing back to the cutters to load up more goods.
What seemed like ages and with people looking exhausted, the last of the boats came ashore and with them came Richard and Shepherd.
Shepherd walked over to Arthur, "These are the last boats, all the goods are now on land", said Shepherd as he handed Arthur a letter".
"What this", asked Arthur, opening the letter reading it with a spout lantern that had been lit as a marker light for the boats. They stood there while he read it, the boats were now retreating to the cutters, breaking through the waves as he looked out to sea and pointed, then made a fist, as the words of the letter sunk in, I could see the expression on his face change, he screwed up the paper and punched Shepherd in the stomach sending him flying across the beach, not for any other reason than he'd lost his temper. I found out from Richard later that the letter was written by Captain Cribb who said he now wanted more shares in what he brought over, or this was the last time he'd work for him bringing over goods as trust had now gone for not giving the captain the full money for the job he'd done, if the boats hadn't left the shore, Arthur would have jumped in one and gone to see Captain Cribb and slit him from ear to ear, instead Shepherd felt his wrath for having him spoil what was for him, a perfectly good day.

The glow of the sun was beginning to show through the darkness, the birds were just starting their morning song as we left the beach behind. All goods loaded, tied down and covered, we made our way back towards Hawkhurst, we were a sight to behold, I couldn't believe the amount that we had ourselves, and the number of carts and people there were. We got Shepherd and Richard to go and count them just so that they would keep out of Arthur's way, I'm sure I heard there were around one hundred and twenty carts and around five hundred and forty five men and women all carrying goods on horses or carts, we were in no rush, just casually making our way back home, selling a few items on the way of course, well we didn't want to miss any opportunity of getting money.

We travelled without stopping, back to Hawkhurst and onto the Inn.

George Kingsmill had stayed behind trying to work out the best places to store the goods and as people reached the Oak and Ivey the people were given different tasks and locations as to where their goods should be hidden, it was long before the village was clear of people again.

The places used were spread all over Kent, it's a good job someone had made a note of it all as we would have never found it again, I took a glimpse of the details written by George, just a quick glimpse. Snargate church, Brenzett, Brookland, Eastbridge church ruins. A barn located near Orgaswick, Fairfield church and deserted barns in fields next to the churches. The list looked endless, there were locations in tunnels in and around Winchelsea, some goods to be stored and hidden at Arthur's house.

Just then George can into the inn and took the list away as more people had just arrived.

"See lad, that seemed easy, that's the way it should be done", said Arthur, coming into the Inn, with a big smile on his face", that's going to be ages before that smile goes, I thought to myself.

"Get Shepard and Richard in here, I want to talk to them both", as he opens the oak door and shouting orders outside. Shepherd and Richard gingerly came back into the Inn to confront Arthur and Thomas.

"Sit down you two", Thomas said pointing to a couple of stools in front of Arthur.

"Right, as you spent some time with Captain Cribb, I want you to tell me all that was said between all of you, and tell me the truth", Arthur's smile had now gone as he'd now moved on from getting the load in from Pevensey.

I let them carry on with their conversation as I was tired and all I could think of was my comfy bed, so I bid them all a good night and headed off home.

I found out a few days later that after the meeting with Arthur, Richard and Shepherd were ordered to go to Ramsgate to find Captain Cribb with a letter of his own, stating that because they had both had to share in the sufferance of the customs men, each are equal to their own survival, both on land and at sea, so as a mark of respect and because they needed each other, Arthur wouldn't grant Captains Cribbs wish, but to accept his new offer of fifty, fifty of all goods sold as long as from now on the captain paid for half of the goods as is only fair. And if this wasn't to be agreeable by the captain then Shepherd had his orders to set fire to Captain Cribbs ship, if this wasn't carried out by Richard or Shepherd then they were to be found and they were to be burnt at the stake for ruining a perfectly good deal in the first place.

Chapter 10
A spy in our midst (1744)

We were doing well according to Arthur, it's the most money he'd ever seen in his life especially after the Large haul from France and now had the reputation of being the most powerful gang than all the others, and there were a few still around trying to do the same as we were to eke out a living, but none as successful as us, no one would dare to try and take it from any of us, we were a team, a family, very close without too many outsiders asking questions, wo betide anyone that did, they run the risk of going against us, for what we were doing was our business and no one else's and anyone asking for information was soon dealt with. Anyone who'd even think of going to the customs men would face our wrath, our reputation had become well known throughout the south and no one was about to take it from us, or so we thought. For several months everything seemed to run smoothly, under Arthur's leadership the Hawkhurst gang had grown and expanded as far as Dorset, from what Thomas was saying, not sure why we needed so many gang members as we were small in numbers but bigger than most in the area, that would have been big enough for me, but Arthur had bigger ideas. He told me he's now able to expand our operations to get more goods in from France, Belgium, Jersey, and Guernsey and was even looking for contacts from Holland, France and as far as Spain, Germany, and India, wherever that was, and anywhere else he can find a contact with.

We were now bringing in Silks, lace, spices, tea, tobacco, spirits, rum, and some select pottery, we were even exchanging goods with our foreign connections and exporting too as we managed to take wool, not buy it, this was taken from the farmers that wouldn't let us use their barns, we managed to get hold of tin from the south west, not sure how Arthur managed to sort that deal out, graphite was also a popular choice but a bit difficult to get hold of at times, it just meant that we didn't have to pay for a lot when using it as exchange. Seems Arthur has a good business head on rather than just being a butcher. The wool was in plentiful supply from Romney Marsh, and we could get a much better deal for the farmers in trading for goods that they wanted and get a much better price for it than they could selling it here, so everyone seemed to be benefitting from what we were doing so the local people helped us in many ways because they too were enjoying the comforts of what we were doing, local people were enjoying the fruits of our labours and were liking what we were doing in helping them.

Arthur always seemed to be busy whenever I saw him, always organising something to get the most for what were officially known as the Hawkhurst gang or Owlers, mostly because most of what we did was at night. We'd seen signs being posted around the village and around Kent for information about us and these were quickly taken down by the villagers. We had by now a lot more members than I could have ever imagined and spreading further than could be travelled in one day by horse back.

Work was going ahead creating more tunnels to hold a greater amount of goods and to act as escape routes in case of nosey customs men, I found out that tunnels were being dug from the Oak and Ivy inn to a location close by, good for an escape route and from the Royal Oak in the Village to a destination along Cranbrook road, near to a small lake another route to smuggle goods into the Inn, from what Arthur was telling me there were a few more tunnels planned, plus hiding places were being looked at and considered in churches in Brooklands, Ivychurch, Snargate and Fairfield, Already the Church in Ivychurch part of the floor was made removable so that goods could be stored below, in a church we can store perishable goods like tea, fine silks and cloth, not a large store but enough to hide a cart load, We even had several churches that had sarcophagus's made and installed and stored with our goods. The number of churches that had got planned to use should be enough to store more and more goods that we bring in, all these places must have been on that list I saw George had written in, along with a map of all the places that would be used to store goods, we'd used anywhere that could store our goods safely without anyone knowing where they were kept. I was told that because I've known them for years and my loyalty to them was more like that of a brother only Arthur, Thomas, George, and myself would be the only people to know the map existed and not to tell anyone of this. I was summoned to the Oak and Ivy inn, I was sure it was for another job of bringing more goods in from France or some obscure country or going to London to sell some goods, this I hadn't had the privilege of yet, never seen London at all, but heard all about it from the others.

The Inn looked different now with the advent of spring, daffodils were showing their yellow faces on the green outside, Blossom on the tree and fresh leaves sprouting from the trees, the days were getting warmer which was better for everyone. I was thinking to myself, when the leaves are fully out this will give us greater cover when moving goods around.
I tied my horse up outside the Oak and Ivy and took a lunge full of the spring air before stepping inside the darkened Inn. I opened the large oak door to find a lot of our members inside, and just managed to hear the end of a conversation.
"I want him found", Arthur shouted.
Arthur looked annoyed and was stomping around, I have never seen him this angry
"I want everyone out looking for him and don't leave any stone unturned, bring him here to me".
Thomas came over to me and told me the news that Richard Palin had gone to the customs men with news about us.
"I want that man dealt with, no one will cross us and get away with it, he's got to go", shouted Arthur once more, "So everyone, what are you still doing here, go out and bring Palin back here? I'll sort him out, there's no way he will walk away from this", Said Arthur, punching the beam
With that everyone unable to finish their ale and left hurriedly to search for Palin.
Arthur came over to Thomas and me, still looking angry.
"With all that lot that came in from Pevensey someone was bound to have a loose tongue, there was a lot there and a lot of hiding places", I said.

"Not from one of our own, what did he think he was getting out of it? The customs men have been around and found some of our goods in one of the tunnels we made, and thanks to Palin telling them where it was they've taken all the goods we had stored there away, but they don't know where it came from or who it belongs to, that much I believe otherwise they'd be here by now with the militia, they've taken it all thanks to him, he'll not get away with it, he will be dealt with, we can't have one of our own going to the customs or have the customs snooping into our business. I'm so angry that I could shoot him right now if he were standing in front of me, or better still cut his heart out and hand it to him to look at as he dies, he's going to pay for this with his life. He's got to be found as soon as we can so he can't say anymore to anyone, he who is dead cannot tell our secrets". Said Arthur.

"He must have been absent of mind or blind drunk", said Thomas, becoming more agitated at the thought that one of our own can go against us.

"How do you know he went to the customs, what proof do you have", I asked.

"We saw him, James and I were on our way to that very tunnel to get the goods so we could sell them, on the way there we saw Palin with a group of customs men going in the same direction as us, he wasn't tied up or anything, we became suspicious and followed them. At the tunnel Palin kept pointing to show them where the goods were kept then they just loaded up the goods onto a cart and left, we thought they might come here so we rushed back to the oak and Ivy to ready our pistols for them, but they never showed up, there was group of five customs with Palin, they left with Palin on the cart,", Said Arthur.

"Good job that tunnel wasn't finished as it could have had more stock down there, but that's not the point", said Arthur hitting the table with his huge fist, causing everything on the table to fall on the floor.

"I want him here, I want to find out what he told them, then I'll deal with him, our way", his lip started to curl, bearing his teeth.
This wasn't what I summoned you here for", said Arthur, calming down now", "I had a job for you but as you can see this puts us all in jeopardy, so I've got to deal with Palin first, I want you to go out with the others and find Palin, bring him back here so he can be dealt with, the sooner we find him the safer we will all be, search all the places he's likely to be".
"Where does he live, I asked.
"He lives in Wadhurst, I've already got men searching over there, so go over there and see what you can do, bring him back alive, and I don't mind if he's bleeding". Said Arthur, now with his knife drawn feeling the sharpness of it.
Thomas and I both left the Inn,
"Let's go together, in case he becomes a handful if we find him". Said Thomas.
"This will help", I said, picking up a leather strap and heavy buckle, shouldn't take long to get there, let's hope someone finds him soon, we will search the rest of the night and return here in the morning".
The following day we came back to the Oak and Ivy after spending the whole night looking for him, with the bad news that we hadn't found him.
As we entered the inn, we were greeted with a scene with Palin strapped to a stool being beaten by Arthur and a few others taking it in turns to punch and kick him, he was covered in blood from head to foot, blood splashed around the bar and across the floor, all the time he was being hit from the front he was also whipped from behind, suffering made worse with rum being poured over his wounds.
"I'll ask you once more, did you tell the customs men anything about us, what did you tell them"? shouted Arthur.

There was a silence waiting for Palin to clear his mouth of blood, "No, I told you, I didn't tell them anything", Palin coughing and spat out some blood onto the floor in front of him,
"According to them someone in the village had noticed something suspicious at my house, they were going to lock me in irons in the gaol till I told them what they wanted to hear", he said, coughing up blood, "the only way I thought of saving myself was to tell them about one of the tunnels, and that I and I alone was responsible for storing it there, in the hope that they'd let me go. It worked, they believed me, you have to believe me Arthur, I'm telling the truth, I would never tell them what's going on here, it was only a small amount of goods that you lost, I'll pay you for the loss". Said Palin, trying to wipe the blood from his eye with his shoulder.
"And what, exactly is going on here? As far as you are concerned and everyone else in the gang, when it comes to the customs men is nothing, you hear, nothing is going on here, it's our business. The goods don't matter, what matters is that you sold us out to the customs. Do you have any name of the person that told the customs men, any idea at all, have you seen anyone paying you special attention, being nosey with your business, anyone been round your house, watching you"? said Arthur.
"No, none at all, I thought I was being careful and keeping myself to myself", said Palin.
"Obviously not, you should have been more careful, let this be a lesson to us all, never take chances, only takes one slip up and they'll be on to us, we can't have that", said Thomas,
"Untie him", we're wasting good rum", Arthur said, catching his breath, his face now very red from delivering his final beating that he delivered to Palin.

"Two of you grab him and tie him to his horse", George and Benjamin grabbed him by the feet and pulled him off the chair, his head giving a loud thump as it hit the ground, his arms above his head he was unceremoniously dragged through the dirt to his horse. They picked him up and threw him over his horse and tied his arms and legs together underneath the horse's stomach.
"Where are you taking me", cried Palin.
"It's one thing to talk to the customs but to sell out the people that have been looking after you, totally wrong", said George, tying the ropes tight around his arms till it dug into Palin's flesh.
"But I didn't sell you out, I told you everything", said Palin now struggling to breath as he was laying across the horse".
"Ask yourself this question, while you're lying there", said Arthur.
"Why did they let you go so easy, surely they would have held you for a lot longer and interrogated you further as to where you got the goods from, it's not a gift from heaven you know, they'd have wanted to know where it came from and what your intentions for it were, just seems you forgot to tell us that part, but we've talked enough, right you lot come with me and bring him along", said Arthur. everyone mounted up and followed Arthur.
We headed off in the direction of the Village, I think this was so people could see this blood-soaked man draped over his horse as a reminder not to go against us, this is what will happen if you do. We turned off the main road into a lane that was covered by trees, further along the lane we stopped.
"This will do, untie him", they untied Palin and stood him up.
"Hold him there", said Arthur.
With that Arthur again started punching and kicking him again till he blacked out.
"Take him over there to that pond, we are going to strap him down". Said Arthur grabbing some rope that he brought with him.

They dragged Palin to a small clearing in the pond, and strapped him down in the water, his face just high enough with the water lapping at his chin, Palin came too and tried to protest but too many arms were holding him down, Benjamin found a large stone and started banging branches that he used as wooden stakes into the mud in the pond and tied Palin's arms and legs down with it.

"Make sure he can't get free; I don't want him going anywhere". Said Arthur.

Thomas looked down and watched as Arthur stood on Palin's head just to push him under that little bit more.

"Looks like it might rain, you'll be lucky as your troubles will soon be over if it does", laughed Arthur

"He'll be dead in the morning", said Thomas.

"I want him to be dead now, but it will be a slow death for this one", said Arthur kicking him in the face, splitting open his cheek,

"He deserves worse going against us", said Benjamin.

"Let's leave him here, we will come back in a few days and move his body before the rats eat it, this pond is deep enough to store more goods, we don't want him stinking up such a lovely spot", Arthur managed a smile, happy that revenge had taken place, satisfied that a debt had been paid.

Two days passed and we'd totally forgot about Palin, no more customs men had shown up, maybe he was telling the truth. We went to move the body of Palin, expecting him to have a slow death and stinking up a perfectly good pond, strange thing was, he was gone, no sign of him, just the straps that held him there, maybe someone buried his body, or he got lucky, and someone helped him escape, that will end up being an unsolved mystery, I thought.

We gave the news back to Arthur that he'd gone, simply disappeared.

"If I see him again a musket shot will make him unlucky, I hope for his sake we never see him again or find out who told the customs on us". Said Arthur with an evil grin on his face as he finished off his ale.

Chapter 11
The Chance encounter (1745)

We had few goods left over from a recent trip that needed selling, so as it was one of those nice sunny days, we went out to the nearby villages to see if we could sell anything. Arthur, James, Jeremiah, Thomas, and Diamond, not a huge amount by any means, we managed to sell almost all of it expect two bottles of rum which we decided to keep for ourselves, our mood was running high, a little bit light-hearted than normal, the bottles of rum being shared around among us. We saw a cart with a lone driver slowly coming towards us taking care not to spill the load he had stacked on the back by avoiding the ruts in the road, going from one side to the other. The cart was laden with goods, he was either going to sell goods or had just purchased them.
"This man coming towards us is using all the road, looks like he's been on the rum as well", I laughed.
The others joined in with the laughter as the men drew nearer.
"Good day, fine fellow", said Arthur, in a very cheerful mood.
"What you got there", said James, finding it hard to stay on his horse.
"Oh, just some straw and oats from my friend who's a farmer, just taking this my fourth load to his barn", said the man.
"Nothing for us then", said Arthur in an inquisitive tone.
"No, it would only be good for your 'orses", said the man, not seeming to mind about the being questioned.
"We shall leave you to carry on your good deed for the day", said Arthur, raising the bottle to his lips and taking another large mouthful of rum before passing the bottle to Diamond.
"Mind the road back there, its full of ruts, mind where your 'orses tread", said the man finding smoother ground for his wheels."
"Why thank you kind sir for the warning", I said, reaching over to grab the bottle from Diamond.

We carried on for a bit longer and saw smoke coming from behind some large bushes.

We stopped on the road to listen, we could hear women and children's voices coming from a clearing further in.

Without notice, Arthur galloped towards the clearing getting his horse to jump the hedge. We followed him by going round the hedge, not chancing our luck by the amount we'd been drinking, Arthur leapt off his horse, well more like fell off his horse by the way he landed and grabbed the first woman he could grab hold of pulling her down to the ground and in the dirt. He tried kiss her, but she put her forearm across her face to stop him, then he made a grab for the hem of her skirt and again she stopped him by reaching down to stop her skirt from being lifted, her arm removed from her face to hold her skirt, her face was now exposed, he managed to hold her head to kiss her.

"Looks like he's got her now", said James, leaning forward on his saddle watching the drama unfold.

Arthur, reached down with the other hand lifting her skirt higher, he got between her legs as she was still trying to fight him off, screaming, and punching him in the face as she did so, not sure he felt anything as he seem to be preoccupied with lifting her skirt and the effects of the rum. The other woman who were standing around started screaming as the children were led away from the sight that was before them, they started calling and shouting, we stayed where we were still on horseback, smiling and watching this funny scene of Arthur fighting with this woman on the ground, as big as he was he didn't seem to be winning against her as she was now beginning to fight back, we could see in the distance what must have been their men who were working in a nearby field realising their woman were in trouble come running down the path towards the camp.

"You should have picked a smaller one", I said laughing at his attempts to pin her down.

The others started laughing at his attempts and the way she was fighting back.
"Maybe she should be in the gang", laughed Thomas,
"Ask her if she wants to join", shouted Diamond,
"Come on Arthur we have to go, leave her" James said, looking concerned at the number of men there were bearing down on us.
"Not likely, not till I've had her", he said as he buried her head into the dirt, dust flying everywhere, as she fought to get his hands off her breasts, the top half of her dress started to rip as he took hold of it.
"I should give up and get up if I were you, there's more of them and they are getting closer", said Thomas taking the last drop from one bottle.
Arthur looked up at the men getting closer then look down at the woman slapping her across the face, tears running down her face mixed in with the dirt. Arthur got off her and stood up over her where she lay and looked at the angry men bearing down on him.
He leapt onto his horse and turned just as the men reached him, the horses tail swishing a few in the face as he caused his horse to buck and kick out its legs, sending a few of the men flying, we all did the same with our horses sending men flying in all directions Arthur managed to grab a pitchfork that was being thrust at him, turned it around and threw it back at the man, catching him in the leg. Thomas as a way of insult threw the now empty bottle of rum at the woman catching her on the back of her neck as she made to get up sending her flying back to the ground. We looked at the scene before us before we turned and leapt back over the hedge laughing as we left them to nurse their injuries.
We asked Arthur what he was thinking as we galloped away, "Well like I always say, if the opportunity is there then take it", we headed off towards Hawkhurst laughing between us as we now knew this must have been Arthur's saying to everything.

Chapter 12
My Prize (1746)

Things became quiet for a while and settling down into what some would call a routine, goods came in and sold to anyone who would pay the price. We established a way of communicating with each other over a distance to save time instead of using messengers, this took more time and not very useful, we used to leave messages in certain trees and on passing would, check to see if any messages were left there. This turned out to be a lot quicker and easier and kept the customs men off our back as they didn't have to see large suspicious groups of us acting in what they say suspiciously, we just went about our business as usual. We'd also get the clergy, farmers or oast house or anyone that had a tall building to fly little flags from various points on church's, or farm buildings, or anywhere that could be seen from a distance, normally a white flag for a meeting to be held at the Oak and Ivy, two flags for the Mermaid, if it was a single red then stay low as customs men were in the area, we also found dead trees to use as a kind of flag pole to use as markers. We had our ways of communicating to help us pass messages along, made our life simpler.

Tunnels were still being dug all around the village, and along to tubs pond where more goods could be stored till, they were needed, houses in Hawkhurst and surrounding villages had many tunnels now leading away from the villages. A lot of churches had now become store houses as well, in certain churches the crypt was used, in Herstmonceux a table tomb was used, anywhere and everywhere that we could hide goods we would use, even some of the places that Arthur and Thomas showed me I couldn't believe, that was the way things were for us, survival of the cunning, just to keep own goods out of the hands of the customs men and stay one step ahead.

I got up early one morning because I had to get to Ashford, off to see a blacksmith there, I'd already sent him a message a few weeks ago to make me a sword, sending him a drawing of what I thought would be a good one, but said I'd leave it up to him to make it the way he felt using this knowledge as a sword maker. The old one I've been using now had a few chips and was heavy in my hand, and I was hoping that by now it should have been made and ready to collect. We could always rely on him to make good swords and not say anything to the customs or magistrates, the blacksmith in Rye was always far too busy, making nails for the ships and shoeing horses and other items.

Ashford is a long way from where I live, it was a bright sunny morning with a light breeze coming in seaward, but that didn't make the trip any shorter, just a little more pleasant perhaps. I came upon one of the message trees as they came to be known, I looked around checking to make sure no one was about to see me before sticking my hand into the hole, it always wary of putting my hand in one of these holes, you never know what's inside, I moved my hands around and to my surprise felt what seemed like paper, I pulled it through the hole, all screwed up, must have been in a hurry I thought to myself. I looked around again to see if anyone had seen me, I unraveled it to read, be at the Oak Tuesday for a meeting, the date on it showed it was for tomorrow, strange I thought as I'd only seen Arthur and Thomas the day before, I'll make sure I'm there tomorrow, so I won't be able to stay in Ashford for very long if I had to get back , I put the message back in the tree for anyone who needed to read it, again looking around so as not to be seen and carried on with my journey.

I finally arrived in the main street of Ashford town, sheep, cattle and pigs were in pens with more being brought in by the farmers and shepherds from the surrounding areas, men were looking at the animals looking to buy the best ones for the right price, the men seemed to make more noise than the animals gathered there, lots of people shouting out prices for the animals this is nothing like Hawkhurst, I had never seen such a gathering of animals and men, I've been to Ashford in the past but I've never seen anything like this, so much busier with lots of things to see and stores to visit, bigger town, better provisions I might be able to take back a few things with me. I decided to look inside the church just to see if there was a place there that could be used to conceal our goods, just on the off chance that we could gain another hiding place in the area, but it was too busy for any of that, we would be seen by everyone in the town transporting it there.

I managed to find a few items to buy for my journey then made my way out of town to the blacksmith.

I could hear hammering in the distance, as I neared his barn, I tied my horse up outside and looked in, it was dark inside with the glow of the fire being the only source of light, the sun was up and beating down on my back, I could make out the silhouette of the blacksmith against the furnace, wielding a large hammer in his hand as it came down into a mass of sparks as it struck home, He stopped, hammering, and wiped his brow, then he turned to see me standing there.

He came out to greet me, he was covered in sweat from head to foot by look of it, how he could spend all day in there next to that roaring fire on a day like today.

"Hello, Will, you made it, any problems on the journey in", he said, now with the sun beating down on him outside seemed to make him sweat even more. He went over to a barrel and lifting a ladle to his lips, took a drink of water, the next ladle of water went over his head.

I watched him as he wiped the water and sweat from his eyes and gave him time to recover before giving my answer.

"Yes, I made it, no problems at all", I said watching the water dripping off his black hair, not sure if his hair was black or just covered in soot from the fire.

"It's finished, and I'm proud of it he said, in an excited way, with a big grin on his face, his teeth had always been perfect, they were really white, not like most peoples, brown and crooked, his were white with bits of soot from what I could see filling the gaps in between.

He ushered me into the barn, I could feel the heat coming from the fire, "follow me", came the excited voice. He started to move lengths of metal and wood from behind the forge and rolled out a few cartwheels that were waiting to be repaired. He picked up the sword that was wrapped in a greasy cloth.

"There it is, just as you asked", he said holding out his arms. I looked at it for a moment, checking out the length before taking hold of it, both had hold of it, like he didn't want to part with this his prize possession, finally he let go once he knew it was secure in my hands, the first time of feeling the weight of it.

"Feels light", I said looking at him, he just nodded excitedly, again showing his white teeth, in this gloom they now stood out even more.

I carefully undid the cloth it was wrapped in, just looking toward the doorway to make sure no one was coming in. The sword unwrapped, we both looked at it in awe as it caught the light from the furnace, one hand now holding the tip of the blade and the other by the pommel.

"This is the most beautiful thing I've ever seen", I heard my voice say, shocked at how good it was, I've never owned a sword of my own, always had to borrow one, until now.

"I can understand why you were excited to show me, I can't believe how good this is, this has got to be your best work, far better than what I asked for", I said, the handle now resting in my grip, I took and few steps back and moved it around feeling the weight.

"I can't wait to show the others, they will be jealous, and they'll want one, you mark my words, you'll be making a lot more if this is your standard".

"You asked for one piece of gold for making this, but this work needs to be paid for, time, effort, I'm going to pay two pieces as I'm so happy with it, but don't tell the others what I paid for it, you might get more out of them if theirs is this good, you've done me proud, I will pass the word on to the others so expects visits in the future.

"Wait to see the faces of anyone who wants to cross me, they'll thank me for dispensing them with this sword", we both laughed, as I moved toward the doorway, it was my turn with the ladle as I was sweating so much from the heat of the forge, with the second ladle full going over my head.

He passed me the scabbard so I could secure it around my waist, that too looked full of designs to show off his work, I placed the sword in the scabbard feeling them mate for the first time, got on my horse who had his head in the trough outside, hot for him as well, I smiled to myself. I looked down at the blacksmith from my saddle as I handed him his two pieces of gold for his work and shook him by the hand.

"Thank you very much for making this sword and scabbard for me, I said with my hand resting on the sword, that's why we come to you, your excellent work, I'll think of you every time its drawn.

I touched my brow as a mark or respect, he waved as I turned and headed back to Ashford, a proud man.

On the way back I decided to stay the night at an Inn in Tenterden as it was getting dark, it was a nice place The Woolpack inn, I befriended the maid in there and she gave me an extra helping of soup and hot chicken with warm bread, just what I needed and the beer tasted nice, she said they have someone local who brews it, I thought they could do with some of ours, not sure if Arthur had sold much this way, but was sure he did, a popular place like this would have been an ideal place to sell to, but I couldn't ask for obvious reason, I didn't want to give myself away.

I seemed to have a warm way with women, I must have, they always gave me extra helpings for some reason, not been with many, never been married, I suppose it was something that I would like, just too busy with Arthur and the others for the time being, I suppose one day, I thought to myself looking at the maid who was cleaning the tankards, she kept looking at me staring at her as I was eating, causing her to blush, I see her running her finger along the top of her dress over her ample bosom then her finger moved to her lip, making her lip curl downwards, baring her lower teeth, in a coy way.

"Come on girl, get this cleaned up, I'm not paying you to mess around, go and cook some more food for our guests or clean up out there ", the Inn keeper barked his orders at the girl, making her rush off and nearly trip over the barrels left on the floor, this added to her embarrassment, before disappearing out of the room.

I finished my meal and washed it down with the nice beer and retired to my room, how nice it was to be able to afford such luxuries now, swords paid with gold, staying in nice Inn's with warm beds, I couldn't do this before, I'd have had to travel through the night to get home to my own bed and be up long before the sun rose, I was enjoying the fruits of our labours for once.

I took the sword off my waist still admiring the work that had gone into it, I kept it by my side as I fell asleep.

Morning again and I continued my journey back to Hawkhurst, feeling refreshed having rested, home first then the ivy to see the others, I thought as I saddled up my horse. I kept thinking as to why we were called this time, no large jobs were mentioned, I'd just have to wait and see. My new sword by my side I headed south towards home.

Chapter 13
Sandwich (1746)

I made my way to the Oak and Ivy as instructed by the note left in the tree, there were a lot of gang members there, most that were there were outside as the inn couldn't accommodate everyone, a lot of familiar faces that I knew anyway and a lot I didn't recognise, I'm sure if they were friends of Arthur's or Thomas, they they'd be alright.

I'm sure if anyone were absent, they would have regretted not being here and seeing this gathering, or at least Arthur would have made his feelings known. A friend is a friend and should be treated as such, and enemy is exactly that and has no place with us, no place at all, I once heard Arthur say.

The atmosphere in the inn was a warm friendly one, none of the usual locals were here, kept away by the vast numbers I suppose so it was just down to us gang members, it was great to see everyone, although the few faces I didn't recognise I'd soon get to know, a lot of them knew who I was and came up to me to say hello, like I was some local hero they'd wanted to meet.

Thomas shouted for everyone to fill their tankards then be quiet and listen to what had to be said. There was a rush to get tankards filled then the seats in the inn started filling with a lot of the members with some sitting on the floor, the windows were opened so those gathered outside could hear what was going on, they'd be updated later anyway.

"All of you listen carefully, we have a two ships coming in with goods from France arriving at Ramsgate two days from now, this is a special assignment as we've had to team up with the Wingham gang as its in their area, I don't like the idea but as we are new to teaming up, we've had to put our trust in them and them in us, we have an agreement, we ourselves have invested a lot in this shipment, a bit more than the Wingham gang so this needs to be shared between the two gangs, with us getting a bigger share", Arthur said filling his pipe with tobacco, probably from our own goods I thought smiling to myself .
"What's on this list is ours, so we want to make sure we get it", said Thomas holding up several sheets of paper, and giving Arthur time for a few puffs of tobacco.
 "Now I'm not too sure about this lot in Wingham, I've asked around about them and I'm not sure if they can be trusted or not, you all know me, I don't trust anyone, not even my own mother", said Arthur this caused a roar of laughter from the men, Thomas looked at him in disgust, not joining in with the laughter at first, then burst out laughing when he saw Arthur starting to choke on his pipe tobacco.
"So, you are all to come with us and make sure that our goods come back with us, or there will be trouble, between this other gang". Said Arthur, catching his breath.
We are all going, and we are meeting more from Folkstone, and surrounding villages, we are expecting around three hundred members if they all turn up.
"Three hundred", Said Smoker, sitting right next to Thomas.
 "Yes", said Arthur, looking round at Smoker.
"There will be around three hundred or more horses and men, and this should be enough to carry all the goods back, and I want them all to be brought back here so we can sort it and get it hidden away, we can divide the goods when you get back here and we will have lists made up of what's to be stored and where, we'll need to do that fast to keep it away from prying eyes", he said, looking around at everyone.

"So, are you expecting any trouble from the Wingham gang? I said cautiously.
Thomas pulled his stool closer,
"Not if they know what's good for them, I've been asking my contacts in the area and they seem reasonable but as you know we can't trust anyone, and besides, you'll all have your pistols so make sure they are loaded and your swords and knives sharp, so if there is trouble then you know what to do", Thomas said, staring down to me as if he didn't need to say anymore.
"We want everything to go smoothly or else we won't be doing business with them again, I've already sent a message to them stating that, just so that they are clear," said Thomas.
"I'll be there, and anyone who crosses us, the Hawkhurst gang, will feel my steel", I said, as I pulled out my new sword from its scabbard.
There was a silence, then murmurs amongst the men as the blade caught the light, everyone wanted to hold it and look at it, some were even swinging it around as it was passed around the inn.
Someone is going to get sliced open if you lot are not careful, I said as I managed to get hold of it and place it back in the scabbard.
"Looky here, he's got some cold steel, you know you'll have to give that a taste of blood don't you", Said Thomas, watching as the sword slid up to the hilt of the scabbard.
"I'll be having a closer look at that sword later, I could do with a new one myself, but now we could all do with a drink", said Arthur.
"Ha ha", laughed Arthur, more drink for everyone", Arthur shouted to John the inn keeper,
"Come on everyone", he said, "drink up, the night is to be merry", Arthur and Thomas laughing loudly now.

We all drank till what seemed to be early in the morning. The inn keeper said we could sleep in the rooms that they had upstairs; this was far more comfortable than sleeping in the barn and stables with the others.
The warmth of the bed soon had me drifting off to sleep, with thoughts of what Arthur had been telling me, and the thought of using my sword for the first time.
The next morning, I awoke feeling hungry, and realising that with all the excitement the night before, I hadn't eaten anything.
I put my shoes on and attached my scabbard around me
I went downstairs to find that Arthur and Thomas had already eaten, and Arthur was filling his pipe again with a large wad of tobacco
"We've got a bit of a ride to get there, we will meet up with the other part of the gang in Sandwich in the Bell Inn, that's where I've told them to meet us, as I've said there will be a lot of us, I want all that's ours to be brought back home, any trouble with the Wingham gang I'm sure they will be dealt with. Remember we still must keep a low profile, any sign of the customs men and we get out of there, it'll be too risky otherwise". Said Arthur.
"Do you have any idea what you are saying, low profile? There's going to be around three hundred men, keeping a low profile is going to be the least of your problems, you are still showing signs of the rum you were drinking last night, and you're worried about a few customs men", I said with a puzzled look on my face.
He looked at me, then realised what he said and burst out laughing.
"It's going to be a long trip all the way up to Sandwich, so we'll make a few stops along the way", Thomas said, we got some provisions together for the journey then went outside to check on the horses, then we mounted up.
"Do you think this will draw attention to us"? laughed Smoker, looking around at all the men.

A few of the men were loading their pistols and the blunderbusses they'd bought along, sharing around a bag of gunpowder, a few were just finishing off getting a sharper edge on their swords.

"This lot are going to hurt someone, including themselves", said Smoker.

"Why do you say that", asked Jeremiah", pulling up alongside Smoker.

"Well, if you look, two of them are smoking a pipe, swords being sharpened giving off sparks and there's a bag of gunpowder being passed around, do any of this lot have any brains". Said Smoker moving further away from them.

"Seems they want to learn about gunpowder the hard way", said Jeremiah.

"Oi, you lot, smoking and gunpowder don't go together unless you want it too, and if you did you wouldn't want to be that close to it", shouted Thomas.

Everyone seemed to be in a quiet mood as we made off.

We headed out of Hawkhurst, then across country towards Appledore then onto the marsh heading for Hythe.

Arthur was right, the trip was long, so we needed to stop at Hythe and get some provisions along the way.

We must have looked a sight there was about two hundred of us maybe more heading across country, people wouldn't be messing with us I thought.

The sun was high in the sky by the time we got to Hythe and going to the street traders to buy some provision, salted beef and hams, bread, onions, and apples, anything that we could eat and store in our saddle bags, then we headed for the nearest inn for some refreshment. The Globe inn was the nearest, as the Three Mariners were always full of fishermen telling yarns about their days at sea, we just wanted to relax and get out of the saddle and not get into any fights along the way.

"So why are you here Perrin, what bring you all the way over to Hawkhurst"? George said, as if curiosity got the better of him.
"I've Known George and Thomas for years, as they are brothers, I used to stay with them, I married a relative of theirs, so I'm a distant part of their family I suppose so when I come over this way, just to visit I like to catch up on old times and go out drinking with them, when either of them come my way they stay with me, we go back a long way.
"That explains a lot then", said George.
Two ship coming in that's a lot of goods that's a lot to offload", said James, looking out towards the sea.
"Is your back hurting just thinking about its James", Smoker said laughing.
"Don't worry, we will have the Wingham lot with us helping to offload the goods so it shouldn't take long, doesn't want to, need to be as quick as we can", Smoker said filling his pipe, just hope those Wingham lot behaves themselves", lighting his pipe from the ashes in the fire.
"Maybe we'll arrive a little late so they will unload it all for us", said James, as he relaxed in the chair, closing his eyes.
"Let's hope they behave themselves, I don't want any trouble", I said.
Arthur looked across to us, "you've got your new sword that needs to be blooded William, let me have a look while we are resting for a while, as I said I could do with a new one, did you get it made specially in Ashford like you were told"? he said taking the sword from me.
"I did, it's so light, and the workmanship that's gone into it, beautifully made, I'm hoping one of the Wingham gang can oblige me in getting it blooded", I said to everyone's amusement.
"You just said you didn't want any trouble", said Smoker.
"I don't, but it would be good to put the sword to good use now that I've got it", I said watching Arthur looking at the sword

Arthur took it out of the scabbard to admire the workmanship, then stood up and started making out he was in an imaginary duel with someone, before looking at it again, then swinging it about to check the weight.

"It's well-made, perfectly balanced, I will have to go and see him to get a few made for the men". He said placing the sword back into the scabbard and passing it over to Thomas to have a look, he also got up and started an imagery duel to test it out for weight, then he swung it around but he needed more room, it caught a rope that was holding a metal ring with candles up from the rafters, they came crashing down next to him, he quickly placed the sword in the scabbard passing it over to me, and bent down to pick it up the candles, luckily the candles blew out once they hit the floor.

Arthur looked at Thomas, "you shouted at the men earlier about gunpowder and tobacco, here you are in an inn, no room, swinging a sharp sword around", laughed Arthur.

"Well, the sword isn't as dangerous as gunpowder", said Thomas, sitting back down at the table.

"All depends on whose hands it's in", we all burst out laughing.

"I told him you'd like it, and said you'd be along to Ashford to pay him a visit, so he'll await your visit", I said looking at Thomas who looked a bit embarrassed by what he'd done.

"I still hope there's no trouble, and everything goes according to plan", I said nervously.

"There you go again, all that worrying is not good for your digestion, you'll spoil your beer," said Smoker puffing on his pipe, "Just relax lad, just relax", he said closing his eyes.

"Besides, we got Jemimah on our side", he said taking more puffs.

"What's so special about Jemimah"? asked Perrin.

"He's got a bad reputation, loves a good killing, especially if he's the one doing it, killed a few men he has, when he was with the Hastings gang, not one to be crossed, but loyal to his friends, so it'll be a good idea to stay on his good side", Smoker said getting smoke in his eyes from his pipe.

"We've seen him in action, seems to enjoy what he does, the more pain he can inflict the bigger his smile gets, do you think it was him that killed that kid that you were talking to Smoker"? I said, looking at the pipe smoke now surrounding Smoker's head.

"You mean that James, when we were in the Mermaid and few years back"? He said wiping his eyes which were watering.

"That's the one, James Marshall, I think his name was, his mum came in looking for him, she was in a right state",

"I wouldn't worry yourself too much lad, what's done is done, if someone was asking too many questions, prying into our business, then they should expect to be dealt with, he was asking too many questions about why we were all there, in the Inn I mean as far as I can remember, that's when Jemimah came over and ushered him outside, I didn't ask what Jemimah was doing, we trust we do things for the good of the gang, that way we can look after each other, we stay safe, I'm sure nothing serious happened to him, he probably got drunk and fell asleep in a ditch somewhere, back home with his mum, you worry too much, pay no heed to them and worry about us, we are your friends not them". Said Smoker.

"Well said Smoker", said James.

"Anyway, you lot, drink up, relaxing as it is here, we had better be going soon so we can get there before dark", Said Thomas, upsetting the lazy mood everyone was getting into.

"Go get the others ready outside Will, tell them we are off to Sandwich, get what they need and be ready".

I finished my ale and went back out into the light, it hurt my eyes at first, all inns seem to have dark interiors adding to the atmosphere and mystery about them, steeped in history of the many drinkers gone before us, I thought to myself. I rounded up the others outside who also fell into the trap of beer and sun, not wanting to move, but move they did to get ready and move on.

Before long they were back in the saddle and heading off toward Sandwich, going through Folkestone and Alkham valley.

It was dark before when we arrived at the Bell inn on the river front in Sandwich, and could hear lots of voices coming from inside, horses were tethered up outside leaving no room for ours to be tied, too many for ours to be tied or for any barn or stables to accommodate.

"I need three volunteers to take these horses, find a field and stay with them till we are ready, it won't be long as it's getting dark, give them hay and water and make sure no one tries to steal them". Said Thomas.

Six hands went up, but only three were picked, they took the horses into a field close to the Inn.

"You can look after the provision, that'll give you something to eat, I'll send out some bottles of rum, don't go getting drunk", said Arthur, getting off his horse and passing the reins over to a volunteer.

We entered through the door of the inn to see more of the gang sitting round the fire drinking beer.

"How long have you lot been here", Smoker asked.

They laughed and said, "Arthur sent a message over by rider saying there are four bottles of rum at stake, the first person to get to the Bell inn first can have all four bottles".

"So, he made you race here"? asked Smoker.

"If that's what you want to call it then yes; Richard over there in the corner was the first to get here so Arthur owes him four bottles of the best rum", they were all laughing.

"Don't drink much you lot, I want you sober for later", said Arthur as he greeted the rest of the gang.

The rest of the gang were mostly from Dover and together they look after the Southeast section of the gang trading with the ports and the sailors coming in as well as helping out in Folkestone making sure that the sailors had for all the rum and gin they needed for their long journeys, it was very lucrative and because Arthur and Thomas trusted in what they were doing, only giving them support when they needed it, they virtually left them alone and up to their own devices.

Chapter 14
The Wingham Gang (1746)

We stayed in the Inn for a while before making our way back outside when it was dark.

"Someone go and fetch the others and bring the horses over", said Thomas.

The others filtered out of the Inn and made their way to get their horses.

"Are we ready", shouted Arthur.

"We are ready sire", Smoker said with a big grin, showing his brown teeth.

I looked round at everyone gathered, it was hard to tell just how many there were in the dark, I think around four hundred now.

We moved out of the town and onto the road towards Pegwell bay, as we neared the bay Arthur stopped.

"Gather round and listen carefully", Said Arthur, only continuing to speak when he got everyone's attention.

"We all know the plan, but just to make sure, we are going to Pegwell Bay not far from here, I'm hoping to get there before the Wingham gang so we can assess the situation, offshore the ships should be waiting, who has the spout lantern", there was a pause. "I have it", came a voice from the darkness.

"Make sure its lit and the front covered up, I don't want anyone seeing the light until we get there", said Arthur talking in the direction of where the voice came from.

Now I've been talking to the landlord of the inn, he said it should be high tide by the time we get there, just right for the ships to get closer to the shore. When we get there I want two teams, one team to continue and the other to hold back just out of sight, as I'm not sure what this Wingham gang are like, we are not sure we can trust them and I don't want to show them all our strengths at once, so one team will hold back out of sight with pistols loaded, the rest of us will go on ahead and meet with the Wingham gang and we will off load the goods from the boats that will be coming in, if you see that there's trouble then come to our aid, we won't move off till they have loaded their goods and gone out of sight. Some the goods are theirs so we will check what we have from the list that I have in my pocket, when they have gone then you can come and give us a hand loading up the carts and let's hope all goes well, oh and if you see the spout lantern then get yourselves over to us quickly", said Arthur.
The men started talking in agreement liking the plan while George and Richard organised who was staying behind.
"Nicely done Arthur", said Smoker, "that's a good plan.
"I have my ways, especially when it comes to trust and money", said Arthur, grabbing the piece of bread from Smoker's hand.
"I was enjoying that", he said, looking at Arthur with annoyance.
"Keep together till we get closer to Pegwell".
We all moved off in the direction of Pegwell bay, the moon was coming out from behind a cloud.
"That's not good, the clouds are clearing, we'll have to get this done quickly so as not to be seen", said Arthur, finishing the last scraps of Smokers bread.
"Right, we are close now so two teams, George and Richard hold back with your team".
The moon was casting an eerie light across the shallows of Pegwell bay, just enough light to see eight small boats out in the bay.

"Are they coming in or going out", I said.
"They are rowing away by the look of it", said Smoker.
"That's not right, they shouldn't be here yet, and why are they rowing away from the bay"? said Thomas looking at Arthur.
"They are too early, let's get down there", shouted Arthur.
With that both teams galloped towards the shoreline to find the Wingham gang already loading up most of the goods onto their carts, we drew our pistols and dismounted and surrounded them.
"What's this"? Thomas shouted at them, "I hope those goods that you've put on your carts are not ours as well".
Looking around at the small number of men that were before them, with a small amount of goods still waiting to be loaded.
"Ah you must be the Hawkhurst gang, you had me worried, I thought you'd be customs men", said one of the gang members, reaching into his coat for a weapon.
But a pistol was quickly drawn and pointed at his head stopping him in his tracks.
"We are the Hawkhurst gang, not customs men, of course you knew that, and why are you loading everything on to all these carts", said Arthur, looking around at the goods already on the carts, he realised there must have been more than was here.
"We were going to load them for you and bring them too you", said one of the men.
Diamond walked up to him and hit him with his pistol grip across the face.
"Don't take us for fools" he said, as the man fell to the ground clutching his face.
Diamond pulled out a knife and grabbing the man by his hair and lifting him high, held it to the man's throat.
"Who's in charge here", I said.
"I suppose I am", came a voice from the crowd of men, now looking uneasy.
I walked up to him, drawing a knife that I kept with me.
"What is your name"? I said, pointing the knife to his throat.

"Jones sir", he said with a gulp, the blade now touching his skin.
"You were stealing our goods weren't you"?
"No, we were only trying to help".
"Help by taking them form us", Perrin sneered.
"Cut him Will", came a voice from behind, "teach them a lesson, not to mess with us".
The men said excitedly.
"It seems to me that you have planned to take our goods from us by the amount of carts that you have, you came prepared, more than you need for your goods, which means to me you were expecting to take more than your fair share, to me it looks like you've almost loaded everything on to your carts, and if we hadn't got here in time there would be nothing left".
"No sir, it's not like that," said Jones.
"Seems to me that I got it right, you were going to steal our goods, that's not nice, even between thieves" I said laughing around to the men.
I looked back to him with a sneering look.
"Where's there rest of the goods"? asked Thomas.
"This is all there is,", said Jones, trying not to move for far that he'd cut his own throat by moving too much.
"Ah, that's what I like, someone who lies where lying shows no worth", said Jeremiah, dismounting from his horse and walking over to Jones.
"We hate liars and thieves", said Diamond, pushing the knife further into the man's throat, blood now trickling down his neck.
"looks to me like you have one way to help yourself survive tonight or his knife will be your butcher, and dispatch you to the afterlife, not just you, oh no, the others will behold the same fate as you, so I'll ask you once more, and as you can see, I'm quite calm at the moment, but that won't last for much longer, where is all the other goods that came off the two ships", said Arthur, getting off his horse as well.

The man gulped as he looked up at Arthur, "well sir, only one ship came in, apparently the other ship was run down and captured by customs men, that ship out there in the bay being faster left them behind as they could only capture the one, there were more goods, but the rest of the gang have taken them back to Wingham to hide it all", he said gulping again and looking at Arthur to see if he's said enough to save his skin.

"How much more did they take to Wingham", asked Diamond, not letting up with the blade.

"These are the only carts that were going to take the rest of what was left so I think around forty horses that were loaded up", said Jones.

"Going by what you said with the other ship being captured, I reckon you got it wrong and looks your goods haven't arrived, not ours", said Arthur.

"Right, you Wingham lot, load up the rest of the goods onto those carts, make sure you load it properly, you wouldn't want anything to fall off on our journey or else we shall cut your hands off, after you've reloaded it back on again", Said Thomas.

"What do you mean, what journey"? Said Jones looking more concerned.

"We are going on a little journey to pay your little village of Wingham a surprise visit and get all our goods back", said Arthur drawing his sword.

"They'll be no arguments about it unless you want to feel my cold steel, the blade pushed right into Jones's face. Right lads, once they've loaded up all the goods on those carts tie them up to the back of the carts, they can walk behind, except you Jones, you'll be tied to my horse where I can keep an eye on you. Smoker, Diamond and Jeremiah follow at the rear so none can make their escape", said Arthur, placing the sword back in the scabbard.

It wasn't long before the goods were loaded up on the carts, the men were tied to the back of the carts with Smoker, Diamond and Jeremiah bringing up the rear.

"Anyone gives us trouble back here, our knives will dispatch that person", said Jeremiah, as they made their way to Wingham.

After a while we stopped on the outskirts of Wingham, the sunrise giving off a warm glow in the east, Arthur grabbed the rope attached to Jones and pulled him up, his arms straining up his back causing him great pain.

"Right, I want about half of you to go to the other side of the village up by the church, wait there and watch, if anything happens, you know what to do, move quietly and quickly.

"Right, you, you know where the other gang members live, and I should think you know where they've taken the goods, I'll give you one chance, so you'll do well not to lie", said Arthur, drawing his knife out.

"Show me", Arthur looking down at him not trusting him to comply.

Jones looked up at Arthur and whispered, "you have my word sir".

They moved forward through the Village with Jones pointing to houses where the other gang members were.

In the distance we heard a man shouting at the top of his voice, "Quick, they are here, rally round, quickly, arm yourselves".

We could see a man running in the distance towards the other end of the village, where the other gang members were positioned, a shot rang out and a puff of smoke appeared as we watched the man fall to the ground.

More men appeared holding pistols and swords from the houses, hearing the alarm, Jermiah, James and the others rushed forward, the men from the other end doing the same, our men still on horseback riding through those on foot sending them flying in all directions, the men jumped off their horses and drew knives and swords, a clash of steel could be heard throughout the Village with pistols being fired in their direction as more Wingham men joining in, shots rang out from a few bedroom windows of the houses along the street, but that soon stopped by the sounds of blunderbusses going off in their direction, taking the windows with them, women were screaming in the streets running clear of the commotion that ensued.

The Wingham gang were heavily outnumbered by us and were soon overpowered, a few of their men lay in the dirt in their own blood, while some of the others were being tortured by our men.

"Tie these men up and take their weapons", I could hear Thomas shouting in the distance, while watching the street in case others appeared.

"Right, grab those men and take them to all the houses, get what you can that's valuable and their horse and carts, it'll be our little prize for taking our goods, the rest of you keep lookout for any trouble", shouted Thomas.

The men grabbed a member of the Wingham gang and lead them off to search the other houses.

"Right Jones, the goods, where are they, show us", said Arthur, who was waiting patiently, watching with the rest of the gang to the east of the village.

Jones led the way to a large building at the back of a large house just beyond a large tree, "that's where you'll find the goods", he said pointing along the pathway.

"They had better be, you lead the way", said Arthur.

Jones reluctantly moved forward past Arthur's horse, Arthur still had hold of the rope, to stop him from running, slowly they moved forward.

Just then a loud bang was heard, and smoke came from inside a tree towards the rear of the building, Jones fell to the floor holding his chest as a shot went right through him missing Diamond by inches and taking a small part of the brickwork of the house with it as it ricochets off into gardens beyond. The men leapt off their horses and fired back into the tree with a blunderbuss, a man fell out of the tree and hit the ground with a sickening crunch along with a few branches, his head and arms contorted on the ground. The men realising a guard was posted to protect the goods moved forward slowly using the trees for cover, a few shots rang out from a window in the building, Diamond drew his blunderbuss and fired at the window, catching a figure full in the face. Seeing this I ran to the door and kicked it open then ran back and hid behind the nearest tree for fear of catching some lead shot in the back, a few of the others from the other side of the village heard the pistol fire and came to join in, they had already reloaded and fired into the open door of the doorway, the others had reloaded by this time and moved forward listening to any noise that might be present from inside. One of the men moved closer as his finger moved to his lips to usher quiet, a man appeared at the door, covered in blood, pistols were trained on him.

The man had difficulty speaking, blood filled his mouth, he staggered through the doorway to see a mass of men looking at him, outnumbered and looking at defeat he threw his pistol and sword to the ground.

Arthur, looked down at him, "is there anyone else in there with you", he said, still in a calm voice.

"No sir", said the man, choking on his own blood.

"You need that new sword of yours to be blooded Will, now's your chance, finish him off", said Arthur, looking at me crouching behind the tree.

"that'll be in cold blood, that's not right", I said, in a cowardly voice.

Arthur got off his horse and walked over to me, grabbed me by the collar to pick me up then hit me right in the face with his big fist sending me flying across the ground.

"You're in this gang, you'll do as I say", he said, that face that I've always feared is now directed at me, the first time I've felt fear as not knowing what he could do, his anger directed at me with everyone watching.

"Take your new sword and finish him, or I'll take it off you and use your blood on it", he said pointing at the sword. This was new, different being on the receiving end of his glare, I was shocked at what was happening, my mind racing, disbelieving Arthur had turned on me in this way, I stood up and looked at him, a tear in my eye from where his fist landed. I wiped my eye and mouth with the back of my hand, looking at my own blood and feeling the pain of Arthur's fist. I looked at Arthur then the man, I slowly drew my sword, and held it up to see the virgin blade catch the light, I looked at Arthur again who was now pointing at the man, I looked at the man again, as I could feel the anger welling up in me, anger towards this poor unarmed man, the feeling of anger grew, till I screamed with full voice and lunged my sword towards him, I could feel as the sword entered his body catching a few ribs as it passed right through him. He was silent as blood now dripped from his mouth and blood started to fill his shirt. He looked at me as he started to fall forward so I pulled out my sword as he fell towards me, lying dead in a pool of blood.

"hooray", went up a cheer from the men with a few pistol shots fired into the air.

"Well done lad,", laughed Arthur, as his big had come crashing down on my back and giving my shoulder a firm squeeze, your sword has tasted blood, you're now officially one of us".

I was shocked and still in a daze as to what just happened, looking down at the man lying in a pool of blood, then up at Arthur, "you're fine, you needed that little push and besides, in front of the men I couldn't have you whimpering now could I, now they'll look up to you", laughed Arthur, as he reloaded his pistol.

We looked inside the building to see a large haul of goods, much more than we thought, a lot more than from any ship. "This must be where the Wingham gang have been keeping all their spoils, not just from the ship that came in, there's a huge amount here", I said, touching my lip feeling it swelling up.

"This is far better than what we had on the ship, we shall take the lot, and that'll serve them right for trying to take us on", said Arthur looking at this vast haul.

Arthur gave his orders to get the goods out of the building and load them up onto the packhorses and carts that the Wingham gang had used, and we made our way back into the street, all the people were running out of village, women screaming and children crying in case there was more trouble. The Wingham gang, what was left of them were sitting on the floor with their hands tied as Thomas was directing the others getting goods from the houses, now they were ransacking everyone's house looking for anything of value that could be taken.

"I can see you have things under control here Thomas", said Arthur.

"No problems here, I could hear you were having fun at your end as well", said Thomas, looking towards the large house.

"Just letting off a bit of powder", said Arthur, grinning to cheers from the men.

"We've rounded up what we can and as you can see, we've managed to get a few extra horses, forty to be precise, we'll get the goods loaded up on them and take them with us". Said Thomas.

"You're going to need a few more horses and carts at the other end as well, we just found a large haul that belongs to this lot", said Arthur.

Arthur looked at the men sitting on the floor, "which one of you is in charge here"?

He got no response from the men, none willing to speak or stand out from the rest, he went over to one of the men and kicked him in the side of the leg, the man reeled in pain, "you, who's in charge? I'm speaking to you", he said drawing his knife out, he wasn't prepared to ask a third time.

"Jones is sir", said the man." But we don't know where he is now, there's no one else".

"I know where he is and he won't be coming back I'm afraid, oh it wasn't one of us that killed him, it was one of your own men. Right, I'll tell you lot now I've got your attention, there will be no more Wingham gang, no treading on our turf, Kent is ours, you've gone against the code amongst thieves, more importantly you've gone against us and that we can't have. Look around you, look at your families running, scared, you've come off worse, you have nothing left to give, we are taking it all, this should be a lesson for anyone wanting to take matters into their own hands and think that Owling is a good way to make money and a living, if we find out that any of you have formed another gang we will be back here, then you can watch as we burn the place down with your families in them, do you understand".

"They all nodded and murmured in agreement".

"I said do you understand"! Shouted Arthur.

"Yes", came the reply from the men.

"Right, you lot, we shall leave this sorry lot to answer to the villagers and families, let's get everything loaded up, we've got places to visit", said Arthur, putting his knife away and mounting his horse.

There was a steady stream of men and carts as they left the village of Wingham to the east back towards Sandwich.

Thomas, Arthur, rode along together followed by the rest of the gang.

"Shouldn't we be going the other way towards Canterbury as the quickest way to get home", I said, pulling up alongside them.

"We should be, but not taking this lot through Canterbury, that would be drawing attention to ourselves, beside, I have been thinking, as this all looks a bit of a coincidence to me….no! before we go, we are going to a little bit of celebrating ourselves, we deserve it, let's go back to the Sandwich and have a few drinks at the Inn, there's someone I need to have a word with, I'm sure the men wouldn't mind a little detour and a little drink".

"I'm all for that said Diamond", as he pulled up alongside Thomas, just catching the end of the conversation.

We made our way back to Sandwich, which didn't take long.

"Right men go in and help yourselves to anything you like, we are not paying for anything", shouted Arthur.

"Why", asked Smoker, looking confused.

"The landlord told me last night as to when high tide was, but he didn't count on us getting there earlier, I reckon he was in with the Wingham gang as he gave us false information allowing them time to get away with our goods, whether he's in with them or not he was unhelpful, so a little pay back won't hurt, won't hurt us I mean", said Arthur, getting off his horse and tieing up the reins to a water trough.

"Maybe he would have gained from the spoils that was coming in off the ship", Smoker said.

"Maybe, most of the Inn's around this area would have benefited from it, that why we can't have anyone cross us, so go in and enjoy yourselves as I'm going to have a word with the Inn keeper and see what he has to say, William go find him and bring him to me". Said Arthur.

The men barged through the door and went behind the bar to help themselves; I saw John handing out bottles to the men as I went to find the Inn keeper the locals that were in there were quick to get out of the way or made their way out through the rear of the building.

I looked around on the lower floor and made my way upstairs, I found him as he was coming down, he saw me and ran back upstairs, I followed and caught him on the landing, "Surprised", I said,

"Oh, I thought it was someone else", he said.

"Didn't think we'd be coming back to see you then, thought we'd be on our way, never to be seen again, thought wrong didn't you." I said.

"I don't know what you mean", he said stammering, as I pulled out my sword.

"See this sword", I said, "I like this sword, I keep it nice and sharp so that it comes in very handy, blunt swords are no good you see, and if you look carefully, you will see some blood on it, it's the blood of one of the Wingham gang that I reckon you were helping them by giving us false information about the tides so that they would get away with all the goods, our goods too. Well, seems you all lost out as you all went against the Hawkhurst gang, not the best thing you could have done under the circumstances, it seems you chose the wrong side, so now as a little pay back we are now downstairs helping ourselves to whatever you got, and that might just include your wife", he went to speak but my sword pushed further stopped his speech.

I dragged him downstairs to jeers from the men.

I looked round the inn and behind the bar where his bottles of drink were kept.

"This is no good", I said, "looks like you have no stock behind the bar, your shelves are empty".

Arthur and Thomas watched on as somehow, I'd found a new me, listening to myself this wasn't me, maybe blooding my sword gave me the inner strength to be more like them, I was handling this situation from Arthur or Thomas, they just drank rum and watched me get on with it.
"Come on lads this is not fair, you can't have an Inn with no bottles", I shouted.
With that I saw George lift a bottle and empty the remains down his throat.
He wiped his mouth and said, "there you go, you can have this one".
All the men started laughing out loud as he placed it carefully on the shelf.
I turned and looked at the Inn keeper, my sword picking at the coat he was wearing,
"You seem to be a little short of stock, if you want to buy some, we have plenty to sell you, but might be a little on the expensive side, well, do you?" I said, pausing for an answer.
The Inn keeper looked at me and said, "I'll be fine now thanking you".
"That's what I like lads…. Manners, go a long way you know, people don't often thank people enough these days when they do a good turn", I said.
But I don't think you quite understand though, this is an Inn, and you need stock, we have stock, so you'll be buying some of ours, that's going to save you a lot of time for when you reopen later, are we clear on that". I said as my sword moved to pick at the buttons near his throat.
Just then a scream was heard from a room behind the bar.
"My wife", shouted the Inn keeper.
Just then the door swung open, Perrin appeared tying up his trousers.
"She's fine", said Perrin, "she's enjoyed herself as much as I did, hasn't had a proper man in years", he said to a jeering crowd.

"I found it, I've found his stash of money", shouted Smoker, clutching a large leather bag in one hand and a handful of money in the other as he returned from a back room.

"Well, well, it seems that you've paid for our stock now, only problem is, our stock was for someone else, so you'll have to wait till we return next time", I said, putting my sword back in the scabbard.

"It's been good doing business with you, you'll look forward to our return.

Right, you lot, take what you got and anything else you like and let's get this lot back home, seems we have a journey to make, besides, this Inn is dry". I said as they all cheered.

"oh, and in future be careful who you lie to, you never know whose listening, I said.

We loaded the inn keepers' stock on the carts and made our way south through Sandwich to the surprise of the onlookers who hadn't seen so many horses or carts for that matter as there were with us.

"You handled that nicely, I was going to kill him for lying to us", said Arthur.

"Not good to kill him when we can get more of his stock next time we are passing", I said, laughing to myself.

"You've come along nicely William, much better than I thought", said Arthur, holding out his hand for me to shake.

We kept good pace to make it back to Hawkhurst, Thomas, Arthur and a few of the others headed off to the Oak and Ivy while we and the others with carts made our way to John's farm by what was now late afternoon, the warm autumn sun, the motion of the carts, the drink along and the day's events were making us all tired.

I pulled back to speak with the others.

"I can't wait to get something to eat", said John, "and a lie down", said George,

"All the excitement of the day has made me very tired", he said yawning.

"We can all rest after we get this lot unloaded and then back to Hawkhurst", I said "we don't want to leave the loads on the carts for fear of it being stolen, you can't trust anyone". I laughed.
"You don't think anyone would, would you," said Richard, playing along with the joke.
"The art is to not trust anyone; Arthur has made that clear from the start and we now have it on first-hand experience from the Wingham gang". I said adjusting my position in the saddle to stop my legs from going numb.
"I reckon you should have cut that inn keeper Will, to show you weren't going to be messed about", said Smoker.
"I think we done enough, he won't be too keen to go against us if we ever need to do business with him again", I said.
"Business with us again, are you sure", Smoker laughing out loud".
"You never know, the opportunity might arise again, by doing just enough will not limit Arthur's contacts should he need them in future, and now they will know not to cross us", I said, getting the blood back in my legs.
We stopped at the junction that led to John's farm and Smoker went down the path to get him. We continued down the pathway to hide behind his barn till he came over.
"Hello Will, Richard, George", said John.
"Hi John, I take it your wife is not back then"? I said.
"No, her sister is still ill, doesn't look good for so the doctor said", said John looking at the number of carts that were drawing up.
"I'm not sure I have the room for all this lot, this is more than Arthur said I'd have to store", said John.
"Yes", I said, "seems we got lucky, I'm sure we can fit most of it in here, don't worry, this lot are good at hiding things" I said looking round at all the carts.

"If there's anything you need in the way of furniture, as you can see, we picked up a few items along the way, just help yourself to anything you want, no charge", I said pointing to two of the carts loaded with furniture.

"Do you have a pond as well, as we can weigh a few half and full barrels in the pond as they won't all fit in your barn, seems we have gathered rather a lot, we had a lucky day", I said.

"I do, it's in the lower field, quite a large lake too", said John.

"Smoker get John's goods off the cart and take it up to his farm house for him as his payment for letting use his barn plus a bit extra, George take a few others with you and move all of the halfers and barrels and anything else that won't fit in the barn onto the carts and take John with you so he can show you where his pond is, make sure they are water tight before you weigh them down in the pond and make sure none are showing before you leave, the rest of you, let's get to work and hide this lot in the barn, the quicker we do this the quicker we rest".

With that everyone was busy, it looked like we had just double the amount of people by the way they were moving about, quickly but quietly and efficiently and before long everything was hidden away.

John came back with George and the others, having placed the goods in the pond.

"What took you so long George", I said.

"There was such a lot that was put in that lake, and I mean a lot, about half of the lake is taken up with our goods", George laughed. "We put some soil on the barrels to help weigh them down, covered them up nicely, no one will notice.

"Go have a look and see if you can find anything in your barn" I said to John.

He went in and after a while came back out.

"There were a few things I noticed, but it's my barn, anyone else just coming to look wouldn't notice anything out of the ordinary", said John.

"That's good then, should be fine if anyone comes looking around, we will have them moved within a few days anyway, I expect Arthur has already got buyers already lined up for this lot, he will have to find a few more now that he has extra", I said to a roar of laughter from the others.
"Come on", I said, let's get going, want to be at the Oak and Ivy before the sun goes down, I'm hungry and thirsty, and I could do with a good sleep", I said.
We all mounted ourselves back on the carts and horses and headed off in the direction of Hawkhurst.
"Northiam to the Oak and Ivy won't take that long", I said to Smoker.
We managed to get back to the Oak and Ivy inn and using the barn to rest the horses, got them fed and watered the horses then went in to look after ourselves.
"That was a good job well done you lot, really pleased with the outcome, that should give the people in Wingham something to think about, I'm sure their wives and families will have something to say about their exploits in future", said Arthur with a big grin on his face.
We all ended up staying the night in the Inn, telling stories of what happened till the early hours of the morning.

Chapter 15
Goudhurst (1747)

The sun was warming me up on my journey and by midday I arrived at Rye and picking up a few provisions made my way towards the Mermaid Inn, I wondered as I passed the Bell inn if I should go in and attract the attention of the Inn keeper's wife, last time I was here she seemed to take a fancy to me but thought better judgment would be to steer clear of married woman.

I could hear Arthur, Thomas and his brother George laughing with a few others as I entered the inn, hello William they shouted, hurry, get yourself a tankard and join in.

"You lot seem happy", I said placing my sack with my provision under my chair as I sat down.

"Thomas is looking for a house now, and he wants to have the same as me, with lots of room", said Arthur.

"So, what's so funny about that, I said, ushering the bar keeper for a tankard of beer.

"I want to get maids and a gardener in as well", said Thomas looking bemused.

"He's gone from rags to riches, thinks he's royalty", said Arthur nearly choking on his beer.

"You'll find something, took Arthur a while to find something, may have to build it yourself Thomas, you should have enough money for it now,", I said.

"Money is not the problem, it's the location", he said, staring into the distance as he was thinking.

"Well, what you could do, is look for a location you want, if there's a house on it then offer to buy it, knock it down and build your own on the land, that way you'll get want you want", I said handing a few coins to the barkeeper as he placed my beer on the table.

"Do you know what", said Thomas, that's not a bad idea, but how about I find this perfect location and make the owners life hell, so they sell it to me cheaply", said Thomas, now even further deep in thought at the very prospect of getting what he wants.

"That's more in line with who you are", said George, watching Thomas in deep thought.

I put my tankard down, wiped my lips and watched all three of them were lost deep in thought, Arthur probably thinking, why didn't he think of that when he decided to build his house, Thomas thinking of the right location for his new house, and I expect George thinking how far Thomas would go to get what he wants.

At that point Arthur said that he was going to step down as leader of the gang for a while and let Thomas take over.

"Why's that, where are you going", I said in a concerned way, looking at him waiting for the answer.

We had the customs men looking out for me, posters going up everywhere and riding officers have been around the village and a lot of the time my name has been mentioned, so I'm going away for a while, you're in good hands with Thomas, and I shall be back once it's become quieter for me.

The door swung open as Jermiah, John Diamond, Poison, Smoker, Barnett Woolett and William Rowland made their way into the Inn.

"Where have you lot been", said Thomas.

"Oh, we've just come back from Goudhurst, been round the storekeepers and left tea with the farmers and got a few riches for our trouble, we didn't get lot from the storekeepers this time, they said they don't have a lot to give as business has been bad", said Jeremiah.

"Riches, what riches"? asked Thomas, now with his mind back in the room.

"Oh, there was some posh chap from Tunbridge Wells, Ballard, I think was his name, he was riding through the village, we asked him where he was going, all friendly like, you know us, always pleasant"? continued Jeremiah.
"Yes, I've seen your pleasant, "said Thomas.
"He told us to get out of his way as he's on an important errand", said Smoker, not having the patient to wait for Jeremiah to continue, and pulled out his riding crop and threatened to hit us with it if we didn't move.
"Now that's not very nice as we were only enquiring", continued Jeremiah.
"Carry on", said Thomas, with a look of intrigue on his face.
"Well, it just happened, we pulled him off his 'orse, and he hit the ground, he quickly got back on his feet and tried to hit us with his riding crop, so we hit him back a few times and knocked him down, well we weren't going to stand for his ways, so as he lay on the floor, we got out our whips and started to whip him to teach him a lesson, as he was lying there, we hit him a few times, then went through his pockets and got money and this nice watch with chain for our troubles, we left him lying there then came here, he was lucky we didn't take his horse for his cheek", continued Jeremiah, rifling through his pockets to find the watch.
"And this was in the village center with everyone watching you do this", said Arthur, looking not too pleased at what he just heard.
"There were a few men, women and children going about their business, but they soon ran off", said Smoker, looking please with himself, taking a bite out an apple he found in his pocket.
"Well, it will show everyone that we mean business, we are not to be mess with", said Rowland, staying quiet till now.
"Aye, that it will, they'll think twice before going against us", said Thomas looking down at the watch paying further notice to the details on it.

"I want you to go back again to Goudhurst next week, and get what's owed to us by them, we do a lot for them, now's not the time to be ungrateful for the thing we get for them, we put our lives on the line for this lot so make sure they pay, business has been bad? I'll show them bad business, said Thomas handing the watch to Arthur.

"And no one is to go to the magistrates or customs over us, they make enough, they can spare it", said Arthur, breathing on the watch and rubbing it on his coat to make it shine.

We sat around drinking and talking for the rest of the evening discussing and reliving the day's events.

A few weeks later, Arthur went off to visit friends in Hampshire leaving everything for Thomas to sort out, just till things became quiet again for him.

Thomas had grown more violent over the years we'd been together, a lot more violent than Arthur had been, this had worried us on occasions, in case it had brought some unwanted attention our way, not good when smuggling goods in and out of the country, news that could have got to our buyers ears and made life difficult in selling our goods, he was told on several occasions by Arthur but now that Thomas was in charge, we could sense a change in his approach to the running the gang.

Jermiah, John Diamond, Smoker and William Rowland were told to go round to collect goods and items from the other villagers that we hadn't visited yet and collect goods and money that's owed to us from them, most of the gang had been preoccupied, otherwise we would normally gone round, on seeing us they normally hand over what we ask for, so that we would leave them alone, otherwise we'd burn something of theirs, haystack, barn, house, just to keep them on our side and to show them who was in charge.

"Before you go, make sure you go back to Goudhurst, this time I don't want to hear that business has been bad, if they don't give us the goods, the next time they ask for tea, whiskey or anything else from us they can pay over full price, they can't have it both ways, that I see as fair". Said Thomas. They returned later that day to the Oak and Ivy Inn, loaded up with goods that they had taken from the villagers, storekeepers, and farmers.

"Is everything alright Jerimiah, any problems"? asked Thomas
"We had trouble with Goudhurst again", said Jeremiah. Dismounting his horse and tying it up to the rail
"Don't tell me they have had bad business again", I said, coming out from the Inn to see what they had collected from the villages.

Worse than that, the villagers of Goudhurst were refusing to let us have any goods from their stores, said they wouldn't let us use their buildings to hold our stock anymore, and they also been to the farmers around the area who put up a bit of a fight when we tried to take their grain and as for taking their horses they said to leave them alone, there was also talk of them smashing open the barrels of our rum in the pond that were had already stored there, to put it lightly the villagers were turning against us. We think it's because of what we had done to that chap, that Ballard, whipping him an' all, some of the villagers said he'd died because of what we did.

"Oh they do, do they, and what about the teas, whiskeys, rum, silks and perfumes they get from us, they'll be getting no more from us, and if they think we won't be able to use their houses to store our goods then they had better think again, do they realise who they are talking to, do they know what we can do to them should they try resisting, you wait, well get back at them", said Thomas looking red in the face on hearing the news.

Back in the village of Goudhurst, a familiar face appeared, someone who was born and raised in the village, happy to have returned from serving in the army and procured with an honourable discharge. Everyone in the village knew his name as William Sturt, most had watched him grow into a man, only in his twenties, a tall upright well-built man. All the villagers welcomed him back, he was back to live a comfortable life in the village he grew up in. It didn't take long for him to fit back into normal life, making the most of what the village had to offer, but news got to him that they were plagued by a gang that used to use their village as a hiding place for smuggled goods, and taking advantage of the farmers horses, just taking them when they needed them with tea or brandy as payment on their return, all this was inconvenience to the farmers, storekeepers and the people of Goudhurst had been threatened with violence and now were fed up with being used by the gang and told Sturt of this, who was sympathetic to their needs. He told them they shouldn't have to put up with these people, they shouldn't be using your barns, or taking goods to get along with them, and I am concerned and deeply troubled by the murder of this man, this can't go unpunished.

The more Sturt thought about this gang the more it troubled him, to have these men come into the village where he was born and treat these people like that, he couldn't just take this lying down, something had to be done to stop these men, but how, he was no longer in the army, but he still had connections and most of all, he had his training.

He left the village again and returned a few days later having been to see his previous superiors for a few favours, those favours he received was a few pistols and some gun powder, then a meeting was called by him to the villagers.

"I've been out to see riding officers in the hope that they can help, but there so few of them that they wouldn't be able to help, plus the fact that the Hawkhurst gang are too well known to them and their ways that they are too scared to get involved, they actually ask me to tell you to just live with it and put up with them till they get tired or move on, that, I'm sorry, is just not me, I want to live here in peace where I grew up and not have to worry about being terrorized by this lot, so I propose to you that we protect ourselves against these atrocities that these men have forced you to endure, we can arm ourselves and fight back, I've been to my commander and he's managed to give me some weapons that they no longer use, with gun powder, our only problem is they couldn't give us any shot, but that's not hard to come by, your roofs have lead on them so does the church in fact, we can melt it down and make our own shot and fight these men", said Sturt looking around at the crowd.

There were mumbles coming for the crowd of villagers that were there and all looking a bit unsure of what was proposed to them.

"We are not soldiers, most of us have never handled pistols before, let alone fired one", said one of the men from the back.

"I can handle a pitchfork", shouted another.

"I will show you; I can show you how to load and fire these pistols, all I need from you is the courage to stand by me and fight as I can't fight them on my own, we have no help from outside we have a chance to rid ourselves of this menace, but I can't do it alone, we need to do this together, this is you village, your homes", said Sturt, trying to get the villages on his side.

"I propose to you that, I will help in training you, helping you to fight back, and with you standing with me, regain your village back to the way it was and give you peace from these men, they'll think twice before coming this way again. If you agree, I will draw up articles, plans, and contracts which I want you people to sign to say that you'll stand by me and fight this abhorrent gang of thieves and ruffians and be rid of them once and for all", said Sturt, looking around at the villagers, he could see a few young men who would take up the challenge, but more middle-aged men, so wasn't sure which way they would vote.
"Can you give us time to think this through", came a voice from the back.
"Yes, we need more time", as if that would change things by not deciding now.
"No we have to work now, it'll take time with the training and getting you ready, time is what we don't have as we don't know when they'll be back to take from you again, and besides, they killed a complete stranger who entered your village, who else might they attack, we start now and surprise them by fighting back", Sturt voice now louder than before as he could see he was winning against the crowd, looking around to see who would be first to agree.
"Count me in, I've had enough of them, we have to fight back, it's our only way", came the voice from the back.
Sturt's expression changed as he heard this.
"And me, they've had a lot from me, almost left me with nothing, may as well fight them", said another.
Then more and more villagers were agreeing to the proposal till in the end there were about 43 of the villagers who agreed to help with a few women saying they could help reload the pistols if shown how to. This was it, he had done enough to persuade the villagers, all he had to do was put it into practice.

The following day the villagers all signed an agreement that had been drawn up by Sturt and they set themselves tasks in preparing to do battle.

Lead was stripped from the houses and the church roof, even the local clergy joined in as he too has had to face the gang head on when they used his church to store goods, so much whiskey and brandy were stored in there at one time that they couldn't use the church for its intended purpose. Everyone rallied around over the coming days, villagers were practicing firing the pistols and the women were tasked with the reloading and melting down the lead for shot, others were enlisted as lookouts in case the Hawkhurst gang were to appear.

Word got back to Thomas that someone was now living in Goudhurst and formed a militia with the villagers with the intent on fighting back, no longer would they put up with the menace that the gang had become, and he was intent on training up the villagers.

"Oh, he has, has he, going to take us on is he, well we shall see about that ", said Thomas, with the others looking on. He punched the oak support the held up the second floor of the inn, the whole room shook as he hit it again, and some plaster came down onto the table.

"I come from Goudhurst, born and bred there, who is this man to think he can take us on, we shall arm ourselves and go there and we shall make them pay for their cheek, how dare they after all we have done for them, we shall kill them all and burn the village to the ground, send a message to that lot, tell them we shall be coming for them on 21st April at 11, o clock in the morning, and we shall be coming from Cranbrook so be ready, to meet your maker, and tell Sturt that I will personally cut out his heart and eat it", said Thomas, baring his teeth feeling the anger well up inside him.

"Should we be telling them when we are coming, surprise would be better", I said.

"With our reputation, they'd be even more frightened if we let them know, share with them our confidence that if we win, they will all die and that village will be scoured from the history books and we will have our revenge, send a rider with a note saying such, that'll send a shock to them, most will probably run at the thought of it", said Thomas,
With that everyone in the inn settled down to more ales thinking about destroying the village once we had defeated them and this Sturt.

A rider came into the village and handed the Inn keeper of the Star and Eagle a letter, and told him, "Beware of us, you've made your choice, now you will pay", before turning round and galloping off.
The inn keeper ran off to find Sturt who was busy with teaching his new militia in a field next to the church.
The note was handed to Sturt who laughed at the note as he read it, then read it out aloud to whoever was in sound of his voice.
"Impudent fools, every military man knows that a battle is won not by the munitions that one has, or the metal of the soldier that wields it, but the element of surprise, if this is true, we now know the date, the time and the direction they will be coming from so now we prepare, but take heed that this could be false information to catch us off guard, whatever may come, we will be ready for them", said Sturt folding the paper carefully and placing it inside his coat pocket.

"Right, gather the men up, let's see a good show of men, get those swords and knives sharpened, fill your pistols full of lead and your blunderbusses ready, we are going to have ourselves a bloodbath with that lot in Goudhurst, make sure you have plenty of lead, and when we get there I want every shot to count, once we are done with this little militia and this Sturt then we shall raze the village to the ground and spare no one, and I mean no one, we don't want any survivors, is that understood", shouted Thomas, rallying the men together. This didn't sound good to me, all that killing Thomas had in mind, these were innocent people who had done nothing wrong, this wasn't what smuggling was all about, but, Thomas was in charge, so we just do as we are told, I sharpened my sword as much as I could before turning my attention to my knives, getting a nice edge on them, then getting as much lead shot as I could, filling my powder bag to the full, struggling to tie the knot to keep it all in, I looked around and seemed everyone was doing the same, this was indeed going to be a bloodbath, I saw Smoker and Diamond and Barnett checking their knives by shaving with them. The time for leaving was nearly upon us, we mounted our horses and headed out to Goudhurst.

Back in Goudhurst preparation was still under way to be ready before the time, the women had bags of gunpowder and shot in bags dotted around the village, these were ideally placed so the men could reload their pistols should they have to fall back further down the hill, then Sturt told the woman to leave and go to the next village and take the children and the elderly with them and wait there with them till they are called. A few teenage boys took up positions on the roof of the Star and Eagle inn, in the church tower and the lower section of the church roof, along the far wall of the church, while a few took up positions in the bedroom windows of the houses opposite the church, the main defence of men taking up position around the church and behind tombstones.

"This is it men, the time of their advance will be soon, don't back down despite their numbers, keep fighting, if you can't reload fast enough then change it for another pistol, make every shot count, we can win this battle,", said Sturt, mustering the men and building them with confidence. Everyone, had gone quiet, nestled behind tombstone were the men, scared that they could meet their maker, but this now seemed like the only way out, the deed had been done and were waiting for their doom.

Sturt was as calm as ever, been in this position many times probably fighting smugglers elsewhere perhaps, he just casually walked around the churchyard checking to make sure that everyone knew what to do, he went to the main door to look at the clock face, "the time is near men, be prepared". He shouted.

Outside Goudhurst the Hawkhurst gang dismounted, by the green, and tied their horses up.
"Take you shirts off lads, and rub some dirt on yourselves, let them see those war scars and tattoos that you have", said Thomas.
This was duly done, and dirt was applied to our faces and bodies to give us a menacing look. Not sure where he got that idea from, seemed a good idea as our bodies stood out in the sunlight, rubbing dirt over us gave us a bit of camouflage.
This was it, we started walking towards the village, carefully at first then sped up to make up ground, we knew we could beat them as they were only villages who turned against us, and now they would pay.

The church came into view, we stopped to look for any movement, none was seen so Thomas ushered us forward and to be quiet. We climbed over the far end wall of the church at Black Lane, a few went round the other side between the grave sites along the road, others were hiding behind the tombstones looking for any signs of movement, we stopped for a moment, then Thomas bellowed at the top of his voice, "Sturt, I'm going to cut out your heart and eat for this, now lads, go"! we all ran towards the side of the church only to be met by pistol fire, as the Goudhurst men open fire at us, sending us for cover, we didn't expect them to be waiting or to offer that much resistance, a few shots rang out from the houses opposite catching James in the leg, George Kingsmill raised his blunderbuss in the direction of the house where the shot came from, and completely laid bare the window and anyone that stood behind it. The Goudhurst men seeing the gang gaining ground across the church yard and along the back wall retreated from the church yard to outside the Star and Eagle Inn, crouching behind the wall, reloading their pistols, shots where whizzing past their heads, then they stood up and fired again, causing the gang to once again waylay their attack and dive for cover, gunpowder smoke filled the church yard obscuring any advance that came upon them, shots rang out from the Star and Eagle roof taking out one of our men, I could see one of our men fall to the ground but couldn't see who it was, The Goudhurst men seeing one of ours had fallen had given them the confidence to fight back even more, but we weren't going to allow that to happen. "Charge, man, kill them all", Shouted Thomas, now with his sword in his hand running towards the church gate, only to be met with another volley of pistol shot ringing past his ears. I stayed behind a grave seeking cover and only firing my pistol when I had a clear shot.

I aimed at the roof of the star and Eagle Inn to fire upon whoever took that high vantage point, then a shot rang out from my right side, ricocheting off the gravestone where I was hiding behind, from the window that George had took out, I trained my pistol towards the window, waiting for whoever it was to reload and come to the open window again, this time another shot came from the roof of the inn to my left side catching the gravestone sending splinters into my face. This was getting too close for any comfort, so I made a dash to a gravestone next to the church out of the way of the rooftop. The others had all made a dash to the edge of the wall firing upon the villagers only to be met by a volley from the men further into the village, sending them diving for cover, these men advance up the hill towards the church picking up pistols reloaded by the women sending out another volley of pistol shot our way as they did so, the men hidden behind the wall had reloaded and firing at us again, I could see the gang running towards the back wall, the person in the windows appeared again to fire another shot my way, I fired back only to hit the wall, I got up and followed the others down the road, running as fast as we could in case they had followed us, back out to were the horses were, the gunpowder smoke followed us as we mounted our horses.
"Where's George", said Thomas.
"We don't know, he was with us, but not when we left, I saw two of our men lying on the ground injured, one of them could have been your brother", said Smoker, catching his breath.
"We need to go back and get him, if he's not dead they'll send him to the gallows, let's go back and get him", said Thomas, Thomas, Smoker, Diamond, and I reloaded our pistols, and went back along the road towards the church.
"We need to find him, bring him back with us, "said Thomas, now with a look of panic on his face.

We reached the back wall as before, I was looking at the open window from where I had been shot at previously, looking for a figure to appear. This time we crept close to the wall and taking things a little slower moved towards the church, hiding behind the tombstone as we went.

We saw a group of the Militia standing over one of our men and picking up the blunderbuss.

"That's my brother, that's George, that's his blunderbuss, they got him, killed him, I killed him, I let this happen, let's get him back. Thomas appeared from the tombstone he'd been hiding behind and opened fire on the group of men, catching one in the leg, this was met by pistol fire from the open window, I fired back as this time I was ready and saw the person fall back into the room as my shot caught him. Then all the militia men's pistols were trained on Thomas, who dived over the back wall of the church yard as shots rang out with all of us following and running down the road towards our waiting horses.

This was a sad day for all of us, two men dead from what we could see and many more captured, a bad day.

Thomas didn't speak to anyone for at least two weeks as he was in full remorse for letting his brother die, everyone else avoided going near the Oak and Ivy or the Mermaid Inn, in case the Goudhurst militia and Sturt came looking to finish what we had started.

A month later after that event we found out that the four men caught attacking Goudhurst were put on trial and hanged for the crime of smuggling, with Bartlett Woolett and George Kingsmill killed during the battle.

Chapter 16
The Three Brothers (1747)

"Right, come on you lot, get this loaded so we can get going", shouted Perin as if he were captain of the ship, or had any right to be raising his voice to them.

The men just carried on loading the large amount of cargo that had been placed on the quayside, at their own speed, as if speed or capture weren't an issue, as far as they were concerned it wasn't their neck in a noose if they got caught loading the goods.

"Let's look lively lads, we don't want to be late for the tide, hoist the sails and make good the ropes when this lot's been loaded, and get someone to tighten the ropes on that foresail, we won't be going anywhere until that is done", said captain Gabe, shouting from the quarterdeck, and looking down at Perin.

As soon as the order was given the activity on board the Three Brothers became frantic, but without chaos, two men climbed the rigging and were making good on the captain's word.

"They'll take no command from you lad", he said looking down at Perin, a puff of smoke came from his pipe then turned his attention to the men in the rigging. "Check those rope", he shouted.

"I just need them to hurry up, it gives me the jitters in case the customs men come by", said Perin looking concerned.

"The men know who's the captain of this vessel, we got lookouts in the streets, we are ready for anything, we'll be fine, look they are almost done". Said the captain Gabe pointing to the quayside.

Perin looked round, what was a large amount that had been placed on the quayside was now gone and making its way down into the hold.

"That's better, at least now I can relax a bit better, I hope we are leaving soon"' said Perin, lifting the collar of his coat as the sea breeze caught him as he turned, at the same time the breeze caught the foresail, forcing it out the of hands of the two men up on the rigging.

"Careful up there you two, tighten it, not loosen it", he said moving off towards the bow to check on what they were doing, giving out more orders.

Two row boats came along side and ropes were thrown down to them, ready to pull the ship out from its moorings and out of the harbour.

"Fetch the lookouts, get them back onboard", shouted the captain, the cabin boy ran down the gangplank and disappeared into the streets to alert the rest of the crew.

Perin made his way below deck out of the breeze that had started to whip up along the coast.

"The wind will help us get across the channel in quick time", said a sailor as he past Perrin on the way to the galley.

Perin didn't hear as his mind was elsewhere. We need to get this load over to Christchurch Bay and meet the others so we could get it offloaded, if we had this crew helping us it wouldn't take that long to unload and get it all on the packhorses and away.

The goods safely stowed away in the hold. The captain gave the orders. "Cast off, bring in the bow and stern lines and man the capstan to warp to the first buoy, the wind and the tide are with us, pull, row harder". The two row boats pulled the stern of the ship away from the quayside while the bow of the ship was warped to the first buoy.

"Take it to the second buoy", came the orders, the row boats now rowing as hard as they could taking the rope to the second buoy, all the time the ship getting further out of the harbour.

"Let out the sails lets catch the wind", shouted the captain, again the men were racing everywhere pulling on the ropes, now with the ship picking up speed the ropes were hauled in from the row boats.

From below deck Perrin could hear the activity that was going on above deck and feel the ship moving.

It wasn't long before they were leaving the relative safety of the harbour and out on the open sea heading towards England, the wind picking up even more.

"The sails are full, we shall be in Chichester in no time", said the captain.

Perrin watched as Guernsey disappear over the horizon, Alderney came into view a short time later, a small island out in the Atlantic, he knew only too well it was another place where he could sell more goods, they were always willing to buy what he had, but this time the cargo wasn't meant for them, they were on their way to Chichester Bay to meet up with the Hawkhurst gang, the members from Hampshire would be waiting for the goods to arrive, and now we had the wind in our sails it wouldn't be long. The sun had risen now to about midday, he sat down on a coil of ropes to take in the view and the warm sun, and generally keeping out of the way, Sailors were still up in the rigging repairing as they sailed, not for me he thought, not with these hands. Perrin used to be a carpenter and a very good one at that, made a very nice living for himself, didn't want for anything, and always had money to spare, but as he got older arthritis in his hands, he could no longer use a saw and unsafe for anyone around him if he were to start hammering, and on many occasions the hammer would simply fly out of his hands, so he was happy to let someone else attend to the sails and the rigging.

It was long before Alderney disappear below the horizon, not long he thought, before the Isle of Wight would come into view, then they'd know they were close to home.

Get this lot unloaded, packed onto the horses, ride home to sleep in my own bed he thought, as he started to drift off with the movement of the ship.

He was woken by the sound of sailors shouting and running about, he rubbed his eyes, not really paying much attention at first.

"Let the sails out, full sail, we'll try to outrun them", shouted captain Gabe at the top of his voice.

Perrin got up to see sailors running around, in the rigging letting out more sails to catch more wind. Perrin ran up to the poop deck to find the captain.

"What's going on", said Perrin, still trying to wake up.

"That's what's going on", said the captain pointing out to sea behind them.

"We rounded off the Ise of Wight to find we are being chased by a sloop of war, running the Royal navy ensign, and I think they are after us, so not taking any chances they'll have to catch us if they can".

"I think I know that ship, I've seen it before, never been chased by it though, can we outrun it"? Perrin asked looking towards the ship heading straight for them.

"No, is the simple answer, that's a Sloop of war and we are carrying cargo of several tons, your cargo, we have a choice to throw it overboard and try and outrun it, but it's still a fast ship and will catch us eventually, we can make a stand and fight, but our guns are not as powerful as theirs, the best we can do is to keep going and not make land, extinguish all candles and lanterns and run in the dark where we might get away, we might just stand a chance of getting away without you losing your goods". Said the captain.

"Do that, that's the better options, at least we might have a chance", said Perrin, still looking out to sea to see if the sloop was gaining on them.

"Get that main topsail yard secured, its running free, let the main topsail loose. We need more sail,", shouted the captain.

Sailors were running up in the rigging, up into the sky to do as they were ordered to get more wind in the sails, the ship listed over as more wind pushed into the sails.

"Check on the load, down below, make sure its secure, we don't want it coming adrift", the captain shouted at me, men were racing about everywhere as if their lives depended on it and if it was a naval ship, it did.

He gave Perrin a telescope, ", look through that and tell me what you see, do you recognise it or anyone on board", said the captain passing Perrin and old leather case bound with string, like it had seen better days.

Perrin put the telescope up to his eye to look through the eyepiece, taking a moment to find the ship and get his hand steady.

"Well,", anything, bellowed the captain, as sea spray came over the deck.

"The ship was rocking about from the waves, so it was difficult to see anything", said Perrin, feeling a little useless at this time.

"Give it here, "said that captain snatching the telescope from Perrin.

"Thats a three masted sloop of war, I couldn't see at first, but now I can, and the ensign, that looks like the Swift, that's the only Sloop in these waters at the moment, we'll never outrun that, but we are not giving up yet.

"Go below deck and double check your goods are tied down, if they come loose, they could list the ship too far, be careful down there, if they come loose, you'll be crushed. Said captain Gabe.

With that Perrin disappeared below deck to make sure his goods were lashed down.

What seemed like ages lashing down the goods and checking on the ropes, Perrin made his way back onto the deck, and looking out to sea towards the sloop, could see in the gloom of dusk the sloop had gained on them.

Perrin felt trapped, the sloop was gaining, the gangs' goods couldn't be landed, Thomas and the gang wouldn't be happy, there was nothing he could do to change the events of the journey which he'd made so many times before without any problems, he could almost feel the noose around his neck, he had to do something, but what?

A stark reality came over him, me, or them, he could easily charter another boat, could easily replace the lost stock, but he couldn't replace his neck, he looked all around, maybe hiding would be the only solution, but after a search he'd be found. The captain in the distance was still shouting orders, as if that were going to make any difference. Perrin needed to think and to think fast, the sloop was gaining he looked out to sea. The darkness wasn't about to slow this ship down and it wouldn't take long before they were all caught.

The sloop was close to a mile out when a shot rang out, missing the masts and the sails, then the ship got closer, someone shouted across the void to lower the sails.

Perrin had to get word back to the gang that the goods had been captured, but how?

Perrin saw a chance, as their attention was drawn to the sloop, Perrin made his way to the port side and with the help of two other sailors managed to lower a rowboat from the side, they managed to get it halfway down before it got stuck, without thinking he got his knife out and cut the ropes, the sails were ordered to be lowered on the Three Brothers thus slowing the speed of the ship as a second shot rang out whistling through the air from the sloop. The two sailors managed to climb down the rope as he cut the second rope to hear the boat run down the side of the ship and splash into the water along with the sailors, he threw a rope overboard and climbed down it into the Icey cold water, then swam towards it, the two sailors managed to climb in the boat, hoping that it was undamaged by the way it hit the water, Perrin stayed in the water moving to the far side and kicking his legs so as to move the row boat away from the ship, just in case someone had seen them, when they were clear enough he climbed inside the row boat helped by the sailors, they untied the oars and placing them into the rollicks looked back to see the Three brothers being boarded by the sailors from the sloop, they slipped quietly into the night to avoid capture and headed for the shore.

Chapter 17
Poole Customs House (1747)

Back in Hawkhurst everyone went about their business as usual, everything was, as far as everyone was concerned, normal, until three riders broke the peace galloping through the village knocking over two men and a woman for getting in their way, straight though the village and out the other side without stopping leaving a trail of dust behind them.
They went to Thomas Kingsmill's house to tell him of the news about the Three brothers being captured.
Thomas Austin, George Austin, and John Cobby had ridden all the way from Poole in Dorset to pass on the bad news to Thomas.
"What's all this", said Thomas looking at the horses covered in sweat.
"The goods, the goods from the Three Brothers have been taken, captured", said Cobby catching his breath.
"What, how, when"? bellowed Thomas. Knowing there's a lot of money that's been spent buying those goods.
"We were waiting at Chichester Bay at the normal place two days prior, and no ship showed up, we saw it as it rounded the Isle of Wight plus, we saw a sloop of war heading in their direction until it got too dark to see anything. The first light of day we saw it heading off toward Poole both ships together, we made some enquiries and found out the captain of the sloop Captain William Johnson has been watching the area and had orders to commandeer any ships that he thought were used for smuggling, and had seen the Three brothers many times before, we reckon he's got the goods, we got other people checking in Poole to see what they do with the goods", said Cobby, breathing a bit easier now that the news was out.
"Hmm", said Thomas, deep in thought, looking down at the ground for some inspiration.

"And what about Perrin, did you see him at all", he said, looking at each of them.

"They must have got him as well, taken him with them, that doesn't look good". Said George, looking at Thomas in a sorrowful way.

"We need to think", said Thomas looking down again.

There was a long pause, just then Diamond appeared.

"Morning all, well haven't seen you three over here for a while, what are you all doing here", said Diamond in a cheerful manner.

"We got problems, big problems, one of our ships have been captured, along with our goods and Perrin as well, and at the moment we don't know what to do, but the more I think of it, all I want is revenge, how can this captain take it upon himself to take our goods, and our man, he will end up hanging him", said Thomas, getting more worked up at the very thought.

"Diamond, get some flags posted up and post letters in the message trees, we meet tonight at the Oak to work on a plan, I want my goods back along with Perrin if we can, said Thomas, now with his fist clenched and punching the frame of his door.

The evening came and it was obvious that the messages got through to the other members as the Oak and Ivy was packed with members all keen to find out what was happening.

A few members were sitting in the corner of the inn openly sharpening their knives with a sharpening stone, it was Shepherd and Jeremiah eager to draw some blood.

Just then a horse was seen galloping toward them along the Hawkhurst road.

"That looks like Perrin", I said, lifting my hands to block out the sun's rays.

"That is, that's Perrin, go and get Thomas out here", I said giving orders to anyone near the door of the Inn.

Thomas rushed out from the inn, pushing past other members as he did, anxious to hear from Perrin.

Perrin, jumped from the horse and gave the reins to Diamond to tie up.

"Get him a drink", shouted Thomas.

Thomas stood in front of Perrin looking at him, waiting for him to catch his breath, a tankard of ale was passed to him, and we all watched as he drank it in one go without breathing, eagerly waiting for him to speak.

"We were captured by the Swift, they boarded us, I didn't know what to do, I had to think fast, I lowered a boat over the side, and made my escape, they took the goods and the Three brothers, I didn't see what happened after that as it was dark, I rowed all night till I made land, stole a horse and made my way here", said Perrin.

Thomas raised his arm and hit Perrin across the face with the back of his hand sending Perrin flying into the dirt, Perrin looked up at him with blood dripping from a split lip.

"You let them get our goods, whisky, brandy, coffee and tea, you do know what that's worth, I should take that out of your hide", said Thomas, losing his temper not so much at Perrin but the fact that he'd lost the goods to someone else.

We watched as Perin pulled himself off the ground and dust himself off still nursing his split lip.

"We ride, we go to Poole and make a plan on the way, mount up, everyone, make sure you've armed and loaded, I want my goods back, get yourself another drink Perrin and a few bottles of brandy and whiskey for us along the way, and get yourself another horse, yours is tired, and you two as well Thomas, George, get fresh horses, it's a long way", said Thomas, looking less annoyed at the thought of getting back his goods.

Within the hour they were making their way out of Hawkhurst and on the way to Poole.

A few days later they stopped, just outside Petersfield picking up a few more members along the way who were more than happy to come along, we totalled about sixty now, more than enough to take on riding officers should they pass our way, we weren't about to be stopped from our goal, what's ours is ours and no one was going to take it from us, the more we rode the closer we got, the braver we got, the more you could see the evil in Thomas's eyes.

Two riders appeared along the road we were travelling, they had just come back from Poole to find us and give us the news that our goods were stored in a safe place, the customs house, along the harbour front.

"This doesn't look good, that's going to by dragoons or riding officers, there was going to be a lot of blood spilled before the day is done", I said.

"We will find out how guarded this place is once we get there", said Thomas looking in the direction of Poole.

We carried on further and as we got closer to Poole it was agreed that only about thirty of us should proceed to the customs house, the others would act as lookouts in case riding officers were in the area, they would take care of them while the rest of the gang got the goods and a plan was made, for whatever happened, by the morning we would all meet up at Ringwood.

We arrived at Poole under the cover of darkness, we had been drinking during the day just to bolster our confidence, for what we had in mind to do.

We stopped just along by the harbour in Poole, in amongst some trees.

"Thats the Customs house over there", said Thomas Austin, pointing to a large building with flags raised on the roof.

"Let's get our goods back", said Diamond, as he made his way towards the harbour front.

"Wait, come back here, look", I said, as I pointed to a sloop moored on the other side of the harbour.

"Isn't that the Swift", I said trying to read the name on the front of it.

"Go and have a closer look Diamond, tell us what you see", said Thomas.

With that Diamond walked along the quayside into the darkness, looking over towards the sloop, then came running back a short time later.

"Yes, it's the Swift, and all gun ports are open, and the canons are facing towards the customs house, said Diamond looking panicked.

"Did you managed to see the Three Brothers as well"? I asked.

"No didn't see it, I wasn't really looking", said Diamond.

"Now what do we do"? asked Thomas Austin, looking at his brother for guidance.

"Not sure what we do, but somehow, we've got to get the goods from that place, sloop, or no sloop, of course they may well be still on the Three Brothers, wherever that may be", said Thomas Kingsmill, not really thinking clearly for any solution as his temper was starting to get the better of him again.

"How about we just sit here and wait, till we find a solution, or check for the Three Brothers and see if the goods are still onboard", said Curtis who had been relatively quiet till now.

"If we wait long enough the sun will come up and all will be lost", said Thomas.

"Actually, not", said Perrin, "the tide runs low here, let's just wait and maybe, just maybe, we will get some luck come our way", he said rubbing his hands together, like he knew what would happen if they waited.

"Tell me", asked Thomas.

"I'm hoping that the tide will go out far enough that the Swifts cannons will no longer be pointing at the customs house, so they won't be able to fire on us.

"That would be good if that happened", laughed Thomas, feeling a little better that his plan might just come together.

Sure, enough the longer they waited the further the sloop went down due to the tide going out, then as the ship hit the mud, we could see the sloop start to list pointing the cannons down further.

"This is it, go fetch the horses, let's make our way over there and get that door open, if the goods are in there, we are taking them", said Thomas.

Thomas Austin, George Austin, and Diamond went to get the horses.

"Curtis", get that door open, I said looking around to see if anyone was around.

Curtis used his knife to pick at the lock and in no time at all we were in.

We searched the customs house to find our goods packed neatly in a back room,

"Come on, let's get this lot loaded and get out of here"", said Thomas in an excited voice.

It wasn't long before the goods were loaded onto the horses, and some loaded onto a cart that was left on the quayside, how lucky were we, we thought as the last of the goods were loaded on the cart.

"Leave that", said Thomas to me as I picked up the last bag of tea.

"Leave this bag of tea", I said.

"Yes lad, we shall leave them just the one bag of tea, as payment for their troubles of looking after our goods and bringing It ashore for us, nice and safe", Thomas now laughing as we rode off out of Poole to meet with the others in Ringwood, happy in the knowledge of what we had achieved. The others couldn't believe our luck when we told them, neither could we.

Thomas Austin said he wasn't going to sleep rough and said he was going home to a nice warm bed as he lived locally, not too far along to Fordingbridge, the rest of us found an Inn and made that our home for the evening. The excitement in the air and chatting and laughing amongst themselves about what happened and how easy it was getting our goods back.

"I'd love to see the look on their faces when they open the doors to the customs house, and realise we've only left a bag of tea for them", said Thomas laughing out loud, when they woke up in the morning, still not believing their luck of the previous night, taking in the fresh Hampshire air.

They made their way following the river Avon till they came to Fordingbridge, the people there were lining the streets cheering and waving, Thomas looked over to us in disbelief as to what had happened.

"Thomas Austin must have told a few people what had happened, and news travels fast in a small town, don't forget he lives here", said George.

We strolled through Fordingbridge feeling like Lords, people were cheering as we started handing out small amounts of tea and passing bottles of whiskey and brandy around, they passed the bottles around so many could have a drink, celebrating our luck I suppose at the audacity at what we had done.

Everyone was feeling good the mood was ecstatic, Diamond looked into the crowd and saw a familiar face and old friend, that of Daniel Chater,

"Hello Daniel, it's been a while since I've seen you, it's good to see you again", said Diamond.

"Hello John, Yes, it's good to see you, it's been a while since you sold your house and moved out, where are you living now, everything good for you now"? said Chater looking up at Diamond sitting on his horse, holding out his hand to shake with him.

"Oh, I live somewhere near Hawkhurst, settled in nicely thank you for asking", said Diamond., reaching down to shake Daniel's hand.
"It's good to see you again, and looking so well too", said Chater.
"What are you doing here now with this lot"? said Chater looking all around him confused at what's going on.
"Oh, nothing much, just getting back some items that belongs to us, now heading off back towards Kent and home, Said Diamond, trying not to give too much information away, too many ears in the crowd.
"Here take this, and look after yourself", said Diamond handing Chater a large bag of tea, then he bid him goodbye and caught up with the rest of the gang.
The others seem to revel in what was being displayed before them with all the people making them feel like royalty.
We left Fordingbridge with smiles on our faces and made our way across country to Chichester, we stayed in an Inn for the night in Chichester, still remarking on what we had gone through.
"Those people back in Fordingbridge, I couldn't believe what they were like, the way they carried on, just so happy to see us", said Thomas, smiling to himself.
"I have no idea what Thomas Austin had said to them, but they were treating us like kings.
"Who was that man you were talking to Diamond,", asked Shepherd.
"That was Daniel Chater, I used to work with him when I lived in the area, we used to bring in the crops and work the land for a local farmer at the time, when I left there, he had just started up as a shoemaker selling and making shoes, haven't seen him in years, said he was doing well and business was good, that wasn't for me, so I left there and came to live in Hawkhurst, I gave him a large bag of tea, thought he'd like that". Said Diamond.

"Generous of you", said Shepherd, gently punching him on the arm and smiling to him, in a playful way.

"Well, we can afford it again", said Thomas, laughing to the others who gave out a cheer.

I was glad that the whole event was over, but to me things did seem to run better when Arthur was around, I think that Thomas's temper somehow distorted his vision of how things ought to be done, Arthur had in some way a more methodical approach on how to do things, only one of our gang members got killed that of George Chapman under Arthur's leadership, now under Thomas, we had two members dead and other members captured and hung from going into Goudhurst and trying to take on the militia.

The following morning, we continued our journey back to Hawkhurst, still reliving the tale that was Poole and the customs house and Fordingbridge.

Chapter 18
Chater and Galley (1747)

About a month or so later Diamond said he was going away for a while on business, off back down to Chichester again, to visit a friend and check out a captain of a ship that might be interested in bringing over more goods from France or Jersey, since we had lost them use of the Three brothers ship the amount of goods coming in were lessoned.
I managed to overhear Shepherd, Thomas, and Diamond talking about getting him to do a delivery for us.
"We need to get him to work with us", said Shepherd.
"I will do my best, "said Diamond.
"I don't think you'd pursued him in the same way that we could", said Thomas looking at Shepherd for agreement.
"I will, I promise, he'll be working for us once I've told him what's in it for him, he'll be happy to work with us", said Diamond.
"Word has it down that way, we didn't know what we were doing and that we let the Three Brothers get captured, that is something you'll have to put them straight on, The Hawkhurst gang is still in business, and if they want proof, we will come down there with a show of strength to prove our point, this area along the south coast is still ours, so you'd better do some pretty good convincing or there will be more blood on my sword", said Thomas.
"I'll go to Chichester and wait for his ship to come in then I'll be having words with him and convince him its worth his while, and while I'm there I'll ask around to see if I can persuade anyone else to take up our offer", said Diamond.
"And if he doesn't", said Shepherd, waiting for a response.
Diamond reached down to his sword and placed his fingers around the handle.
"That's good, show him some steel, that always does my convincing", said Thomas.

A few days later Diamond had his order and headed out on his recruitment journey to Chichester.

Time went by slowly after that, there wasn't many goods coming in, we were just selling what we had for the time being, getting it all from the hiding places in and around Kent, until Diamond or someone had sorted out another ship, all the others that we had been using up till now were busy doing their own deliveries and keeping their head down now that the swift was patrolling the waters to the south, we had plenty to sell and decided to let things calm down for a while, we still had ships coming in from Belgium and northern France coming into Whitstable and along the northern part of Kent, but we still needed the big ships to come in from France and other European places with their exotic goods, like spices and silks.

About two weeks later John Hammond came by delivering a message, he told us the bad news that Diamond had been captured,

"The customs men had somehow found out that a member of the Hawkhurst gang was in the area asking question about ships out to France or Guernsey and had lain in wait for someone of his description to turn up. Apparently waiting along the quayside and jumped him as he talked to ship owners and captains, trying to get them to work for him, putting propositions their way. They jumped him and carried him off and entered into Chichester gaol, I didn't think he'd be in their long as they had nothing to hold him on, but I did ask what they are holding him for, they just said it was for the Poole Customs office break in that they were holding him responsible for the whole thing". said Hammond.

"They can't hold him for that, it was more than him involved, he was one of about thirty of us", I said, looking concerned.

"Well, why don't you go down there and tell them that", said Shepherd, getting his face close to mine.

"Word has it that because he gave a bag of tea to someone in the crowd in Fordingbridge that knew him that this person is now the only witness they have and they will do their utmost to keep him in gaol and interrogate him to get other people named, and if he can be identified they are certain to hang him by the neck, a lot of people saw him shake a man's hand and give him a large bag of tea and that was from the gang that rode through Fordingbridge, so it doesn't look good, and they are going to get a magistrate and this man that he gave the tea to go to Chichester and establish him as a witness, if this man identifies him then that It'll be the end for Diamond", said Hammond.

"I'll have to tell Thomas about this and see what he will do", I said trying to think of a way to tell Thomas without getting him into a rage.

I passed the message onto Thomas, and I was shocked, he didn't seem concerned in the slightest,

"What's done is done, oh well we will have to find someone else to look for ship and corrupt captain", he turned and look at Shepherd, "do you want to go down Chichester or Portsmouth to find a ship and a corrupt captain to work with us", said Thomas.

"I'm fine here, send someone else", said Shepherd.

"Seems there is no one else, so might have to be you Shepherd", said Thomas, a bit sterner and a little put out by being answered back, this was new for him.

"There's Will standing there, why don't you get him to go"? said Shepherd.

Now these two were both strong willed and both have a nasty streak, with Thomas being the most aggressive and the one person who you couldn't predict, so I was standing back just in case swords became drawn at Shepherd refusing a command from Thomas.

There was a pregnant pause and Thomas held his finger to his lips to stop anyone from saying another word while he was thinking.

"No, he said, we will send Hammond, he's here, he knows the area, he can go back that way and do a better job of it than Diamond can, sending Diamond was a mistake as he doesn't know the area, Hammond knows the area and can use the back streets to hide and avoid detection, yes, we can send Hammond, Said Thomas, looking like he'd just solved a puzzle.

Seeing the look on Thomas's face, seemed he was slowly finding leadership in Arthur's absence, but not very well, he shouldn't have sent Diamond and now he was caught couldn't really be bothered about rescuing him out of Gaol, yet it was fine for his stock to be rescued out of the customs grasp, I was beginning to see Thomas in a different light, I knew from the beginning there was always something about him that I didn't like, and now I was seeing him for the real person that he was.

Hammond agreed that on his return to Chichester that he would seek out any captain that wanted to join us and make it worth their while in doing so.

Hamond rested the for the night and was gone by first light. I asked Thomas in the morning if we were going to rescue Diamond from the gaol, His words cut me deep, for him to be saying this about a friend.

"Everyone is expendable, our goods are worth more than any individual's, we have to think of the rest of the gang not just on one person", said Thomas. As he turned and walked away to avoid any arguments.

I was left stunned at what I'd heard, Diamond was a good friend not just to me but to everyone,

I didn't know where to look or what to do, I was stunned as I watched Thomas just walk away as if Diamond didn't mean anything to him.

I just left and went back home angry at Thomas's words.

Back in the Fordingbridge and member of the Magistrate by the name of William Galley went to where Daniel Chater was working and on seeing him asked him if with a reward for his time would accommodate his person and accompany him to the Gaol of Chichester to see a Major Battine a Justice of the Peace and a Commissioner of Customs at Chichester, where upon identifying the said John Diamond, who had given him an amount of tea and going by the name of Diamond or Dymer as he was often known, act as a witness against the crimes that were done to the customs house in Poole, for reasons of which a large bag of tea was passed to his person from the said Diamond.

To Danial Chater this did sound official by the way it was portrayed to him and with the aid of a reward decided that friend or not this was too good an offer not to turn down, so with agreement he said yes, not really knowing what the circumstances that lay ahead for his friend Diamond in doing so.

Sunday 14th of February was set as a day to leave and Galley and Chater set out to visit the magistrates in Chichester.

They passed through Havant to visit a friend a Mr. Holton who had been acquainted with Chater for many years along the way through to Chichester.

Mr. Holton told them that the Major wasn't at Chichester, he was in East Marden so directed them both to go by the way of Stanstead near Rowlands Castle, along the way they passed through Leigh and decided that they would stop for refreshments at the New Inn to rest from their weary journey and to ask for direction so that they may continue with their journey to Rowlands Castle then onto East Marden.

There they met three men by the names of George and Thomas Austin and Mr. Jenkes, who they found out later was their brother-in-law,

"Excuse me gentlemen", said Galley, in a very polite manner. "Do you know the way to Rowlands Castle"?

"We certainly do", said George Austin.

"Could you possibly point us two gentlemen in that direction so that we may continue our journey", said Galley.
"We can do better than that, we are going that way ourselves so you can follow along with us, and we'd be glad to have you with us as company", said George Austen.
All then men then rode off towards Rowlands Castle with George Austen now riding beside Chater,
"So where are you off to if you don't mind me asking"? Said George.
"We are off to East Marden to give a letter to Major Battine, then we will return back to Fordingbridge by way of tomorrow", said Chater, not really caring about what he said to who, as far as he was concerned it didn't matter to anyone what he told them.
A short time later they arrived at Rowlands Castle and entered the White Hart Inn.
"Hello", said Galley, to a woman in the Inn.
"How do you do", said the woman
"I'm William Galley and this is my friend Danial Chater, we were a little lost and helped by these three gentlemen of good standing, to arrive here, do you mind if we come in for some refreshment and a chance to rest our horses", said Galley.
"Hello and welcome, I'm Mrs. Payne, but you can call me Elizabeth or Liz for short, you are most welcome to come and, rest your feet and I'll get someone to tend to your horses, while you are here". Said Payne, looking round to get someone out to tend the horses.
"What refreshment would you like"? said Payne, looking at them both.
"I'd like a rum, said Galley,
"And for you"? now looking at Chater.
"Make that two glasses of rum please", said Chater.
"Come a long way have you deary", she asked placing the drink on the table.
"We've only come from Fordingbridge", said Chater, reaching for some coins to pay for the rum.

"Where are you supposed to be going then if you are lost, "she said, looking at them and waiting for an answer.
"Oh, we, we were supposed to go another way, but seem to have got lost along the way, we are headed for Chichester, and if it's not too much trouble, once we've rested could you direct us in the correct direction". Said Chater, now trying to sound like he had a better upbringing and match his tone to that off Galley.
"And why would you two gents want to go to Chichester for"? she said.
Galley wasn't about to go into too many details as this was a private affair and trusting someone with information that's not for their ears was not a thing he was about to do, given the way she was questioning them about their affairs.
"Oh, we are just going to visit friends", said Galley, butting in, in case the wrong thing was said.
"It's alright deary, just enjoy your stay, and rest while", said Payne, the smile leaving her face, as if she had just been told to mind her own business.
She went back to behind the bar and in the kitchen, to see her sons to find out more information about the two that were now sitting in her Inn and to her mind now acting suspiciously through their answers. She spoke to George and said they acted strangely when she asked them where they were going.
"Oh, they did say on the way up here, now what was it"? said George scratching his head.
"Oh yes, that's it, they've got to deliver a letter to a Major, umm, Major Battine, on official business, that's it, I asked that Chater chap, who told me were they were going, so nothing special", said George.
"Well, I don't like it, I don't trust them at all", she said turning back towards where they were sitting.
She peered through the kitchen doorway at them sitting there and saw Galley reading a letter that he had got from his pocket, looking round before opening it and reading it.

"I don't like it,", she said, turning round to look at George.
"There's nothing to worry about, nothing at all, seems perfectly innocent in what they are doing, you worry too much ma", said George, looking at his mother, who didn't seem interested as to what he had to say.
"Send out Thomas to go find William Jackson and William Carter and tell them to come quickly, I'm going to give them some more rum on the house so they can stay longer while you're getting them". Said Payne staring at them through a crack in the door.
She went back out to see them and offered them more rum.
"There you go deary, because you got lost and as its quiet in here today you can have this rum on the house, just to show you our hospitality and for your regrettable circumstance". Said Payne, moving round their table quickly.
"Why thank you, that's very kind of you, we appreciate your fine hospitality, we weren't lost, just needed pointing in the right direction", said Galley lifting his glass to Mrs. Payne.
Payne again disappeared to the kitchen to look through the window to see if anyone was coming, then after a while went back to peer through the door, Galley and Chater were looking agitated, so she went out to the main room again to where they were sitting.
Galley got up and came over to her.
"I do beg your pardon Madam, do you think that you can find someone to ready our horses, as it seems the day is moving on and we have to be going", he said in a timid sought of way.
"Unfortunately, that's not possible at the moment as the person who looks after the horses has gone out and locked the stables and taken the key with him, I'm so sorry but you'll just have to wait for his return, he's never done this before you understand". Said Payne.
"That is unfortunate, oh dear we shall just have to wait", said Galley, losing his demeanour.
"I can offer you another rum if you like", said Payne.
"No, no, it's fine", said Galley.

"It's on the house, said Payne", now with a smile on her face, "it's the least I could do for the inconvenience".
"Alright, if you insist,", said Galley, now smiling back at her. She brought the drink s over to the table and went back to the kitchen, to be met by George Austin.
"George, I need you to go away from here, I don't want you here when the others arrive, you're too good and I don't want you to get into trouble", said Payne.
"What trouble", he asked with a puzzled expression.
"I just need you to go and don't ask any questions, come back in a few days, then I'll explain everything to you, but you need to hurry as they will be here soon", said Payne in an anxious voice.
"Alright I'll do it for you ma", with that he put his coat on and went through the back door to the stable to get his horse, then she watched as he rode away.
Just as George disappeared in the distance then William Jackson, William Carter and William Steel entered into the yard.
"We got your message that you wanted to see us", said Jackson.
"Yes, I did", said Payne, now looking a little relieved to see the three of them.
"those two men sitting out there have got a letter and are taking it to a Major Battine, if it's the same person I know he is a justice of the peace, when I asked them what they wanted with him they just said they were visiting friends, no one I know would want to be friends with Battine she said, so I'm a suspicious of their answer and think they will do us harm by way of that letter they are carrying", said Payne, now looking back through the crack in the doorway.
"Are they still here"? asked Jackson.
"Yes, I've been giving them rum and told them the stable door was locked so they couldn't get to their horses". Said Payne.
Mr. Jenkes and Thomas Austin entered the yard and into the barn to check on the horses.

"Liz, go in and get one of them out here so we can find out what they are doing here", said Jackson.
She did as she was told and disappeared back to where they were sitting. Moments later coming back out to the yard with Chater.
"Where is it you are going and what are you going for, and has your journey got anything to do with a Diamond", asked Jackson, holding Chater by the lapels of his coat so that he couldn't break away.
"I believe that Diamond is in Gaol, and a rather unfortunate affair, of him being captured", said Chater looking concerned to be asked that question.
"So, you do know John Diamond"? asked Jackson.
"We believe that letter that you are carrying for Major Battine would seal Diamonds fate and convict him of his crimes and get him hung, all for what, is there a reward that you are seeking"? said Jackson, now becoming angry at the thought of it.
Galley suspecting that his colleague might become indiscreet about the information he was holding, came out to see what had happened to Chater and ask him to return back inside the Inn.
Jackson, turned to face Galley and punch him with such force as to knock him down.
Galley rushed back into the Inn with Jackson following him.
"I am a Kings officer and cannot put up with such treatment", said Galley, checking for signs of blood on his lips.
"You a Kings officers", said Jackson, "take a care as I'll serve you again", he said laughing.
Galley and Chater became uneasy by the situation and wanted to leave and continue their journey.
They all entered the Inn together Galley and Chater feeling concerned by the situation, and said they would like to leave, but the others persuaded them to stay.

Please stay, I'm sorry for what I did, and can't apologise enough for my behaviour, I mistook you for someone else", said Jackson being very apologetic.

"Galley said that he would except his apology and that perhaps mistakes had been made and drinking with the men in a more friendly atmosphere would make them feel more at ease around them. So, Thomas Austin, Jackson, Carter, and Mr. Jenkes, along with Chater and Galley continued drinking until Chater and Galley were drunk and fell asleep.

While Chater and Galley were left in their drunken sleep the men got round them and searched in their pockets for the letter that Mrs. Payne had seen them with, they found and read the letter and realised that it was in fact a letter which would incriminate John Diamond and put him in the place of the Poole customs house when it was robbed of smuggled goods. They made a committee to decide what should be done with these two men, now knowing that the letter they had would incriminate Diamond.

"Should he go before the magistrates they would surely condemn him as a smuggler with this information, and as a participant with breaking into the customs house in Poole, to which the outcome would be certain death". Said Carter, who read out the letter aloud to the others.

John Race, Richard Kelly and Edmund Richards then came in and were told the story about Chater and Galley by Jackson.

"What are we going to do about them, asked Kelly.

"We take them both to a well far from here, murder them and throw them in", said Steel, rubbing his hands together in a joyful manner, thinking he had found a solution to their problem.

"Not a very good idea", said Kelly. "How about we just send them to France, without the evidence Diamond would be set free".

"And if they come back in time, they could still condemn Diamond with their evidence", said Jackson.

Just then the wives of Jackson and Carter came into the inn, and overheard the discussion, they said "Hang the dogs for they came here to hang us".

"That Chater was supposed to be a friend of Diamond, and look at him now, just for a reward he is willing to turn against him, I say let them hang", said Mrs. Carter.

"They should pay for what they've done, or what they were going to do", said Mrs. Jackson.

"We could just lock them up till after the trial", said Wiliam Carter, quiet till now but trying to turn his wife from the violent thoughts she was having.

"On doing so we could all afford three pence a week for their upkeep, till Diamonds trial was over.

"I'm not paying anything to these dog's, they want one of us to hang for money, they are not getting mine", said Jackson. With these words still ringing is the ears of the others he stood up and kicked open the door and immediately run his heavy spurs on his riding boots across the forehead of each of the men waking them up, then dragging them into the kitchen of the inn whipping them with a horse whip with them streaming with blood from their wounds. Not satisfied that he had done enough and with Jackson still in a rage, both men were dragged outside to the courtyard where they were placed on a horse one behind the other.

"Bind their hands and legs together, tie their legs around the horse's belly, then bind their legs to each other, make it uncomfortable for them", said Carter.

"Take those coats from them, they need to feel this, whip them lads, cut them deep, make them pay", said Jackson, being the first to lay punishment upon their flesh, catching Chater across the face with the first lash.

Edmund Richards now fired up and angry by what he was witnessing, pulled out his pistol, and pointed it at everyone present.

"I will shoot anyone in the head should anyone of you here present mention what you've seen or heard on this day".

"I can't go with you, I don't have a horse", said Race.
"You'll just have to stay here and mind the inn with Liz while we are away". said Carter looking down at him.
As they journeyed on, Jackson called out again, "whip 'em lads, cut 'em, slash 'em, dam them both".
The roads were bad, so the going was slow, as the whipping and punishment continued. The whips striking their face, eyes, shoulders, body, legs, anywhere they could do them harm.
No longer could the two men take so much punishment and stay conscious, they both rolled to one side and fell under the horse's belly, now the situation had changed for now the horse with every step struck each one of them in the head as it walked. After a while on seeing that the men were in a poor state, stopped the horses and managed to put them both upright in a sitting position as before.
"Let's lift them back on the horse", said Jackson.
The others helped in lifting the men back into sitting position and checked the ropes to see if they had become loose, but it was the blood from their bodies that had made the saddle slippery.
With this duly done they continued their journey and their whipping on these two men, striking them again in the face, eyes, arms legs as before, and still with the horses going at a slow pace.
They made their way for several hours all the way to Rake, still whipping the two men across all parts of their body till they were almost dead. Again, the two men fell under the horse with their feet up in the air. The men tried to put them back upright but now they were so weak they couldn't sit upright at all.
They cut their bindings and separated them both, they sat Galley behind Steel and got Chater to sit behind Little Sam. Then continued with their lashing on their bodies.

"Ouch, you've got to stop, you're hitting them so hard that you are hitting me with those lashes,", said Steel looking at the cuts on his arm.

The men stopped near Lady Holt Park.

"I'm going to kill you Galley", said Jackson pulling him from Steels horse.

Galley looked up at Jackson standing over him with his pistol in his hand.

Please kill me, put an end to my misery.

"What? if that's the case and you can still speak, you must have more to say, God damn your blood, put him back on the horse", shouted Jackson.

"Whip them again, whip them till their flesh peels from them for we are not done yet, strike hard lads, make them pay", said Jackson, intent on making every lash cut deeper than the last.

This carried on for a while till Galley became so weak that he fell from the horse and landed in a heap on the floor, the dirt from the road going into his wounds mixing with his blood. Carter and Jackson lifted him up again, but he was so weak that he was no longer able to sit so they just lay him across the saddle. Richards walked along side of Galley's horse holding him as not to fall from it but became tired of this and again let him fall to the ground.

They lifted him again from the ground and put him over Steels horse and set his legs across the saddle, a leg either side with his head up by the horse's mane and this time, Jackson took a turn of helping him stay on the horse, all the time torturing him by squeezing and punching his balls as hard as he could covering ground of about a mile and a slow pace.

"Galley cried out please stop, please shoot me through the head and end this misery".

"Stop your moaning, this is nothing to what awaits you" said Jackson punching him across the throat to stop his whining.

They continued into the village of Leigh and neared the Red Lion inn, it was early in the morning and hard to wake up the landlord, who it seems was a friend of theirs and often served as a place to store their smuggled goods.

Scardefield was the owner of the inn and was shocked to see Chater in such a pitiful state covered in blood with Galley laying on the floor looking likewise.

The others went into the inn and plied themselves with more drink, as Jackson told their story to Scardefield, to waylay any concerns.

"This man had an engagement with some officers who he fought and won against them, killing them in the process, and we are here to tend to his wounds that were inflicted on him by the officers, during this brave and selfless act", said Jackson, giving Scardefield a specious tale of what happened. After more drinking, Jackson and Little Harry left with Chater and placed in an outhouse of a man called Mills, who they knew and often used his outhouse as a store for their smuggled goods, a little way from the inn, the outhouse was locked with Chater inside chained up on a three yards long chain bound by one ankle so as not to escape, then they returned to the Red Lion to continue drinking and to discuss what to do with the men next.

They went to the outhouse of the Red lion Inn and found a spade, they got Galley dragging him out into the yard across the gravel and onto a horse and threw him over the saddle, led him a short distance into the country.

Again, they tied Galley to Little Harry, who wasn't so please to be tied to him in case the others started whipping him again, the ropes became loose and with gallery suffering too long from his punishment fell off the horse and hitting his head on the ground with a crunch, the others thought that he had fallen in such a way as to break his neck.

"Right, you lot, bury him by the side of the road, I don't want to pick him up and carry him anymore, he's dead anyway, let the dog suffer in his grave and be dammed with him", said Jackson, still holding his pistol while giving out the orders to the others.

It wasn't long before they had Galley laid to rest in his grave and threw his coat and belongings further along their journey to rid themselves of any wrongdoing towards Galley.

Then they returned back to the Red Lion Inn.

While they were sitting in the Red Lion Inn Richard Mills came in and joined in the discussion as to what to do with Chater and now Scardefield, as he was too, evident to their goings on and could bear witness to what has happened.

It was now Monday and still they had sat around drinking and wondering what to do.

"I know what we can do, Scardefield is one of us and I'm sure he wouldn't say any words about us for fear of any reprisals, for he that knows the Hawkhurst gang, knows what they can do, so I propose we leave Scardefield alone, we all go home to our respective houses, back to our wives and make it known to our neighbours that we are there, get seen by them, talk to them so that it doesn't create suspicion or otherwise of any event that's taken place, we can also seek advice from the other gang members on how to proceed with Chater, Little Harry as you live in the country you can go and stay with Chater to make sure he doesn't try and escape and keep him from calling out for help. On Wednesday evening we meet back here at the Red Lion and finish what we have started.

Wednesday had arrived and as agreed the members returned along with a few others that had been consulted.

"We need to dispatch Chater so as not to draw suspicion to us and to make his body somehow undiscoverable", said Jackson, again taking up the position of being in charge as he's become accustomed to.

"I know, there is a well not far from here, we could throw him down it so that no one would find him and hide what had been done to him, and we can be free of any guilt less someone should talk", said Benjamin Tapner who came along to help find a solution.

This was agreed by all as this was the best way to rid the gang of Chater once and for all.

"There will be no loose tongues for what you know, no loose tongues by any of you gathered here as to what has happened, for if any of this is repeated, anywhere or anytime you shall suffer the consequences to you and your families, do we strike an accord to this agreement", said Jackson, placing his hand inside his coat to hold his pistol.

"We all agree", came that many voices in the inn.

"Let's get Chater and get this done before the night is over. They went to Old Mill's and to the outhouse to find Little Harry guarding Chater.

On seeing Chater, in the condition he was in, rather than take pity on the poor man it just renewed their anger for again they gang set about him kicking him and punching him.

Tapner pulled out a knife and look at Chater, his face full of rage.

"God damn your blood, down on your knees and go to prayers, for with this knife I will be your butcher", said Tapner. Looking at the man covered in blood before him. Chater terrified as to what was going to happen to him, every moment could be his last in the company of these men, he took a while but eventually got to his knees, while he was in this position making prayers to end his suffering, Cobby got behind him and kicked him hard, recovering on the floor from being kicked and through his suffering Chater still gave a thought and the asked about his friend.

"What, what have you done with Galley", came the voice of this suffering person.

"Damn you, we have killed him, and we will do so by you, who are you to ask us, damn your blood", said Tapner, with this and without any provocation Tapner drew his knife across Chaters face, over his eyes and nose with such violence he almost cut through both eyes and the end of his nose now hanging free, held on only by a small piece of skin.

Tapner still not done and still in a frenzy lashed out again with his knife aimed at the same wound but hitting too high and opened a deep wound on his forehead.

Tapner stood back to look at his handy work that be done to the poor wretch kneeling on the floor before him.

Blood was streaming from his wounds, his body with deep lashes from the whipping, his eyes almost removed as well as his nose.

Just then Mills who's outhouse they had been using to commit such an atrocity came in and upon looking at the scene told them all not to kill him here, "murder him somewhere else", for an older man to have shown no care of the scene before him shows just what these people were like, the scene of this ferocity should have made anyone feel sorry for what had been done to him, but such was the nature of bearing witness to one of their own, and to aid his guilt would not change the hearts of these cold hearted men.

"Get him out of here and do it quick, I don't want him here when he dies", these cold words coming from old Mills, was enough to bring the men back to their senses.

Chater was dragged from the outhouse and again placed on a horse and led towards Harris's well. Tapner still sensed with anger towards Chater, continued the journey whipping Chater across the face and eyes, again making the wounds bleed more and more.

"That my horse you are on Chater, if you drip blood on my saddle, I will destroy you and send your soul to hell", said Tapner again sending another lash across Chaters mouth slicing open his lip.

They came to the edge of the well, they looked at Chater, totally disfigured and unrecognisable from what they saw when they first set eyes on him, a young man, in his prime, full of life, and with everything to live for to the shadow of his former self and now begging his captures to let him die at their hands, what had he done to these men that could cause him such harm, such brutality, men wouldn't treat animals in this fashion let alone a fellow human, but here he was on the edge of his life, barely hanging on to it.

"It's about thirty feet deep in that well, that should be deep enough", said Tapner, throwing a stone in to see how long it took to reach the bottom, there was no splash.

"Good, no soft landing for him", said Jackson.

The only light they had was a lantern as it was now dead of night with no moon to help their way.

The well was surrounded by a metal railing that had been put up to stop cows from falling in.

"You'll have to climb over the rails", said Tapner, pulling out a cord and forming a noose out of it placed it around Chaters neck.

Chater saw an opening through the rails, weak from his condition and blood dripping from his wounds he managed to crawl through to get through the other side, now standing on the rim of the well. Tapner reached over and grabbed the rope that was tied around his neck and tied the other end to the rails.

The others got behind Chater and pushed him into the well, but the rope offered no real length and only Chaters knees were overhanging into the well.

They left him hanging there for a length of time, watching him slowly choke, but his body not offering weight to aid his death, and the others became inpatient.

"Get him up, he's not dying quick enough, "said Jackson.

They pulled his legs out of the well, Tapner untying the cord from around the railings threw him down to the ground and turned him around, The others got together to lift his limp body over the well by his legs, and dropped Chater head first into the well, they heard him hit the bottom of the well with a sickening thud, and waited for some time to make sure their deed was done, they listened over the well for any noise that came from Chater, they could still hear him breathing, then start to groan In agony.
"He's still alive", exclaimed Tapner, "we should have killed him up here and threw his body down there, that way we would have been sure to have sent him to hell".
"We will certainly be discovered if he's not finished", said Carter, now looking more worried at than fact than to the horrors that he's just witnessed.
"We can get a long ladder and one of us can go down there and dispatch him with a knife", said Carter.
"Look, go and see if you can find a ladder, that way we can be certain"", said Jackson to Carter.
"Where are we going to get a ladder this time of night", said Carter.
"Look for one, look around, ask someone", said Jackson.
Carter went off to find a ladder leaving the others to wait for his return. After a while Carter returned with a ladder long enough to get down the well.
"Where did you get this so late in the night", asked Jackson.
I went to a chap Called William Combleach who is gardener, I had to wake him up and begged a favour from him to loan me his ladder, as I told him a friend of mine had fallen in Harris well and I needed to get him out, as this was a charitable action, he decided to loan me the ladder so my friend could be rescued", said Carter.
"You actually told him that"? said Jackson. "You were drawing attention to this very well where Chater is down there dying"?

"Well, I had to tell him something, what else could I say"? said Carter.

They tried to get the ladder over the railings six strong men struggled for a while to no avail, the ladder was too long and too heavy, to get over the railing and send down the well so this idea was given up.

Again, they listened at the edge of the well to hear Chater still groaning below.

"let's look around to see if there's anything heavy that we could throw down the well that would finish him off, like large rocks or logs, see if you can find anything, "said Tapner.

The all scattered around in the dark looking for anything heavy that could be thrown into the well.

Two large logs that used to be gate posts were found along with a few large rocks and these were bought to the side of the well, and helping each other, threw the logs and the large rocks into the open hole of the well. No sound came up from below, no breathing, no moaning, their deed had been done, Chater was finally no more.

The men, getting back onto their horses realised their work was still not done. There were still two witnesses that could lead the Customs officers to us, that of Galley's and Chater's horses.

"They would surely bring us to task if the horses were ever found, surely convict us of the crimes of these two men, people had seen Chater and Galley riding them before they had reached us, what should we do", asked Carter.

"We shall have to do away with the horses, if we let them go someone will surely identify them as theirs, there's no other way, we should kill them and that'll be that.

Tapner grabbed Galley's horse by the reins and stabbed it in the neck, while Jackson hit it over the head. Galley's horse fell to the ground, where the gang proceeded to skin it and cut the flesh up into little pieces and disposed of, then they cut the horse up dismembering it and left it for the foxes and other creatures to feed on.

"Let get Chaters horse and do the same, it's still back at the inn at Rowley's Castle", said Carter.

They travelled through the night only to find that the horse had got free and ran off, to where no one knew.

They all went off in different directions, back to their homes and their lives in the hope that the unfortunate affair of Galley and Chater be forgotten through time.

Now the absence of the two missing men would not go unnoticed for very long, letters were sent to Major Battine asking if he had spoken or even seen any of the men as that seeing him was the cause for their journey, as time went by the mystery disappearance of the two men deepened. At first thought a suggestion that they had met the Hawkhurst gang on their travels and upon taking and reading the letter had sent the pair off to France out of the way till the trial of Diamond was over, that was the suspicion for a while till a large, bloodstained coat was found by the side of a road between Rowland Castle and East Mardon, with the assumption now that they had met their doom along the journey. A proclamation was immediately ordered by the commissioner of customs along with a reward for any information leading to the discovery of William Galley and Daniel Chater along with a Kings pardon that would also be granted, should information come from nefarious means.

After about seven months with no information as to the whereabouts and still no indication that they had returned home a letter was sent anonymously, within the letter had been described the location of one of the men of whom the proclamation named buried within a certain place in the sand near to the village of Rake, and that's where they will find said person. He also mentioned that he didn't feel it prudent enough to make himself known.

People went in search and after many hours found one of the men, this was Galley, who it seems was still alive at the time he was buried as his hands were still covering his eyes.

After Galley was found another anonymous letter was sent claiming that William Steel might have had something to do with the disappearance of the two men, to which he was found and taken into custody.

Steel wasn't the strongest of men and seeing that there was a possibility to be let off either for the murder of Galley and Chater he decided to tell everything he knew about what had happened to the men in the hopes that he would cheat the gallows for the information that he was to give.

After information was found forthcoming from Steel, a search was made of the Harris's well in Lady-Holt Park, to which the body of Chater was found. His body was brought to the surface and gazing upon him found a rope still attached to his neck, his eyes had been plucked out with his nose had been cut from his face, only one leg was still attached and the other brought to the surface afterwards.

Word had got out about the accounts of the two men and the crimes that had been committed against them, turning the tide of the Hawkhurst gang's goings on.

John Race was the next one to turn Kings evidence in the hope of clearing his name of the atrocities that were now being made public.

The names of men involved were beginning to come to light and their whereabouts were soon located and brought in for questioning.

John Hammond was apprehended and gave evidence to the crimes along with John Cobby taken to Horsham Gaol, Benjamin Tapner was also committed to the same Gaol, after being captured outside Chichester. Richard Mills Junior, others that were with these on the same night were also apprehended for their part in the murders of the two men along with William Carter and William Jacksom who it seemed were the ring leaders of the Hawkhurst gang in Hampshire, these two were taken to London and after a trial were sent to Newgate, for the murders of the two men and for the crime of smuggling.

A list was drawn up and posted in villages for the arrest of all those involved.

Wiliam Steel.	William Jackson
John Hammond	William Carter
John Cobby	Edmund Richards
William Tapner	Thomas Stringer
Henry Sheerman, alias Little Harry.	Richard Mills

Daniel Perryer alias Little Daniel.
John Mills alias Smoker
Samuel Howard alias Little Sam

Major Mills was also apprehended in his role of the murder of the two men, his part was to say that he didn't want the men murdered in his house, to take them elsewhere and murder them. Most of the men that were on the list of offenders were detained in gaol being hung by the neck for all to see.

The news of what had been done reached Thomas over in Hawkhurst, he was not happy to hear that all those men had been captured and hung for their crimes against Chater and Galley.

"They should have just got the letter off them and left it at that", said Thomas thumping his fist down on the table, tankards were sent flying in all directions.

"Well unlike you they were concerned about Diamond being locked up, if you had done something about him, they wouldn't be in that situation would they", I said shouting at him.

"What should I have done, he was in gaol, I couldn't just go in there and get him out", Thomas now standing up to face me.

"You just ignored the fact that he had been caught, out of sight and out of mind, as far as you were concerned, it didn't take much to go and get your goods from the customs house in Poole, even though the odds were against you, you still went, it seems this was the start of all your problems, if Arthur had been here he might have been better to judge the scale of what you were doing and maybe, just maybe have a plan to get Diamond released", I said, standing up to Thomas,

This wasn't me, what was I doing, maybe watching Thomas mess things up too many times had got to me, I was defending Arthur who had been my friend for years, I know he would have handled everything differently, been more prepared going into battle against the Goudhurst militia, the customs house, and now this, a lot of men's lives died for no reason other than pure greed and the hope of keeping the Hawkhurst gangs reputation alive and well, and now with growing animosity against us will find it difficult to get more goods in the country and even harder to get items sold, the Hawkhurst gangs name will go against us.

"What would you have done, could you have done it any better", shouted Thomas.

"I doubt it, but at least I would have been a bit more subtle about some of the things you've done", I said.

"Are you challenging me and my authority, is that it", he said, now moving his hand to his sword.

"I'm not saying anything anymore, I'll leave you to soak up my words so that the next time you decide you want to go and take on another village you might want to think ahead and think of the consequences of your actions". I said, moving away from him.

His hand left his sword and he lunged forward at me, with his fist finding its mark on my chin sending me flying.

I woke up looking at Smokers face, wondering what had happened, he was looking down at me, his black teeth showing through as he was grinning from ear to ear.

"He caught you good and proper with that punch, he said, he was holding a glass of rum.

"Here get this down you, looks like you need it", he moved the glass to my lips for me to drink.

"Where is he, I said moving the glass away from my face.

"Leave him be, he's gone, that's a big shock to take in all those men, our friends being hung, you argued with him at the wrong time", he said, drinking the rum that he bought for me.

"Well, we are all annoyed at what has happened, I can understand why they did it, according to some of the things that I've been hearing it was one of the worst murders that have ever been brought to justice, I just can't understand why they would have tortured them for so long when really they hadn't actually done anything", I said, wishing now I'd had the rum.

"No, they hadn't done anything, but their intension was to act against Diamond and send him to the gallows to hang, said Smoker.

"I suppose you're right, do me a favour Smoker, go get me another rum, and let me sit here for a bit and rub my chin, feels like its swelling up", I said, feeling around my face for signs of more injury.

"I'll have another one as well, you were lucky he said, he only hit you the once", said Smoker going off to get the rum.

Chapter 19
The trial (1748)

A short while after the events of Galley and Chater we all had some goods new, that Arthur was back home after a long stay away, he had been moving around avoiding the customs and the magistrates.

He eventually arrived back at the Mermaid Inn to tell us all about where he had been, he had a bit of a tan to his skin, so I knew that for a while he hadn't been in this country.

He told us that while he was away, he had contacted a lot of people who were willing to do business with us, they wanted to buy the wool from the farmers sheep and were willing to trade in other items, they in turn were doing business with other countries getting more and more luxurious goods in from India, China, and they said they could get us anything we wanted as long as we could sell it on, so we would be expanding a lot further around the world and not just Europe.

"that's why I've come back, I've cut my journey short to come back and tell you all about this fantastic news and what I've been doing, I can't wait to get things organised.

We were all excited and happy to see him, Thomas didn't look to happy about his arrival as now he knew he'd have to take orders from Arthur again, being in charge for a while had changed Thomas, he saw himself as the chief, not Arthur, even with the mistakes he'd been making he still thinks of himself as the brains in the outfit.

Arthur didn't mind Thomas being in charge for a while, but the news soon got to Arthur about all the things that had been going on, what with George Kingsmill dead along with Barnett Woolett who was with us at the time, not to mention the ones that got caught for being in Goudhurst, Diamond in gaol and the lot from Hampshire, being in gaol and facing the death penalty, he must have thought his little empire was crumbling, the size of the Hawkhurst gang had somewhat diminished during his absence and in what seems a very short time, he had his doubts as to whether Thomas should be left in charge again, maybe seeing Thomas more as a liability than an asset to the Hawkhurst gang. He was only good at taking commands not giving them, this is the way that I saw it, not sure that anyone would actually listen to me, but having been punched for saying my piece I was going to stand back and see what happened in the future.

Things seemed to go back to the way they were for a while, more and more trips were being organised on the continent again, that's the one thing that seemed to stop when Arthur was away, now all was about to be resumed.

The other gang member were also happy to hear of Arthur's return as now they could be selling more goods to the locals.

"I suppose we shall have to stay away from Goudhurst now after what's happened" said Arthur to Thomas.

"I wouldn't go there not after, you know, losing George and Barnett Woollett", said Thomas, the way he said with his head down, it was almost like he didn't want to be reminded of the affair, to erase it from his memory, bad decisions, and bad judgements, he didn't want to be reminded of the fact.

"We shall have to find another village that would do business with us then, said Arthur looking at Thomas sternly.

"You might want to wait a bit longer for that as word has got around to the other villages, if you're going to do that then we may have to travel a bit further out as a lot of villagers know and seem they too have turned against us", said Thomas.

Arthur didn't like the sound of that, he had worked hard to build it up only to be knocked down, he wasn't prepared to start all over again, all Arthur could think of was his money-making scheme had taken a knock by what Thomas had done and made things hard to build it us again.

"Don't take it too hard Thomas, we built our gang up, we made it work, we are rich are we not? we can build it back up and make it stronger, we won't sell to the locals anymore, they don't want to buy our stock, our rum, whiskey, tea, let them buy their own at full taxation prices, it won't be long before they come asking us again, and when they do, well it'll cost them a lot more than it did before.

This was the thinking of a man in charge, someone who could think rather than do, Thomas was all about attacking with a sharp sword and a blunderbuss, whereas Arthur was using his brain, I sat there listening to them talk and I got the same impression about the both of them as we carried on drinking through the night.

A few days after arriving William Fairall and Richard Glover were again asked to travel to France to organise the purchase of goods that had come all the way from India and China, they were to travel to Le Havre again and bring back the goods from a man who they have met before, Pascal Moreau.

"I hate going over there, can't you get anyone else to go", said Fairall.

"Why would I do that, said Arthur, stopping what he was doing and looking at him straight.

"It seems while I've been away you've been answering Thomas back, and arguing with him, changing his mind and to be honest being a bit unruly, do you think you'll get away with it with me, because I'll not have you answer back to me", said Arthur, the more he spoke the more you could see his face change.

"It's just that I thought you could get someone else to go, give them a chance to see what's involved", said Fairall.

"I thought that we had sorted things out here, I'm the one that does the thinking, besides, I know that I can trust you in all things French, you know what Pascal looks like, how he behaves, you've had dealings with him before, so tell me, why would I send anyone else but you, when so much money will be involved".

"Alright but please, make this the last time, I'm beginning to hate the French". Said Fairall.

A big smile came on Arthur's face, and he slapped Fairall on the back and dug his finger is deep.

"You make me laugh Will, you sounded just like a kid", said Arthur as he walked away while Fairall gritted his teeth and clenched his fists.

The day arrived that Fairall, and Glover were to depart for France and came to the Oak and Ivy for final instructions a list of goods required and to get money off of Arthur.

"Where is Arthur, he should be here", said Glover.

Maybe he's just stopped in Hawkhurst to get something, remember he has been away for a while", said Smoker.

"Could be the reason", said Glover.

Just then Thomas arrived.

"Where's Arthur asked Thomas.

"He's probably gone to the village to collect some items, he's been away for a while", said Glover assuming that could be the reason.

"Well, he needs to be here soon, we need that list and money from him, I'm not paying for all the goods in France with my own money, it's bad enough going there", said Fairall.

'Let's go inside and have a drink while we wait for him, I'll pay", I said, hoping that this will ease the tension that had built up between me and Thomas.

"That's a first", said Smoker, putting his arm around my shoulder as we walked in.

The mood between everyone seemed to be a lot more light-hearted now that Arthur was back, even with the past events, the mood was picking up.

We sat, and talked and waiting for what seemed ages, still waiting, with no sign of Arthur.

"Smoker, go to Arthur's and see what's happening, don't forget to look out for him along the way", I said.

"Yes, he may be laying in a ditch somewhere, drunk, said Thomas laughing to himself, no one seemed to be joining in with his laughter, as if it were true that would truly mess up any plans, we have of getting business back up and running. Smoker got on his horse and made his way back to Hawkhurst looking out for Arthur's horse as he did, well you never know Thomas could be right, Arthur did like a drink most of the time.

I wasn't at the Inn when Smoker returned, I too went into Hawkhurst, and he must have passed through the village as I went into the stores there.

I got back to the Oak and Ivy to see everyone looking gloomy, Smoker rushed up to me and said that Arthur had been taken by members of the magistrates and customs officials to gaol, for the murder of Thomas Carswell and for smuggling goods into the country, avoiding the Kings taxes and they have got William Rowland as well he was visiting Arthur at the time.

"Are you sure, how did you find that out, what gaol", I threw all these questions at Smoker, not giving him time to answer any, my mind racing with the thoughts of this can't be true.

"His sister told me, that's why he never showed up this morning, they came and got them late last night William Rowland was visiting him at the time to get some goods from him that were hidden in his house, his sister is distraught and doesn't know what to do", said Smoker, with that concerned look on his face.

"His sister, I said.

"Yes, Arthur's sister, she's been living with him", said Smoker.

"This can't be true, but why say he killed Carswell, he wasn't there at the time, he didn't Kill Carswell, we wouldn't know who did, many shots were fired that day, it could have been anyone", I said.

"They say he was responsible as he is the leader of the Hawkhurst gang, they've been waiting for him, waiting for him to return", said Thomas.

Suspicions were running through my head, Arthur's return, Thomas wanting to be leader, it all looked very suspicious, how did they know he was back, unless someone told them customs officers, I need to find out more before I started accusing anyone, but for now that was the least of my worries, but Arthur being arrested was.

"Where did they take him Smoker, does anyone know where"? I asked looking at Smoker who seemed to be drowning his sorrows with one rum after another.

"Newgate Prison, his sister asked where they were taking them", said Smoker.

"What, all the way to London"? I said.

"Under a heavy guard apparently, according to his sister. That squalid place, he won't survive the sentence let alone the rope", said Smoker, his words being slurred from the rum.

"Go home Smoker, go home before you say something that you might regret, before you drink too much and fall from your horse", I said in a stern fashion, not wanting to hear bad things against or about Arthur.

The mood had changed again, from sad to happy now gloom, we all sat drinking thinking deeply about the news and if there was anything we as a gang could do. As we drank, I kept my eye on Thomas to see if there were any signs that he had something to do with this, I was still thinking that someone must have told them, Arthur has been away for a long time and for the customs men to suddenly appear did seem strange, I will ask the others one at a time, when the time comes.

"I'll take him home if you like", said Fairall, moving towards Smoker as if he was about to fall off his chair.

"He's alright, let him be, said Thomas, stroking his chin whilst pondering the predicament set out before them.

"No, I'll take him home, before he says something or hurts himself", said Fairall, with that he got up and helped Smoker onto his feet and almost dragged him outside.

I continued to watch Thomas, to see if there was any evidence that I could gleam from his behaviour that he had a part to play in this, remove Arthur so he could be in charge of the gang, I wasn't sure if he were thinking of helping Arthur out of this situation or thinking about the next lot of contraband that was being shipped over, his face and emotions wasn't giving anything away.

"Can someone give me a hand getting Smoker on his horse"? Said Fairall, poking his head around the door, Smoker has passed out of the laying in the dirt".

"Where he belongs", said Thomas, "give him a hand Will".

I went outside to see Smoker lying in the dirt under his horse, "Right, grabs his arms, lift him up and throw him over his horse", said Fairall.

This we did, with a bit of a struggle, and then we tied him to the horse so he wouldn't fall off.

"Alright, hand me the reins and I'll lead him home", Fairall led Smoker and his horse away from the Inn, and I made my way back in to watch Thomas and wait for his next move.

"You go Will, go to London, they have to have a trial, go there, see what's happening, if they need help in anyway, be a witness to say he was with you at the time of Carswell's death, tell them it must have been another gang as Arthur would know nothing about it, get the blame put of the Wingham gang, or the lot over in Aldington, Hastings, anything but the Hawkhurst gang, we've got to do something, I can't go as my face is too well known but you can get away with it", said Thomas, taking control again.

"What do you mean I wouldn't get noticed, I was there when Carswell got killed, and the dragoons, plus the Wingham gangs' demise, my face has been put about enough", I said, my turn to punch the table now to let off some steam.

"Yes, but I don't see your name put on posters with any reward for your capture anywhere", said Thomas with an evil look on his face, burning right through me.

"Look, you'll be the best one to go, we could have sent Smoker, but he'd give himself away, no, we need someone to go and help if there's a chance to get them free not hinder their chances". Said Thomas looking at me, waiting for me to resign that fact that he indeed was right, I was their only chance.

"I'll get myself ready and go in the morning", I said drinking another glass of rum.

"I don't think you should be waiting that long, go tonight, in fact, go now and get there as soon as you can, we don't know when the trial is or where it is, finding out that information will take time, so go now and do whatever you can to free those two but whatever you do just don't incriminate yourself, we want you back, the way things are going we'll be running out of men soon", said Thomas, with a more positive tone In his voice.

"You're right,", I said, finishing off Smoker's rum that he hadn't drank, "do you know where that gaol is, draw me a map and I'll find it"?

"Good lad, and I hope for their sake that you can find some way of helping", with that Thomas too drank his rum in one mouthful, then pulling a piece of cloth out of his pocket and going over to see John for a quill and some ink to draw out a map.

I went outside to ready my horse and set the saddle for a fast pace to London.

I kept replaying Thomas's voice, he seemed keen for someone to help, he did make sense with me going not just to get me out of the way, Thomas seemed genuine in his remarks, maybe I was wrong about him, and he didn't tell the customs men that Arthur was in the area, if he didn't tell then who did, who else told them, these thoughts would be with me for the entire journey as I set off to London.

I got to London close to just over a day's journey by horse, I didn't realise the country was that big. London was big, now I had been to Brighthelmston along the south coast, and I thought that was big, but London was far bigger than anything I'd known or seen before, so many people, horse and carriages were everywhere, I had to stop on many occasions to ask for help as the map just showed me how to get to London, I should have checked with Thomas before I left, I think he didn't know the way either. I managed to find my way to Newgate after my weary journey. Someone had posted notices on the outside of the gaol, after reading a few of them one notice was for a Judith Butler, announced as a thief, John Taylor for assault then I read Arthur Gray's and William Rowland's, I read it, to my horror, it read.

Here in this gaol lie two smugglers, tax avoiders and murderers from his Majesty the King in the County of Kent, with a trial set for 20th April 1748, all are invited for standing room only for the trial.

This was tomorrow, I had to be there it was set early in the morning, I had to find a place to eat, sleep and be there to get a place to see if there was anything I could do, this was serious, I had to do my best. It was lucky that Thomas told me to go, I would be on time.

I managed to find an Inn close by and spend the night there but found it hard to sleep as I kept thinking about Arthur and William placed in that horrible place, hard to imagine what they were going through, and all the time still thinking who could have told the customs men about them in the first place, if it wasn't Thomas, maybe it was Fairall, Thomas's close friend.

Sunlight streamed through the dirty window as the reality of the new day came to me, I tipped some water in a bowl to wash my face and run my wet hands through my hair trying to look a little more respectable and wash some of the dirt off me after my long journey, even though I had money I wasn't about to waste any on luxuries I just needed a place to stay, my thoughts went to Arthur and what he'd have this morning and if he even slept that night, I'd be worried as well.

I got back out into the busy streets and headed to where the trial was to be held, I got a place near the front close to the door as a queue and crowd built up behind me, and it wasn't long afterwards that we were allowed in.

The walls of the courthouse were covered in wood, with lots of seats that were beginning to fill with people, people of good standing, dressed in their finery, I was standing at the back along with all the others that were allowed in, then the doors were shut, the courthouse was full. The judge arrived,

"Please stand for the Right honourable Sir Robert Ladbrooke, Knight and Lord mayor of the city of London", came a loud voice at the front.

Everyone seated stood up as two large wooden doors swung open to reveal the judge in what looked like some funny wig, I'd never seen the likes of before, he sat down then everyone else followed.

"Bring on the first case, that of Judith Butler, engaged in theft, the trial went on for a little while, I sat mesmerized at the whole proceedings. After a while some people got up and left the room, I spoke to the person next to me to ask what was happening.

"Is that it, is it all over for her", I said.

"No, said the man, that lot are the jury, they are the ones who decide if they are guilty or not", he said with an accent to his voice.

"So now what happens, I've never been inside a court room let alone seen a trial or even what happens", I said, I must have looked excited not stopping to realise why I was there.

"When they come out after having a long discussion about the case, they pass their verdict onto the judge and he decides their fate", said the man

After a wait, the jury came out and handed a piece of paper to a person in the courtroom.

The judge spoke to the jury.

"How do you find the defendant, Guilty or not guilty"? asked the judge

"We the jury find the defendant not guilty", one woman from the jury called out.

There were screams and cheers as the verdict was read out. That's good, looks like the jury are in a good mood today", shouted the man over the noise.

The next case was then heard, that of a man called John Taylor.

These were the names of the people that were on those notices outside the gaol I thought, I was beginning to understand, if these people were in a good mood today then maybe they'd let off or go easy on Arthur and William.

"John Talyor you have been accused of Assaulting Mary Foster", I didn't hear much after that as my mind turned to why I was there, somehow I had to pluck up the courage and offer some evidence to help Arthur and Will out of this situation, I'm not sure I was the right one to do this, I have the motivation, just lack the courage, what if this crowd turned on me, what if I ended in their position for just helping, my mind racing with thoughts.

John Taylor stood in front of the judge and pleaded guilty to the crimes he had committed.

"He's done for now, he's surely going to hang, confessing like that, not good", said the man, turning to look at me, I must have looked white with fear for my fellow smugglers.
Taylor carried on telling the court in a moving manner, he would not give them any trouble. Mrs. Barham, and Mrs. Foster the prosecutrix, recommended him to the court to intercede with his Majesty for mercy, and accordingly when the report came to be made, his majesty extended his royal clemency, this was done, and the judge proclaimed that his sentence of death had indeed been changed into that of banishment or transportation for life.
"Well, I would never have thought that, never have thought that at all, that's good then that two out of two that have got off, not good news for the hang man", said the man folding his arms and resting them on the wooden railing overlooking the courthouse.
A man walked up to the judge and handed him a piece of paper.
"Bring out the next case".
I looked up and saw, Arthur and William chained together one chain around their neck and another around their ankles.
"Ah now this one looks good, these will hang, you mark my words, normally when they come in chained like that, they'll be a definite hanging", said the man rubbing his hands together and smiling.
Cheers went up inside the courthouse, one man shouted, "hang them, hang them till they are dead, scum". The cheering got louder; they wanted these two dead even before they'd heard any evidence.
"Silence! Silence in the courtroom or you'll all be removed", shouted the man at the front.
Arthur looked pale standing there before the judge, and William was visibly shaking, both had their heads down, not sure if they'd they would have seen me anyway as there was too much on their mind.

"Then a hush came over the courtroom as the crimes were read out, it wasn't just about Carswell's death, somehow, they had a long list of crimes that had been committed over the years going back to Dungeness, the Wingham gang, even Shoreham was mentioned with what had happened there and the disappearance of the two customs men, and how the two got nearly burnt alive, this did not look good for either of them.

"Ah this is good, this is what I come to see, two horrible men getting justice served to them, I'd even hang them myself", said the man, waving his fist at them.

There was no way I could speak up, no way I could help these two, now they didn't look like my friends I could see what they were really like, having heard their crimes read back to the courtroom, our crimes and of what we did, we did all this for money and here was the outcome, these two men were on the verge of losing their lives for this money, all greed, not just from our part but by the part of the king and his government putting up taxes, no way could I or would I speak up to help these two, I would have surely ended joining them, I moved further back into the crowd just to hide in case one of them looked up to see me and called my name.

The jury left the room and came back after a short time of being away to weigh up the evidence and passed a piece of paper to the judge.

There was a silence in court.

I looked through a gap in the crowd that stood around me at Arthur, looking at his face, looked nothing like he used to, a shadow of the figure I knew and in just a few short days, the fear for his life was showing.

"After hearing the evidence against you both, the Jury has found you guilty of all the crimes set against you, I hear pronounce that you Arthur Gray will be sentenced to death by hanging on the morning of the 11th day in the month of May the year of our King, 1748, where you shall be taken to the gallows where a noose shall be placed around your neck and hung till you are dead at Tyburn, from there you will be gibbeted at Stanford Hill for all to see as a deterrent for crimes against the King, and sir may God have more mercy on your soul, more than you had for your fellow man.
As for William Rowlands because of your lessor crimes of smuggling the order for your execution must come from the King, and this so duly done you have also been sentenced to Death by hanging, and may God have mercy on your soul too. Take them away, if there are no other cases to be heard then this court is adjourned.
I watched as both these two men, my friends and at most part, my family were taken away and led back to Newgate gaol where they were to spend their time counting the days they had left.
I decided to stay in London for a while, see the sights and smells that were all around me, trying to block out the guilt I had for not helping, I ended up talking and arguing with myself over what I could have done, what I never did, over hearing that man in the crowd, hearing the cheers from the crowd, everything was being played back to me in my mind, so much so that I went to all these places in London and never saw a thing, such was the way my mind was working.
I needed help, I needed someone to talk too, I wasn't helping myself. I found another inn to stay in and drank rum all night to bury and rid the thoughts I had in my head.

The days passed by quickly and the day of the hanging was soon here, the day I wasn't looking forward to, I can't imagine what was going through the minds of Arthur and William. I left the Inn and made my way to Oxford Street where a crowd had started to gather in the streets and made my way towards the gaol. I looked back towards Marble Arch, to see a crowd had already gathered at the gallows with people lining the street.

I walked up as far as the church of St Sepulchre looking at it and wondered if anyone was looking down at me and my friends in our hour of need.

Just then the large doors of the gaol opened up to the cheers of the baying crowd.

Hooray we are going to see a hanging", shouted several people from the crowds.

A horse drawn cart was led out through the gates, this had a locked cage mounted on it and sitting inside was Arthur, looking weak and frail, not the man I used to know, far from it, where he could knock anyone down with one punch, he looked like he couldn't even make a fist, this was followed by a second cart with William sitting inside.

Vegetables were being thrown at them by children running alongside the carts, I ran alongside the carriage as well with me knocking a few children out of the way.

"Arthur", I shouted, he didn't hear me above the crowd, who had started to gather behind the procession and follow it along.

"Arthur", I shouted again, he looked up but couldn't see me, then he put his head down again resigned to the fact that all hope had now diminished as they reached Tyburn.

The cages were undone, and the men led out to the gallows, their legs still in chains, they were led up the stairs to face the hangman, the crowd still cheering, no way would he be able to hear me calling to let him know that he wasn't dying alone, a friend was here for him, a face in this lonely crowd baying for his death. I was shouting at the top of my voice to be heard over the crowd. I saw Arthur hand the hangman a few coins in the hope that it would be a quick death, they weren't alone not really as another twelve men woman and teenagers were led up the gallows to make up the number of fourteen, the woman were trying to stay strong as you could hear the teens crying, it'll be alright my dear, it'll be over soon, you'll soon be asleep, said one woman to a one young boy standing next to her, the men were trying to look brave and you could see them mouthing the words in prayer, staying strong as a cover was placed over their heads, I saw Will and he was still shaking as the noose was tightened around his neck, the material over his face caught his breathing in and out becoming faster as the end grew near, Arthur was the same, his breathing quickened as he sensed the end.

The crowd, were still shouting and screaming and a tomato left the crowd and hit one of the woman on the head, leaving a mark on rope as it struck home to cheers from the crowd. These were animals, I was thinking to myself, I'd heard the judge reading out Arthur's crimes, and they seemed insignificant to what I was witnessing here, there were youngsters up there about to be hung, and the crowd were cheering.

The hangman put his hand up and the crowd drew silent, listening, waiting, for any neck that would snap as it hit the end of the rope. A few that were up there had wet themselves though fear, to laughs from the crowd. The lever was pulled and they all fell to the end of the rope, a few necks had snapped in the process, they were the lucky ones, that had paid a bit more to the hangman, but most, especially the teenagers were left to dangle including Arthur and William, although William and Arthur had paid money to the hangman for a quick death, someone said in the crowd they won't get it easy as they were murderers, and the hangman doesn't like murderers, so it wouldn't have mattered how much they paid, it was going to be slow for them.

The crowd were rapturous from the spectacle that lay before them, they couldn't get enough and still tomatoes were being thrown at those that were left kicking as the rope tightened.

I watched for a while at the sickening spectacle, watching the legs kick out and the bodies going into spasm, the life being drawn out of them by this final act till at last all the kicking and movement had subsided and all that were hanging were left to swing in the wind.

Saddened by the horrors of what I had seen, and tears now welling up in my eyes I went back to the inn to find my horse and headed back to Hawkhurst as fast as I could go, to find Thomas to have it out with him about who told the customs men about Arthur arriving back home, this wasn't going to be easy but now I had the inner strength to face him

Chapter 20
Cook (1748)

A few days later I got back to Hawkhurst and straight to the Oak and Ivy to confront Thomas. Now Thomas was a much bigger man than myself, so I drew my pistol before entering into the inn, I wanted to be sure I was armed before facing this man, if only I had the strength, I found now to face Arthur's accuser when he needed help, a coward I was then now freed from its constraints and I burst through the door.
There in the gloom, sitting in what was Arthur's seat was Thomas, my pistol pointing right at him.
"Put your hands on the table where I can see them, "I said, not taking my eyes off him for one second for fear he might try something, I looked around the room quickly to see who was there, then back to Thomas.
"I want to know the truth, I want to know if it was you who told the customs men that Arthur was back at his house, I want you to tell me you knew all about it, just so that you could be the head of the gang and get control of all the money, and so help me if you are man enough to tell me the truth and say yes, I will end your life with one pistol shot". I said still not taking my eyes off him.
He sat there relatively quiet and listened to what I had said, he thought for a while before answering.

"I take it you weren't man enough to stand up to the crowd and help Arthur and William out, defend their part to the crimes they had committed, unable to speak up for them in their last unfortunate hours when they needed help, and here you are coming here with pistol in hand trying to be the man you failed to be when they needed you most, you are the most sad spectacle, taking out your anger on me, why would you think I would play in any part towards Arthur's demise, we were friends, friends stick together not stab each other in the heart, we don't go against each other, never have, never will, we've been together for years building on what we had together, so ask yourself, do you think that is something I could do to a friend", he calmly moved his hand to his glass of rum, lifting it and placing it to his lips, he closed his eyes, as he drank the last drop, swallowed hard, opened his eyes and looked at me as he placed the glass back on the table.
"I thought not", he said.
I lowered the pistol, my thoughts again running through my head.
"It must have been Fairall then",
"And what make you think that"? said Thomas, still being calm about the whole situation, me still with my pistol in my hand.
"When the news first came to our attention from Smoker, I remember he was the first one to offer help to Smoker when he was drunk, like he couldn't wait to get out of the inn, avoid any unnecessary questions, I was betting it was either you or him that told the customs men where Arthur was, he couldn't get out of here quick enough", I said, still looking dazed, Thomas could have easily reached for his pistol by now and blown a hole right through me and I wouldn't have even seen it coming with my mind full of questions.
I placed my pistol inside my belt, keeping it handy in case it was needed.
"Wiliam Fairall is one of us, what reason would he have of removing Arthur", said Thomas.

"Only so that you can become head and him second in command, like he was taking your place when Arthur was here", I said, sitting down opposite Thomas, he was likely to hit me if I was to get too close to him for pulling my pistol out on him, but I needed to find the truth, someone here told on one of our members and had to be dealt with.

"Have a drink, you're tried, eat something, rest a while, London is a long way to have travelled", said Thomas.

"If you like you can sleep in one of my rooms upstairs", said John the bar keep, still wiping the tankards with a dirty rag, "I'll get you something to eat as well, that'll keep the dog happy, you can have a friend", he said as he went back into the kitchen.

My anger broke as he said that, and a smile came on my face as I looked over at the dog curled up on the floor by the fire, then over at Thomas who also was smiling at what John had said.

"What is that dog's name Thomas", I said feeling tired now.

"You know in all the years I've been coming here I've never known what its name is either", said Thomas.

"Look I'm sorry for pulling my pistol on you Thomas, but I needed to know if you were with the gang or not, and by your answer I think I can safely say that you are with us, but that still leaves the fact that someone must have told, how else would they have known to be there", I said.

"You're right Will, and we will find out who it is and deal with them accordingly and it won't matter who it is either they will pay the price.

John returned with a large lump of beef, vegetables and potatoes and a bottle of rum.

"There you go Will, get that down you, the rum is your stock so share it between yourselves, it must have been hard in London with Arthur, still you're back here now lad, enjoy your meal, I'll get the wife to sort out your bed upstairs", said John, placing his hand on my shoulder as way of comfort.

"Thanks John", I said taking a mouthful of beef.

As I started to eat this meal that John had brought over, another friend appeared at my feet, to sit and look at me. Thomas and I both burst into laughter, either by the situation, the dog, or the fact of just shear relief that I was back home and the tension for now had gone.

The following day I again met with Thomas.
"I've been thinking about what you said yesterday in the Inn, you know, about someone must have told the customs men, we were the only ones, besides his sister that he was going away, and we were the only ones who would know of his return, so it must be one of us, most of us stick together and as you say Fairall seemed to leave us be and dodge questioning, I'm not saying its him that told but we need to ask him, specifically I need to ask him, if you do then he'd probably kill you", said Thomas, looking as puzzled as I was the night before.
"I'll get a few rums inside him to loosen his tongue then ask him, see if he knows anything, now I'm on my way to Arthur's house to see his sister who lived with him and pay my respects and I also need to get some papers, that list that he should have given me and the money, would you like to come", said Thomas, moving his arm out for me to lead the way, seems I don't have a choice in the matter.
We rode though Hawkhurst to Seacox, the home of the late Arthur Gray and his sister.
We walked up the steps to the large door and pulled on the lever that was hanging outside, a bell could be heard ringing inside.
"I'm not looking forward to this, is this the first time that you've been here", whispered Thomas.
"Neither am I, and no, I've been here before just after it was finished, haven't been inside since though, haven't seen what he did with the place", I whispered back.

"Did his sister or any of his family know what he was doing, ever ask him where all this money came from", I said, feeling more open towards Thomas.

"Yes, she knew, I think, how could she not with all the goods that were stored here", said Thomas.

We could hear footsteps approaching, then the lock turning on the door, the door swung open to reveal a sweet looking woman, in a nicely presented dress, which I could only describe as a bell-shaped skirt silhouette, in solid dark blue and ivory floral fabric. She wore a white apron, frilly sleeves, and flowery headdress, and she looked stunning, although her faced showed she had been crying.

"Hello Thomas", she said, giving a little curtsy as she spoke. Such a gentle voice I thought, totally the opposite to Arthur.

"This is William, I'd like to introduce Elizabeth, Arthur's Sister", said Thomas.

I'd never seen Thomas this courteous before, maybe he was taken back by her looks.

"I'm overwhelmed by your beauty if I may be sold bold", I said reaching out for her hand that I may kiss it.

"Thank you, you are so kind sir, please, would you like to come in", Elizabeth said.

"Thank you, most kind", said Thomas.

As we stepped inside, I thought this was the first-time I'd been here with it now fully furnished, since it was finished, so here is where a lot of the goods have been stored, I think with the size of the place even I'd have problems trying to find anything. We were led into the drawing room, to be met by an equally stunning woman, sitting on a large chair, and dressed very similar as the first only in a light blue dress.

"Who are these two fine gentlemen dear sister", she asked raising herself from for the chair.

"This is Thomas, and this is William, may I introduce my sister Jane", said Elizabeth.

"I am pleased to meet you both, I take it you were close friends of Arthur", said Jane.

"We have both known Arthur a long time, growing up with him, I've seen you two when we were all younger and how we have all grown, I didn't recognise you both", said Thomas.
"You flatter us with you fine words sir", said Jane. "And yes, I do remember you, you were always coming round to see Arthur, how have you been all these years"? asked Jane.
"I have been better, given different circumstances which I shan't dwell on", said Thomas.
"Quite, it is a rather unpleasant situation, that's why we are here to look after my brother's estate. May I ask of your business here now that Arthur has gone". Asked Elizabeth.
"Yes you may, firstly we would like to extend our condolences to yourselves and your family on the untimely loss of your brother and to collect some paperwork that he would have left for me, they would have had my name written on the front, he used to keep them in a large set of draws in his room, third draw down, if you would be so kind as to get it for me, or if you wish I could get it myself and save you the trouble", said Thomas.
I was loving this, watching Thomas, seeing him like a little kid in front of these two, I could see why Arthur went out of his way to keep these two adorable sister away from our eyes, and by what I was hearing even Thomas hadn't seen them in years either, yet he had been round to visit Arthur on a few occasions, maybe they were in a different part of the house when he arrived, Arthur must have shut them away, not sure yet as to which one was staying here yet but a little bit of prying would gain that information.
"It's alright Thomas", said Elizabeth, "I can fetch it for you, third draw down you say"?
"That is correct", he said.
Elizabeth disappeared with a swish of her dress catching the furniture as she walked.

"So, Jane", do you have family of your own", I said, I wasn't sure how that question would go down given the situation, seemed like I was trying to court her from the way it came out.
"Oh no, I am living here with Arthur, Elizabeth has her own family but she's staying here for a while so that we can grieve our loss together and comfort each other", she said lowing her head, as she was made to dwell on their loss again.
"Please forgive me for asking such a question", I said.
"Thank you, William", it's hard not to ask questions that would otherwise be normal given different circumstance, so really there's no need to apologise.
"Theres a man lurking outside in your garden", Thomas said, then rushed outside through the main door.
"Thomas, no, came back, that's Cook, he is the servant, he's been here a long time", Jane called to him.
Thomas stopped in his tracks.
"Servant? Arthur never mentioned he had a servant", said Thomas looking bewildered.
"Arthur always wanted to live the life of a lord, although that could never be, he always said, if I can't be a lord, I can still have the lifestyle and the trappings of one, and he employed Cook as a servant, feeling sorry for him I suppose he lives at the gatehouse, tends to the gardening and generally looks after the place, he's a servant and a good friend", said Jane.
Elizabeth returned with Thomas's paper that he instructed her for.
"Thank you, Elizabeth", said Thomas placing the papers inside his coat
"Would you like to stay for tea", asked Jane.
"That would be so nice but, on this occasion, we need to be going, need to sort these papers out", said Thomas tapping his pocket where the letter was placed.
"We shall make it another day perhaps, under much happier circumstances", said Jane, again bowing her head, remembering her loss.

"That would be nice, we'd like that", said Thomas, heading towards the door.

"Thank you for your condolences and remembering my brother, we are thankful that Arthur had some lovely friends, do come again, you'd be most welcome", said Elizabeth.

"Thank you for your offer, good day to you both", I said, I could see Jane peering over Elizabeth's shoulder and wave before shutting the door.

We both looked over at the servant that was in the garden, kneeling over a flower bed.

"Servant", said Thomas, whatever next. "Come on, I've got what I've come for".

With that we made our way back to the Oak and Ivy

"What meal has your good lady wife made today, John, I'm starving"? I asked.

"Not a lot, sliced beef or one of our chickens, potatoes and carrots, nothing special", he said.

"Better than what we've had, which is nothing", I said.

"I will get the wife to bring some out, would you like rum with that or beer", he said, kicking the dog out of his way.

"Best make it two beers when you are ready", said Thomas.

"Would I be correct in saying that the sisters didn't know what Arthur was up to from the conversation that we had" I said, to Thomas.

"It would seem that you are correct, I don't know how he kept it from them, he was surely a sly person", said Thomas.

"Sly and very astute", I said.

With that William Fairall arrived in the inn.

"Just in time am I"? he said, shaking his coat.

"Time for what", said Thomas. He looked at me as if to hint, don't say a word.

"I need to ask you some questions Will, get yourself a beer and come over here and sit down", said Thomas, moving his hand inside his coat, to which I can only image, his hand was on his pistol.

Fairall came over and placed his tankard on the table", "what's this about, what questions"?
"I don't want you to get annoyed Will, I'm going to be asking everyone, so don't go getting all excited and doing something stupid, I'm not having that, it's only a question and I want you to answer it honestly", said Thomas, his toned changed to one of being stern.
"Ask away, I have done nothing, or do I have anything to hide", said Fairall, now looking at where Thomas's hand was.
"Oh, it's like that, with your hand on your pistol, do you think I'm going to do something like go for mine, this question sounds like it's going to have some repercussions, so I do hope you're ready for an answer that you may not like", said Fairall, now the atmosphere in the inn had certainly changed.
"Do you have anything to do with this"? Said Fairall looking at me.
I never said a word as he turned to looked back at Thomas.
"Well, let's have it", said Fairall, his tone changed completely.
"Did you have anything to do with Arthur being caught at his house, informing the customs men that he was there", said Thomas.
"Is that it, the big build up and you come out with that, what are you mad? Do you think I'd have anything to do with his capture? You've got to be joking", he said, putting a smile back on his face, Arthur was a good friend; I would never dream of going against him, I'll tell you this, when I was broke Arthur gave me two hundred pounds, that was the most money I'd ever seen, he even said I don't need to pay it back, is that the kind of man that I could inform on? Now I feel bad about telling you of my problems". Said Fairall.
Thomas looked at him, looked into his eyes to see if he was lying and relaxed his grip on his pistol, picking up his tankard and taking a mouthful, swilling it around inside his mouth while he was thinking.

"Alright, but listen, if it wasn't you, or any of us, who do you think could have done it, the customs men were waiting for his return", said Thomas.

"It would have had to have been one of us, or someone close to him", I said.

"Surely not those adorable sisters of his", said Thomas, the mood becoming better.

"Ah, you've met them both, they are staying at his house looking after each other". Said Fairall.

"You've been there and met them"? Asked Thomas taking another drink from his tankard.

"Of course, I have, only briefly though, I went round there as I knew his older sister Jane lived with him, went to pay my respects, and offer my condolences for their loss, and met the pair of them, is that the kind of man who would inform of someone, and go to them paying respects", said Fairall, raising his voice slightly to get the message across.

"Did you know he had a servant; we saw him in the garden, we couldn't believe it, what with Arthur wanting to be a lord and all", said Thomas, at that point, John came over with the food that his wife had made me.

"Are you talking about old Cook, Arthur's servant", asked John.

"Yes, we are, what do you know about him", I said taking the first mouthful of food.

"He's been with him for a while. Look Arthur often had encounters with the officers of the customs as you know, and the soldiers who assisted them, the many fights he's had with them, he beat and wounded the officers and soldiers so badly. Cook lives with Arthur as a servant, and several times prevented murder; in particular, he said his master Gray cut a soldier so badly when he was in a rage, that he nearly died, if Cook had not intervened and got proper help to dress the poor fellow's wounds he surely would have, he never liked the way Arthur treated people, he used to say the master didn't treat him with respect and on certain occasions had taken a beating from him, and on many occasions when I've met Cook in the Village and spoke to me he wanted master Gray to stop all this smuggling and violence against others, I don't think he knew what he was talking about half the time". Said John before returning to his duties.
I took another mouthful but stopped chewing halfway through as it dawned on me of what John had just said.
I looked up at Thomas, and Will looked at me as well.
"Cook", we all said at once.
Without saying another word all three of us ran for the door of the inn and in another few minutes was racing towards Arthur's house.
We arrived at Seacox, leaving our horses just by the main gateway, went inside to the rear of the garden and waited for Cook to appear.
"We don't want to alarm the women, we can't be seen by them, we just want Cook to be on his own", I said looking around to see if I could see him.
"Go and look in the outbuildings Will", said Thomas.
Will Fairall, pulled out his knife from under his coat and moved cautiously towards one of the outbuildings, on hearing a noise, he stopped and moved a bush, then waved his arm for us to follow, this we did to catch him up, he moved a part of the bush so that we could see.
"There he is, he's in there", said Will.

Thomas moved round and went straight in the building and grabbed him around the neck and mouth to stop him shouting out.

"We want to ask you some questions", said Thomas, "now be a good boy and don't struggle because if you do, I'll squeeze the life out of your body and end it all for you now".

"What do you know about the customs men coming here, waiting here for Arthur", I said grabbing his hair to lift his head up.

"He looked at me, I used to be an Owler myself, going out in all weathers, every day, every night, the threat of being caught was like a game, a game of chance, taking your own life in your own hands, what with the customs men, dragoons and magistrates, and after a while I became very good at it , like Arthur was, but the killing, I didn't kill anyone and didn't approve of Arthur killing, to Arthur it was more than a game, I never liked the way he dealt with people, killing them and the like, I thought if I mentioned him to the customs men that he might know someone who smugglers goods in the country, it might be that it serves as a warning to him with them asking questions and all, frighten him a bit, that he might stop and give it all up, I never for a minute thought they would take him away and hang him, that's not what I wanted, just to serve as a warning so that he'd stop, that was all. Said Cook.

"Well, you thought wrong didn't you and you got him killed", said Fairall pulling out his knife, placing it under his chin and thrusting it up through his head, and out the top of his skull just missing Thomas's face who was still holding him around the neck.

Cook gurgled then went limp In Thomas's arms. We picked him up and carried him out to the front of the house to where our horses were, throwing his limp body over my horse and tieing his arms to his legs so as to not fall off.

"You two go, take my horse and Cook, leave my horses back at the inn and I'll walk back, it's not that far", I said.

"What about the sisters"? said Thomas, "they'll be wondering what has happened to Cook, if he's not around".

"If they ask, we can say we saw him in the village and because Arthur is no longer at the house, his services would no longer be required so he left to go traveling while he still has time in his life", I said.

"Sounds good to me", said Fairall, wiping the blade on Cook's coat and replacing it back in the sheaf inside his coat.

The two rode off into the distance through a wooded area to dispose somehow of Cooks body, as I looked around to make sure we hadn't been seen, then I made my way on foot back to the village.

Chapter 21
William Fairall, (alias Shepherd), (1748)

Now it seems that all the time we had been going as a gang, we hadn't up to now considered just how rich we had become, we got richer by the day, money just seemed come to us, we took it for granted about the worth of it, we could buy anything we wanted, and of course this wasn't going to stop us at any point soon. Poverty of the people was at that time everywhere, only the rich just seemed to revel in the fact that they had more than anyone else, they would take more and more from the poor in taxes while they lived of the fat of the land, while they watched the poor suffer, people were, as I once heard a so called gentleman of the time, described as peasants, low life's and people to be discarded like rubbish, we were never like that, we knew that we started life as the lowest, trying to find money to pay for bread, life was hard, carpentry wasn't the answer to my problems, and I'm sure that whatever the others were doing, we soon found fortune as an Owler, this is what we had heard us being called, only because we were out most of the nights bringing and moving our goods around, I suppose we got called a lot of names behind our backs. We didn't care because we managed to find a way to escape that time in our life and make things better for ourselves, maybe not that way others would it as a living. We gave money to the needy, those poorer than ourselves, people struggling through life, we gave to them, not as expensive as the government would charge, we weren't greedy by any means, we also gave money as well, and by doing so, gave us power, the people trusted us, they also knew our connections and it was these connections and our reputation that we put down to saving William Fairall's life.

The story goes like this, and this was first-hand from John Mills who was with William Fairall at the time, this all happened while getting goods from a pond that they had stashed away previously. William was apprehended in Sussex and John Mills had made his escape, after being chased on horseback across country for a while.

Mills double backed to where Shepherd was, that was the name Fairall liked to be called, and saw that Shepherd had been captured. Mills followed him and his captures to Lewes. A court date was set and Mills who was not identified or assumed would turn up at a place of court for fear of being found out, saw the trial of his friend Shepherd.

The justice of the peace at the time, a James Butler having realised who William Fairall was and the reputation of the Hawkhurst gang could put the Jury in the trial in danger of reprisal and could even sway their decision to let this powerful man go.

So, a decision was found to take William Fairall to London for a trail where the Jury were not so much in danger and could be protected in a somewhat better fashion, this was done, and another date was set. The tale gets taken up by Fairall himself, as he was taken to London by armed guard as they thought there could be an ambush to free Shepherd on the way to Newgate Gaol, but the journey went without incident. The party stopped that evening at an inn close by to London bridge, where he said they were going to spend the night, so they settled down at the inn ready to continue the journey to Newgate the following morning. He thought this a bit strange as they were only about 3 miles from Newgate gaol and could easily have made the journey that evening.

Now while in the Inn, it seems that they took a liking to Shepherd and began to share drinks with him whilst in the inn and they took note that he told them he couldn't run because of a wound that he had was causing him some distress. They believed him and continued till they drank themselves just a little bit too much and with this they forget to clamp leg irons back on him after showing them his wound. While his captures were distracted or whether they had planned to let him go we will never know but make his escape he did. He ran out of the inn and through the back streets of south London, on seeing a horse tethered there, jump on the horse and scattered crowds of onlookers as he galloped through London. About three days later and much to the surprise of gang, especially of John Mills who thought it would be the last time he would see Shepherd again as he was sent to London under such a heavy guard, but there he was telling his story to the others almost to their disbelief. Although he was grateful for returning to Hawkhurst unharmed, one thing was on his mind, revenge of one James Butler.

So, it was put to the others for a means of how to exact revenge on Mr. Butler, so a few of the men got together to go over a few plans of how and what should be done.

First it was said to kill all the deer on his estate and level all the trees as well turning it into a wasteland devoid of any trees, this was agreed to at first but some of the others including, Mills, Thomas and Fairall didn't think this would satisfy them enough as a revenge. Someone suggested that his house should be burned to the ground with him it, an argument ensued as a few of the men thought that it wasn't right to kill a gentleman of standing and that it could bring more trouble their way should it happen.

They argued through the evening trying to come up with a plan, but none was found. After the others had left, Thomas, Fairall, Mills and a few others took it upon themselves to go to Butler's home and kill him, they each had a brace of pistols and together went to wait at Butler's home, they heard he had gone to Horsham and would be coming home later that night. As it transpired Butler was delayed and didn't return until the following day.

The gang disappointed that they hadn't got their man decided that they would return in a month's times to exact their revenge.

Butler lived in a quiet hamlet and the Hawkhurst gang were seen waiting at Butlers home, this was informed to him. If these men want to come back, then care would be taken to apprehend the men and make sure of their capture.

The month passed but Fairall couldn't find many people to come with him to act of his revenge on Butler this annoyed him, Thomas said you were denied your revenge, but you still have your freedom, revenge can be taken another day.

Chapter 22
The Chase. (1750)

Well, it seemed that while Fairall was trying to catch Butler to take out his revenge on the fellow, the customs, magistrates as well as the dragoons didn't like the idea that he had escaped their clutches and were seen in the area in and around Hawkhurst asking questions and the whereabouts of William Fairall, and all this was going on while the rest of the gang were planning their next shipment that was coming in from Guernsey.

I was at the meeting while all this was being discussed, there were going to be another three cutters worth of goods, months of planning meant that the goods coming over were tea, coffee, rum, whisky, silks from China and India, spices, all paid for and was going to be here on the south coast within a month, this would have made us all very rich, we had to pay around fifteen thousand pounds for the pleasure, I just thought it was Thomas's and Fairall's way of trying to compete with what Arthur had managed a few years prior, to see if they could organise it just as well as Arthur.

"The Staymaker is going to succeed with this shipment, another month and we'll all be really rich", Thomas shouted and everyone around him held their tankards high and cheer.

"Maybe you'll settle down after this one", I said.

"Never, all the time the money is coming our way, why stop"? said Thomas looking at Fairall for approval. "We have the buying power, the ship captains like us, the French like us, and soon the rest of the world will get to know us and want to do business with us, there's no stopping us Will", he said looking at me and holding his tankard in my direction for me to cheer with him.

"I'll let you lot organise what needs to be done, I need to go to Hawkhurst and get some food in as I don't have anything, I'll be back later, and you can tell me all about it.

"You should stay and enjoy the moment with friends", shouted Perrin from the rear of the Inn.
"Don't worry I won't be gone long, if I don't get something I'll just go hungry, and drinking beer with no food inside you is", I got stopped in mid-sentence as Glover shouted.
"The best way to drink it", shouted Glover.
"Just keep my place warm for when I return", and with that I left them inside the inn to work out more details.
I mounted my horse and decided to take a leisurely stroll off towards Hawkhurst, the sun was out and gave me a nice relaxing feeling, I was thinking of all the goods we were getting and what was I going to do with my share of the money, I rounded a corner only to be confronted by dragoons, lots of them.
"Theres one of them, get him", shouted one of the customs men.
The sound of his voice brought me back to reality, as I saw the dragoons dig their spurs into their horses and bolt towards me.
I turned tail and got my horse to galloping speed in no time and headed back in the other direction with the dragoons hard on my heels, now all my thoughts were set on how to get away, there was a lot of them, but weighted down by what they had to carry as a uniform I could easily outrun them. I got my horse whip out and was egging my horse to go faster and create some distance between us both. I went racing past the Oak and Ivy just as the others came out the Inn.
"Hawkhurst is that way", said Glover pointing towards Hawkhurst and laughing out loud".
I never said a word, I looked behind as a lot of the dragoons stopped to turn their attention on the Inn, I just kept going in the opposite direction and ended up in Rye.

I needed to hide, I couldn't stay at the Mermaid, they would come here and ask questions as well, I just wondered what happened with the others, I'm sure they wouldn't have surrendered easily, they have put up some fight, but there were a lot of dragoons, all this was going through my head as I was continuously looking over my shoulder, half expecting to see dragoons coming up to get me.

I know, I'll stay at the Olde Bell Inn again as I did the last time I was here.

I made my way towards the town and up the hill towards the Inn and opened the door.

The girl that was here before was still here handing out drinks to the sailors that were there.

She was looking just as pretty as the last time I saw her.

"Can I help you", she said.

I looked at her for a moment at her smile, lost for words by her beauty.

"Um, err, I'd like a room please", I said.

"I remember you", she said, you came in once before, I never forget a face, not like yours anyway, handsome, how have you been"? she said, with a big grin on her face.

It was my turn to blush now from what she said, no longer coy I thought to myself, must be all the sailors that come here, made her like that.

"I'm fine, I've been keeping busy", I said, turning around to look at the door, hoping it wouldn't open.

"I'd like a room for the night please, if there's one available, that is", I said, looking back at her.

"For you, my dear of course we have, and is there anything else you'd like, hot meal perhaps, I do have something cooking in the kitchen", She said, pointing to the kitchen.

"That would be nice, and do you think it's possible that your husband can look after and feed my horse for the night", I said looking around for him.

"Husband, what husband"? she asked looking at me in a puzzled way.

She looked at me then started to laugh, "that's my older brother not my husband my dear, that's made my day, never been married, never felt the need, I own this Inn and I just employ him to help run it", she said, turning to head for the kitchen still laughing to herself,
She brought me a large tankard of ale and placed it on the table, she lent down and kissed me on the cheek.
"What was that for", I asked as I touched my cheek.
"Because you're good looking and you just made my day", she said, now she seemed to have a spring in her step as she went into the kitchen.
She brought out a large amount of chicken, potatoes, carrots, and peas.
"There you go, just for you", she said.
As she turned to walk away, I grabbed her hand and she turned to face me.
"Thank you, you are so kind, I don't even know your name, to thank you properly".
"You don't have to do that, "she said, "anyway my name is Mandy", still with a big smile on her face.
"Thank you, Mandy", then I kissed her on the cheek to return the favour.
She touched her cheek, paused, then walked over to another table to clear the empty tankards that were there, looking back at me, blushing as she went.
She went through to the kitchen again to call Stuart, her bother, to help with my horse, and get him bedded down for the night.

After a while, all the sailors left the Inn, and I was left on my own with a glass of rum feeling I've escaped capture once too many times. If I went back to the Oak there might be someone watching and waiting for any gang members that might return, if of course there were anyone watching, I'm sure that Thomas, Fairall and the others would have fought hard and not give up too easily, is was the uncertainty of it all, not knowing what had happened, and thinking for a while I decided that I would leave it for a few days and let things die down, the goods weren't supposed to be coming in for at least another month anyway, so plenty of time still.
Mandy walked over to the door and bolted it for the night.
"Would you like another", Mandy appeared with a bottle in one hand and a glass in the other, she filled my glass.
"Do you mind if I join you, you look a bit lonely over here all on your own", she asked pouring herself a glass of rum.
"Can I ask you your name as you now know mine", said asked politely, taking a sip of rum.
"Oh, I'm sorry, I should have introduced myself before, but my mind was elsewhere, its Will, William", I said watching her play with the rim of her glass, her legs were crossed showing off her ankles under her skirt.
"I know your mind is elsewhere", she laughed, "most men's minds are when they come in here", she said.
"Well, I hope you don't mind this being too forward of me, but you are a very beautiful woman", I said as I watched her blush.
"Why thank you Will, a lot of people have told me that but the way you put it, made it sound so sincere, she lifted her head up to look at me, her hair falling onto her shoulder, and she flicked it back behind her to give me a better view of her face.

She was not like other women that I'd met or even spoke to, something about her that I found alluring, she was bubbly, always smiling, happy, she held my attention all night as we chatted till it was very late. She said that she's had a hard day and if I liked I could carry on with our conversation in her bedroom, to which I agreed would be the best way to spend the night.

We spent the next two days talking to each other and getting to know each other, unfortunately I couldn't tell her the truth of who I was or what I had been doing, so most of what I told her was a lie, I had to keep secrets from her, after all there was nothing serious between us, just an acquaintance, so in a few days I bid her goodbye for a second time and decided to try my luck back at the Oak and Ivy.

As I got close to Inn, I headed for the fields opposite to see if I could see any movement, there were no horses tied up outside which to me looked very suspicious, if dragoons were in there, they would hide their horses elsewhere so as to hide their presence. I tied my horse to a tree in the field and made my way closer, hiding behind trees and bushes, when I got close, I peered through the window. Nothing, I saw nothing the place was empty, not even John the bar keep was in there, so I moved to another window, still nothing, I went to the rear of the inn and there was John and his wife tending to his garden, he looked up and saw me, then looked at his wife before coming over to me.

"What happened to you, where have you been", he asked.

"I got chased by those dragoons they saw me and came after me, what could I do but get away as fast as I could", I said.

"They came after Fairall, wanted him back for escaping, then they saw Thomas and the others, said they were looking for them as well, something to do with Poole I heard one of them say, they had the place surrounded armed with muskets, pistols, and blunderbusses, and swords drawn, the others didn't have a chance. Before they could even go for their swords two shots were fired at them just missing them, wasn't a lot they could do, took them all they did", said John, rubbing his chin.

"Took them where", I asked.

"Said something about Newgate", he said looking worried. "Good job you weren't here Will they'd have had you to, if you know what's best, you'd keep away from here and don't go travelling up to Newgate either, keep well away in case you are recognised, the magistrate did ask after you, but no one said your name, no one", he looked at me to see what I was going to do.

"It's alright John, are you and your wife alright"? I asked.

"We were asked a lot of questions and I think we convinced them that we knew nothing of any gang that resides in the area. They just wanted Thomas and Fairall from what I could hear", said John.

"I'm going to Newgate, got to see what's happening, find out why they want them so bad, as if I didn't know already, I will be alright, don't worry about me, I will hide in the crowd like I did before with Arthur", I said looking worried for them myself.

What was I thinking? Here was the perfect opportunity to break away from them, the gang was now gone, behind bars, I could see no way that they could escape their fate especially as they had gone to Newgate, there was only one way out of that place and it wasn't the one they'd be hoping for, and here I was going back there putting myself in danger just to see what's happening, they may get off but who knows.

"I need to borrow a horse John, can you look after mine, he's over there in that field next to the Inn, I need a fresh one for the journey", I asked, as I walked over to his barn, he walked into the field to get mine, and bring him over to the water trough.
"Best of luck Will lad, you're going to need it", said John patting my horse.
I adjusted the saddle, got on and made my way towards London, again.

Chapter 23
Out in the sweet air. (1750)

A few days later I was back in the hustle and bustle of London, I was beginning to get used to the crowds, the noise and the smell that was in city life, not for me though I thought, I much prefer the country. I found my way unaided this time to Newgate, and again read the list that was posted outside. Here in this gaol lie seven smugglers, tax avoiders and murderers, and for the disturbance and theft at the Poole Customs house from his Majesty the King in the County of Kent and Sussex, with a trial set for 5th April 1749, all are invited for standing room only for the trial.

This was to be in three days' time, I went to find the Inn that I had stayed in before, but it seems that a lot of people had arrived in London to watch some more hangings, I had to look elsewhere in the hope of getting any room, eventually I found somewhere. This place was so dark inside, tobacco smoke had ingrained in the woodwork, the windows were filthy and hadn't been washed in years, the chair legs were broken and found it hard and uncomfortable to sit on and the smell of the sewer just added to my pleasure, but this seemed to be the only place left were to get a room, I was dreading seeing what the room was like given the state of the main room, I kept wishing I were back in the Olde Bell in Rye, back in that cosy surroundings.

I spent most of my time outside looking at all the places that London had to offer, reminding myself that I wasn't there to see sights but to find out what was going to happen to Thomas and the others.

I found myself next to the river and looking over the parapet at the water, the tide must have gone out and created a small beach next to the water's edge, there were rats everywhere, a man walked past, "Don't fall in they'll eat you alive", he went away laughing.

I had no intentions of falling in or going anywhere near them, I looked around to see some of the rats running along beside the buildings, there seemed to be more rats than people, how could anyone live like this and say it's good to be in London. I kept myself pretty much busy for the next few days, trying to avoid as much as possible of going back to that dirty place, then the day came of the trial, I had to get a place to stand in what was called the gallery again so I could see. I didn't want them to see me in case they called out my name.
Their names were called, and the judge asked for silence as there was a lot of cheering and booing at those standing before the judge.
Thomas Kingsmill, alias Staymaker, William Fairall, alias Shepherd, Richard Perin, alias Pain alias Carpenter, Thomas Lillywhite and Richard Glover, were called out.
I was lucky that my name wasn't on that list as these were the men that were in the Oak and Ivy when the dragoons arrived. The trial began and I was fascinated to hear all the so-called evidence that was being read out and then the witness came out to speak against them one by one.
The customs house in Poole was spoken about along with many other details that they said were carried out by Thomas, Fairall and the rest of the Hawkhurst gang.
Silence was ushered over the court room, the judge lifted his head from what he was reading, then spoke clearly;
"For far too long have you got away with crimes against King and country so much so that the people that you thought were your friends have long since had enough of the goings on of such vile and violent men, it would seem they have turned against you in the hope that it would bring some justice to their lives as you set about to make theirs a living hell, and to put right many wrongs that have been committed by you and your so called gang for far too long, and believe me, justice will be served on you should you be found guilty of the said crimes".

The judge continued to read out their crimes, while Fairall sat smiling and looking round the room as if taking pleasure on hearing it.

Thomas Lillywhite hadn't really been part of the gang and during the time he met his brother-in-law and was threatened by him to join in to rob the Poole customs house, it was thought that he was innocent and was acquitted,

That was good, I thought, maybe the judge was in a good mood, or maybe scared of the Hawkhurst gang, if their reputation had in fact spread this far.

After a lengthy trial with many witness coming forward and speaking against them all it didn't bare well from what I had heard, the jury got up and left the room.

All the time the trial was going on Fairall was laughing at the witnesses as they were giving evidence, the judge tried to reprimand him, but he just ignored him and carried on laughing.

I overheard from a man standing next to me about Fairall and Thomas and what they said the night they were brought to Newgate. The man said he heard Fairall shouting, "He did not value being hung, let's have a pipe and some tobacco and a bottle of wine, as for I am not to live long, I am determined to live well in the short time I have left".

The jury came out of the room and sat back down, one of the jury passed a piece of paper to the usher. This didn't look good for what I could see, and once again Fairall was laughing and smiling at the jury and even smiled at the judge as they were all handed the death sentence, but it was what he said to the judge in his response to him.

As the judge passed sentence he said, "and may the lord have mercy on your souls".

"If the Lord has not more mercy on our souls, that the jury has had on our bodies, I don't know what will become of them", Fairall boldly replied.

The judge looked at Perrin, "You are to be hanged and afterwards you shall be taken by your friends and family and buried at a place of their choosing.
The judge turned to Thomas and Fairall, "you two are the perpetrators of all that is evil, and your conduct in this court tells me so, therefore you two will be hanged by the neck until you are dead, then you will be hung in chains for all to see as a deterrent against any more wrong doers.
Fairall looked across to Perrin and said smilingly, "We shall be hanging up in the sweet air when you are rotting in your grave", this was for all to hear.
They were all led away in chains.
A few days later I found out that Glover had a received a pardon from the King, but not so for the others, the day was set for their execution which was set for the 26th or April, again I would have to endure watching my friends be put to death and all the time racked with guilt that I too should be joining them for I am as guilty for my crimes as much as them but somehow I couldn't quite bring myself to confess or offer any assistance as a witness for them, it was for me to remain in the shadows.
I watched as the party left Newgate gaol, in iron cages under a heavy guard, along with seven others that were tried for their crimes on the same day as Fairall and Thomas, they too were to go to their graves on this day.
They each walked along the scaffold to a rope, it didn't look like the hangman cared as to who was who as long as you got a rope, only two were given their own rope, and they looked like they would suffer the longest, with no broken necks, just a long choke.
Black cloths were placed over their heads and the noose tightened.

The crowd were laughing and cheering all the way from Newgate with rotten food, fruit and eggs being thrown at them such was the indignity they were being put through. I looked at Thomas, he was covered in eggs and tomatoes as was Fairall, he had more than Thomas, including a few eggs to the face, rotten eggs were still being thrown from the crowd as they all are waiting with a rope round their necks.

Then the hangman put his hand up, the crowd again drew silent, they knew not to make a sound, they were waiting to hear necks snapping from the long drop.

Then the lever was pulled, I only heard two necks snap and the others were left to dangle and kick till they were dead. The crowd were rapturous and applauded the hangman for his days' work.

I couldn't help thinking that Thomas was only twenty-eight, just slightly younger than Arthur, it was the life they chose and for many years they had got away with it and became rich on the proceeds, there wasn't many of the gang left now, I even found out that Smoker had been hung and a lot of the others from Hampshire that had something to do with that Galley chap and Chater, they were all hung for what they had done. Jeremiah Curtis escaped and headed for France to get away, hiding in another country and joined the French Legion army to get away. Seemed like only me left, oh and John from the inn, which reminded me, there's a shipment coming across in a few days' time, it was now down to me to organise some men to get the load off the ships and hidden.

With the sad sight that stayed with me, I left the baying crowd back to my room, packed my meagre belongings and headed back to Hawkhurst.

Chapter 24
The last one. (1750)

I got back to the Oak in good time to see John and ask for help in offloading goods from three cutters onto carts, he said that he would, and it'll be like the old days. He told me that Arthur had always trusted him, but never let on to anyone that he was a silent member of the gang, but he knew all there was to know about owling, and in particular knew where and how to find the rest of the gang, Arthur also made him keep a record of where the goods were placed, it was in a leather bound book, this was needed in case anything happen to the rest of the leaders, so it wasn't long before John had organised a large amount of people with carts and we made our way to Fairlight cove, where we had been many time before. We got to the cove to find that indeed the ship had been during the night and offloaded our goods, it was all stacked up along the cliffs kept away from the sea, there was a lot of it, we didn't think we would have enough carts, three of the men went off to find a few more which they did, found three more horses and carts from a local farmer. All in all we had about thirty carts now, just enough to carry all the goods inland, many of which were hidden throughout Kent, in churches, graveyards, barns, cellars, in places where no one would suspect packages or casks to be hidden, it took five days to hide it, another two months to sell some of it on, we gave some of the goods to those that helped us out, and a lot more was sold through our contacts. I shared the money between myself, john the bar keeper so he could do up the Inn and John the farmer for all the inconvenience of having to store our goods other the years. It couldn't have been good for him to worry the way he did whenever we come round, it was just his nature not to refuse and old friend.

I myself decided that that was the last job of the Hawkhurst gang, no more would people hear the clatter of hooves late at night, no more did they have to hide their faces and fear when we came past, they were in fact the good times but now it was ended and I had to think that with all this money I could buy myself somewhere nice to live, somewhere bigger than I had now, I often walk past ,my old house, the one with the leaking roof, spending many days and nights trying to keep warm, and I remember the look on Georges face when he looked down at his lack of buttons on his coat, the faces of the old gang, sharing times drinking till late, these memoires will stick with me for the rest of my days, some good and some bad, but for me now, I need some new memories, start a new life somewhere and get away from this place just in case anyone came looking to pick up stragglers of the Hawkhurst gang.

I said to John that his services to the Hawkhurst gang were paid in full and told him that I was going to do something with my life and move on.

He looked at me and held my arm as he placed a small book in my hand, "You might need this, everything is in here, all the goods that we've had, all the hiding places we've used to store all of it, all the contacts that we have gathered over the years are all in this book, "Arthur made me keep records of everything that we did, he was meticulous in his way and made me write everything down, and after you've read it you'll soon come to realise that there's still a lot of goods still out there ready to be collected and sold on, go find them Will and build an even bigger life your yourself".

I gripped his hands tightly, then placed the book inside my coat, I thanked him for the pleasure of his company throughout the years as I turned to mount my horse and headed for home.

A few days later I plucked up the courage and rode to Goudhurst, enough time had passed between us being there for the fight that ensued with the loss of George and Willett.

I came to the green in Goudhurst and stopped to look at the remains of Thomas Kingsmill, to pay my respects quietly, not to draw attention to myself, who was entombed inside the gibbet, swinging away in the wind, to think he was once the leader of the Hawkhurst gang after Arthur.

I searched around the graveyard but was unable to find George and Willets grave, I looked up in the church register but still couldn't find their graves.

The vicar told me that because of who they were and what they did, carrying out murders and smuggling, that it was the wish of the people of Goudhurst that they be placed somewhere unmarked away from the other villagers, so it would be hard to find where they were. I travelled on further down the hill to the pond and as I passed, I wondered if we had left any half ackers at the bottom, if we had I'm sure the villagers would have had them by now, I made my way to Horsmonden to pay a visit to Fairall who was also gibbetted, I found him, just like he had said, swinging in the sweet air, still locked up high for all to see, I looked and could see where some eggs had been thrown at him by the local kids or villagers who still took their anger out on his body for what he had done.

Chapter 25
A new life (1750)

Life had become a bit dull since the last shipment had come and gone, I spent a few days at the inn with John going over a few stories but, in the end, we became tired of listening to them and reminiscing on the things we did, life was turning back to normal, but now as my carpentry business was gone, I had plenty of time to do my own things. I visited Arthur's sister at Seacox who still looked remarkable even though she was older than Arthur, gorgeous Auburn hair running down her back, and dressed in such finery, she had indeed looked the part that Arthur was always craving, here she was now living the life he was always chasing.

"You should get out and explore the world, you are and man of substance now, a gentleman in your own right, you should take the trouble in finding someone to settle down with, someone to share your life your dreams, you've got plenty going for you, you are a good looking man Will, if you don't mind me saying so, I have always admired you, you're quiet and trusting person, you'd make someone a fine husband I'm sure of it", said Jane with a big smile on her face.

"You are right Jane, that's what I need, someone to care for, to make our dreams together, get away from all this, start again", I said holding her hand, a big smile appeared on my face as I looked at her.

"You are single as well I'm sure you would make someone a fine wife, but as much as I admired you Jane you could never be mine as you are too close to Arthur, too many memories of what's gone before". I said trying to be humble.

"Not me, silly, I wasn't talking about us getting married, I was talking about you finding someone, someone to share new memories, a new life, away from us, this house, I have my own memories, enough to keep me going for a lifetime, go out and find her and treat her well, whoever the lucky girl will be", she said this while holding my hand and leant forward to give me a kiss on the lips.
She tasted very nice, but I had to restrain myself, she had made it known that we weren't to be.
"I think I might travel abroad for a while, just to get away and you never know, I might find my future wife there, and good fortunes as well", I said to her.
"That's a bit different, will we ever see each other again", she asked, looked sad.
"Of course, we will, I'm not staying away, just looking, I might even bring you something back, as a gift", I said, moving her hair from her face.
I said my goodbyes to her and left her to her own memories all alone in that big house.
I made my way back to Rye in the hope that I could find a ship to sail on, somewhere unheard of, I asked around and a few sailors told me that the "Lady Endure", was sailing to Jamaica in a few days' time, wherever that was and that if I wanted adventure, I should look for captain Webster and pay for a place on board his ship. I tried all the Inn looking for captain Webster, in the hope of getting a place on his ship, I didn't try the Mermaid Inn as I might have been recognised by anyone in there as to who I was, I stopped to ask someone who was passing if they would be some kind as to ask for me, but they just laughed and walked away. In the end I gave up and went to The Olde Bell Inn where I knew I'd be welcome. As soon as I opened and closed the door, Mandy threw herself into my arms.
"I've missed you, I've done nothing but think of you, where have you been", she said, then started kissing me all over my face spending a lot longer on my lips.

I held her in my arms for a while feeling the warmth of her body close to mine, I held her at arm's length to look at her, she looked as gorgeous as the first time I met her, she now had a pink flowing dress on which touched the ground, a white apron around her with a few beer stains on it, her hair was a bit ruffled from where she had been working but other than that she was perfect.

Why would I want to go around the world looking for something that's right here, happiness can be right under your nose if you took the time to look.

It wasn't long after this that I moved in with her, much to the annoyance of her brother. It was better for me here, now, away from Hawkhurst, away from all that had been, this was the start of the future that I'd hope to start, and now I'd finally found the person I wanted to spend my time with.

Two years later we got married, yes, I finally did it, I convinced her to sell the Olde bell Inn, her brother bought it, so it still remained within the family, it seems he had plenty of money put aside as well, I wonder where he got that from?

We ourselves built a large house overlooking Rye, with sea views to brighten our day, we had a gardener who looked after the grounds of the house and then decided to start a family, we had three sons and a daughter, who grew up respecting the law and all it stood for, needless to say that my past was kept from them, and the book, well that was kept in a secret place away from prying eyes, it still held secrets of where goods had been stored in case there was a time that I needed some more money, but as it was we had plenty enough for all of us.

From where we lived, I could see out beyond the coast to the many ships that passed by and stopped to wonder if they were carrying anything that they shouldn't be, and every time the memories kept coming back of our past but secret life.

May the past stay in the past for if it should rear its ugly head, all would be done for. The end.

A SMUGGLERS SONG

If you wake at midnight, and hear a horse's feet,
Don't go drawing back the blind, or looking in the street,
Them that ask no questions isn't told a lie.
Watch the wall my darling as the gentlemen do by!
Five an twenty ponies,
Trotting through the dark-
Brandy for the parson, Baccy for the clerk.
Laces for a lady: letters for a spy.
Watch the wall my darling as the gentlemen do by!
Running round the wood lump if you chance to find,
Little barrels, roped and tarred, all full of brandy-wine,
Don't you shout to come and look, nor use 'em for your play,
Put the brushwood back again - and they'll be gone the next day!
If you see the stable door setting open wide;
If you see a tired horse lying down inside;
If your mother mends a coat cut about and tore;
If the lining's wet and warm - don't you ask no more!
If you meet King George's men, dressed in blue and red,
You be careful what you say, and mindful what is said.
If they call you " pretty maid," and chuck you 'neath the chin,
Don't you tell where no one is, nor yet where no one's been!
Knocks and footsteps round the house - whistles after dark -
You've no call for running out till the house-dogs bark.
Trusty's here, and Pincher's here, and see how dumb they lie
They don't fret to follow when the Gentlemen go by!
'If You do as you've been told, 'likely there's a chance,
You'll be give a dainty doll, all the way from France,
With a cap of Valenciennes, and a velvet hood
A present from the Gentlemen, along 'o being good!
Five and twenty ponies,
Brandy for the Parson, 'Baccy for the Clerk.
Them that asks no questions isn't told a lie -
Watch the wall my darling while the Gentlemen go by!

Bibliography

General sourced reference. No parts taken in context only as a reference.
Richard Platt: Smuggling in the British Isles. History press 2011
Christopher McCooey. Smuggling on the South Coast. Amberly 2012
John Dawes Publications, Hawkhurst England: Smugglers Murders. First printed and published 1749
10th Edition by John Dawes Publications of Hawkhurst, 1999
Peter Faulkner Lost Churches of Romney Marsh.
https://theromneymarsh.net/lostchurches
Charles G Harper. The Smugglers. The Gutenberg eBook:
https://www.gutenberg.org/files/45856/45856-h/45856-h.htm
The Weald of Kent, Surrey & Sussex:
https://theweald.org/N10.asp?NId=3928
Georgian Britain. Published 14.10/2009:
https://www.bl.uk/georgian-britain/articles/crime-and-punishment-in-georgian-britain
Smugglers Britain:
http://www.smuggling.co.uk/history_buying.html
https://spartacus-educational.com/LONnewgate.htm
https://www.ncbi.nlm.nih.gov/books/NBK379345/
TNA, T 64/262; ASSI 23/6, ASSI 31/2; West Sussex Record Office (WSRO), Goodwood MSS 154; Old Bailey Online.
https//www.facebook.com/hawkhurstsmugglersgang
https//www.facebook.com/dayofsyn

© 26/06/2021 ALL RIGHTS RESERVED.
FRONT COVER BY COLIN DIXON
MANY THANKS TO ANDY STROUD FOR COVER PHOTO.
ARTWORK BY COLIN DIXON.
WHITECLIFFSPHOTOGRAPHY.CO.UK
IGSTER PRODUCTIONS.

To Karen

I hope you enjoy the book

[signature]

3/6/25

Amazon ASIN: B097X5VTS2

https://colindixon19.wixsite.com/the-hawkhurst-gang
Links to the book to enhance your reading.

Printed in Great Britain
by Amazon